EVENT COGNITION:

An Ecological Perspective

RESOURCES FOR ECOLOGICAL PSYCHOLOGY

Robert E. Shaw, William M. Mace, and Michael T. Turvey, Series Editors

EVENT COGNITION:

An Ecological Perspective

Edited by

VIKI MCCABE
University of California, Los Angeles

GERALD J. BALZANO
University of California, San Diego

LEA LAWRENCE ERLBAUM ASSOCIATES, PUBLISHERS
1986   Hillsdale, New Jersey   London

Lawrence Erlbaum Associates, Inc., Publishers
365 Broadway
Hillsdale, New Jersey 07642

Library of Congress Cataloging-in-Publication Data

Event cognition.

   (Resources for ecological psychology)
   Includes bibliographies and indexes.
   1. Perception.   2. Change (Psychology)   I. McCabe,
Viki.   II. Balzano, Gerald J.   III. Series.
BF311.E86   1986   153.7   86-13369
ISBN 0-89859-811-7

Printed in the United States of America
10   9   8   7   6   5   4   3   2   1

Resources for Ecological Psychology

Edited by Robert E. Shaw, William M. Mace
and Michael T. Turvey

This series of volumes is dedicated to furthering the development of psychology as a branch of ecological science. In its broadest sense, ecology is a multidisciplinary approach to the study of living systems, their environments, and the reciprocity that has evolved between the two. Traditionally, ecological science emphasizes the study of the biological bases of *energy* transactions between animals and their physical environments across cellular, organismic, and population scales. Ecological psychology complements this traditional focus by emphasizing the study of *information* transactions between living systems and their environments, especially as they pertain to perceiving situations of significance to planning and execution of purposes activated in an environment.

The late James J. Gibson used the term *ecological psychology* to emphasize this animal-environment mutuality for the study of problems of perception. He believed that analyzing the environment to be perceived was just as much a part of the psychologist's task as analyzing animals themselves, and hence that the "physical" concepts applied to the environment and the "biological" and "psychological" concepts applied to organisms would have to be tailored to one another in a larger system of mutual constraint. His early interest in the applied problems of landing airplanes and driving automobiles led him to pioneer the study of the perceptual guidance of action.

The work of Nicolai Bernstein in biomechanics and physiology presents a complementary approach to problems of the coordination and control of movement. His work suggests that action, too, cannot be studied without reference to the environment, and that physical and biological concepts must be developed together. The coupling of Gibson's ideas with those of Bernstein forms a natural basis for looking at the traditional psychological topics of perceiving, acting, and knowing as activities of ecosystems rather than isolated animals.

The purpose of this series is to form a useful collection, a resource, for people who wish to learn about ecological psychology and for those who wish to contribute to its development. The series will include original research, collected papers, reports of conferences and symposia, theoretical monographs, technical handbooks, and works from the many disciplines relevant to ecological psychology.

Dedication
To James J. Gibson, whose pioneering work in ecological
psychology has opened new vistas in psychology and
related sciences, we respectfully dedicate this series.

Contents

**13. Kinematic Specification of Gender and
       Gender Expression**   **259**
Sverker Runeson and Gunilla Frykholm

14. Epilogue: Cognition and Ethics   **275**
Viki McCabe

INTRODUCTION: EVENT COGNITION AND THE CONDITIONS OF EXISTENCE

Introduction: Event Cognition and the Conditions of Existence

Viki McCabe
University of California, Los Angeles

CONTENTS

*Once the whole is divided, the parts need names
There are already enough names.
One must know when to stop.
Knowing when to stop averts trouble.
Tao in the world is like a river flowing home
to the sea.*

—Lao Tsu

The central question of cognition, what it means to *know* something or somebody has concerned me since I was a child because my father seemed to be repeatedly misclassified—people typically took him for Thomas Dewey, the governor of New York who lost the presidential election to Harry Truman in 1948. Mistaken identity raises interesting questions about the most useful unit of analysis and the clearest form of information for the cognition of ongoing *events* (such as a

3

person's life) (Gibson, 1975).[1] For example, what kind of information specifies my father's *identity*, and what is the relationship between that kind of persisting information and the sort of information that specifies my father's membership in a *generic class*—his similarity or *equivalence* to someone else?

One possibility is that, having seen Tom Dewey before, people constructed and internalized a schema of him through which they perceive and misclassify my similar father (Bartlett, 1932; Bem, 1981; Taylor & Crocker, 1981). A core assumption underlying theories of schematic processing is that the important relationship between equivalent instances is that of similarity. Similar criterial attributes in some way combine to form equivalent instances (Bruner, 1962; Rosch, 1978). From this view, the unit of analysis for cognition is a schema and/or category, and the information used specifies the criterial attributes from which such schemas and/or categories are constructed. But, theories of equivalence based solely on similarity provide neither constraints on, nor objective criteria for, the choice of pertinent attributes from which to make such constructions; this can lead to arbitrary and inaccurate classifications (e.g., tables and cows both have four legs and crows and bowling balls are both black yet neither pair is equivalent; Ghiselin, 1981; McCabe, 1984).

In addition, the cognitive processes thought to subserve schematization and/or categorization—abstraction, generalization, classification, and storage— tend to culminate in somewhat static generic categories; such categories may not adequately specify particular events (such as my father's life) that change over time. Without constraints or dynamics, schematic processing (in the traditional sense) does not necessarily provide adequate knowledge about the world as it changes around us, a questionable outcome for a species that coevolved with and adapted to the environment in which it lives (an environment it needs to know in order to survive). Perhaps, however, "mistaking" my father for Tom Dewey occurred because the pertinent information that specified my father also specified Tom Dewey, and as a species we evolved with a predisposition to attend this type of information.

MOTION EVENTS

Things in motion sooner catch the eye than what stirs not.
—William Shakespeare

Human beings evolved to rely most on visual information with priority given to visual motion that produces *dynamic geometric patterns* (Bertenthal & Proffitt, 1984; Gibson, Owsley, & Johnston, 1978; Johansson, 1964, 1973; Lappin,

---

[1]An *event* is defined here as a coherent and meaningful unit that has properties that persist and properties that change as the event occurs over time and space. It could be as short as a raindrop or as

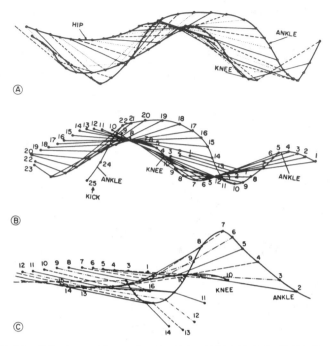

FIG. I.1.   Side views of three swimming kicks: (a) Dolphin kck, (b) Schollander Fly kick, (c) Van Kennan crawl kick, from Stanley Plagenhoef, Patterns of Human Motion: A Cinematographic Analysis, 1971, pp. 125, 126. Reprinted by permission of Prentice-Hall, Englewood Cliffs, New Jersey.

Donner, & Kottas, 1980; Mace & Shaw, 1974; Riddock, 1917; Sekuler, 1975). Instances of these patterns are available when anything moves; they are etched across the spatial and temporal dimensions of any motion event by the systematic transformations of the moving structure one is watching. Consider, for example, the patterns produced by kicking the legs during swimming (see Fig. I.1). Different styles of swimming kicks produce unique yet similar dynamic patterns that specify both kicking in general (although kicks vary, they are all kicks) and each unique kick in particular. In short, each kicking style is a variation on the general pattern of kicking (see Chapter 3 on the concept of generator). The patterns that specify kicking (like those for any movement) fall out of the interaction of the swimmer's biomechanical structure and their particular action or movement pattern (see Chapter 13, this volume).

---

long as evolution; it could be as fast as the wink of an eye or a slow as the formation of a mountain; it includes entities such as organisms, objects, and activities—lives that develop, physical structures that shift and erode, and activities with beginnings, middles, and ends (see Warren & Shaw, 1985, for a more complete analysis of the concept of cognitive events.)

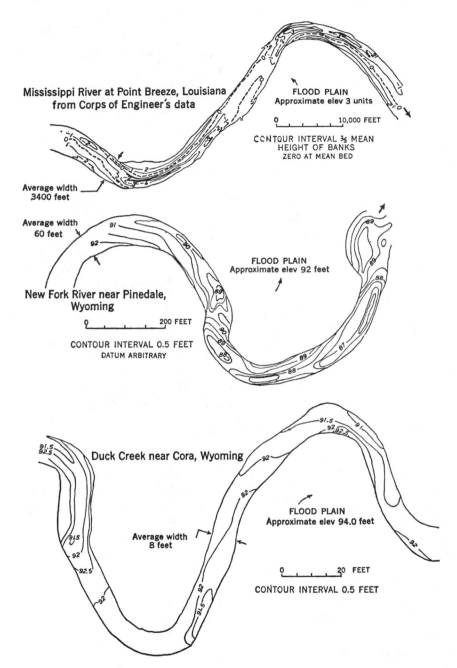

FIG. I.2. A comparison of three waterway patterns: (a) 8' wide Duck Creek near Cora, Wyoming, (b) 60' wide New Fork River near Pinedale, Wyoming, and (c) 3400' wide Mississippi at Point Breeze, Lousiana, from Luna B. Leopold & M. Gordon Wolman, (1960) River Meanders, *Bulletin of the Geological Society of America, 71,* p. 775. Reprinted with permission of the publisher.

When something moves or appears to change in any way (even by a change in the observer's perspective or through slow development over time), *it can be identified by the patterns produced by its own dynamic structure.* Similar to kicking patterns is the *meander* pattern of flowing rivers that is produced by the interaction of centrifugal force and gravity (Stevens, 1976).

The meander both *specifies* and *is* the flowing river; this patterned information is comprehensive, specific, and permanently "stored" at its origin—the river itself. Because the meander pattern is perceptually available, it may be unnecessary to abstract and represent it. A key point is that all waterways (similar to swimming kicks), no matter what their size or location, are specified by the *same* lawful pattern; each particular waterway, like a melody played in different keys, is simply a variation on the same basic theme (Stevens, 1976).

The similarity between the three rivers in Fig. I.2, however, is not an arbitrary mental construction but is the result of physical law (Leopold & Langbein, 1966). Our perception of such similarity, whether it be of the identity of a particular river (or person or kick) or the equivalence between different variations of these phenomena, must in some sense be a function of our own cognitive evolution under the same physical laws (Campbell, 1985; Shepard, 1984). The world, however, is not built in; rather, we are capable of coordinating with its lawful properties (see Chapter 5).

As Quine (1973) wisely points out, "our innate standards of perceptual similarity show a gratifying tendency to run with the grain of nature . . . since good prediction has survival value, natural selection will have fostered perceptual similarity standards in us and in other animals that tend accordingly" (p. 19). An assumption that takes account of Quine's insight about the grain of nature turns the equivalence/similarity equation on its head and suggests that *equivalent things are not related because they are similar, rather, they are similar because they are related.* For example, living things are either homologous due to common ancestry (fins and limbs), or analogous due to common conditions of development (wings of butterflies and birds) (Ghiselin, 1981; Hildebrandt, 1982; Luria, Gould, & Singer, 1981).

STRUCTURAL CHANGE EVENTS

The active maintainance of normal and specific structure is what we call life, and the perception of it is the perception of life.
—J. B. S. Haldane

Both homology and analogy characterize slow events that occur over time and space. The transformations characteristic of slow events produce the same type of patterned information (although it lasts longer) as the faster events of visible motion (Shaw & Pittenger, 1977). As we see, homology implies common genetic, ecological, and physical constraints that subserve the ongoing event of phylogenesis, and analogy implies common physical and ecological constraints that subserve the ongoing events of development and adaptation. Although homology is a function of historical lineage and therefore is thought to primarily involve identity, whereas analogy is a function of environmental press that produces equivalence (Ghiselin, 1981), both identity and equivalence are subject to the same constraints and tend toward the same types of structural similarity. These constraints, according to Cuvier (1812), comprise the "conditions of existence"—physical, mechanical, and biological laws such as gravity, motion, and phylogenesis—that order the world in which we all live and produce the forms we perceive (see also Chapter 4, this volume).

THE CONDITIONS OF EXISTENCE

The truth is, it is no contingent fact about us that our bodies are the size they are. We ourselves, are not as Descartes suggested purely mental creatures. We are not tentatively considering possible incarnations.

—Mary Midgeley

Biological, physical, and ecological constraints on natural forms "run with the grain of nature" and provide the grounds for persistent, nonarbitrary, and accurate specifications of, and connections between, stable objects and organisms; such constraints reflect the "conditions of existence" that limit what things can possibly be and consequently what we might possibly know (Cuvier, 1817, reviewed in Russell, 1916; Futuymo & Slatkin, 1963; Jacob, 1982; Pantin, 1969).[2]

To sample how some of the conditions of existence serve as persistent connections within and across both homologous and analogous events, consider the following constraints:

---

[2]The use of the word constraint here should not be confused with constraints on predication such as the M constraint (Keil, 1981, 1983). For cognitive theory, the M constraint provides a large step in the direction of informing language based studies with ecological validity. It is not, however basic to knowledge acquisition. Because the M constraint is purportedly based on ontological knowledge (see Carey, 1983 for a critique), it must itself be constrained by the properties of the phenomena predicated; these properties are in turn constrained by the conditions of existence. Linguistic predication reflects the possibilities that we can express; it does not, however, constrain the possibilities themselves.

1. *Possible* adaptations are constrained by *actual* structures. Species morphology (that must have some origin) tends to adapt within the constraints of common ancestry—*the event of phylogenesis*. Thus, our ability to hear came from an ancestral jaw internalized and miniaturized by newer and more efficient chewing structures; "evolution the tinkerer" recycled this jaw cum ossicles as vibrating structures—the three bones of the inner ear that transduce sound waves and subserve hearing (DuBrul, 1969; Jacob, 1982). Nature never starts from scratch. For the cognition of similarity, phyletic relationships can provide the type of lineage that supports the notion of a series of related items (Cassirer, 1953) or of the resemblances within a family of related organisms (Wittgenstein, 1953).

2. The *parts* of things *necessarily* constrain and thus constitute one another to produce an integral *whole—the event of intrinsic development* that functions to preserves identity within the necessary compromises of adaptation. Thus change in one part of an event such as an organism requires reciprocal adjustments in other parts (Hildebrandt, 1982). Cuvier (1817, quoted in Russell, 1916/1982) states:

> The different parts of each being must be co-ordinated in such a way as to render possible the existence of the being as a whole, not only in itself, but also in its relations with other beings, and the analysis of these conditions often leads to general laws which are as certain as those which are derived from calculation or experiment. (Cuvier, p. 6, Russell, p. 34)

What we typically conceptualize as an organism's "parts" may be conceptually distinct but they are not ontologically separate; parts both constitute and get their meaning from their relationship to one another. These relationships are the working structures from which an integral whole develops. If we actually (rather than conceptually) abstracted parts to construct wholes, we would violate their intrinsic reciprocity and change the nature of both the parts and the whole (McCabe, 1984).

3. *Gravity* governs both *the event of organic growth* and *the event of physical development*. All structures, whether animal, vegetable, or mineral transform systematically under the gravitational pressures of compression, tension, and shear or else they would fall down (Gordon, 1978; Thompson, 1917/1962; Williams, 1981). "In order to maintain the same structural characteristics a difference in size must be accompanied by a difference in shape" (Stevens, 1976, p. 10). Living bone, for example, adapts its structure to changes in biomechanical load (Kummer, 1972; Saha & Lakes, 1979) and in turn, complex morphological structures remodel their proportions to accomodate such increases in size (Thompson, 1917/1962; Todd & Mark, 1981). "We grow. This is size. We grow up. This is proportion" (Krogman, 1972, p. 3). And we perceive these

proportional changes as growing up or increasing age-level (Mark, Todd, & Shaw, 1981; Pittenger, Shaw, & Mark, 1979).

4. Species and organisms develop within the *reciprocal matrix* of their eco-system—*the events of speciation/adaptation, resource utilization, and reciprocal behavior* (mother and child, predator and prey, plant and pollinator): "Let it be borne in mind how infinitely close-fitting are the mutual relations of all organic beings to each other and to their physical conditions of life" (Darwin, 1859, p. 80). The upshot of this is, given two similar ecosystem, similar animals will fill similar niches.[3] For example, kangaroo rats in Western North America and jerboas in Africa and Asia show striking parallelism. They both live in hot, sandy deserts and have adapted in nearly identical ways. The result is although they are not genetically related, they look almost identical (Hildebrandt, 1982).

The conditions of existence provide invariant constraints on how things combine, grow, relate, persist, and change. These constraints provide some of the "necessary connections" that support our perception of similarity between the "instances" and "items" we tend to *conceptualize* as temporally and spatially separate.

Given the constraints imposed on cognition by these conditions, mistaking my father for Tom Dewey is understandable. Although the following account is anecdotal, it suggests that there are many nonarbitrary ways in which Tom Dewey and my father are connected. For example, their physical properties (in spite of a lack of direct kinship) indicate a large measure of shared genetic material (condition 1) that reveal a common ancestry persisting in the present. They could both be considered part of the same "genetic series"; their shared properties reflect the "necessary connection" between the members of that series.

Their short stature, stocky build, gender, and age combine (by the second condition of existence) to produce equivalent integral structures that produce the same movement patterns. Complying with the third condition of existence, their morphological proportions reflect the same gravitational constraints on their growth pattern; as for the fourth condition, in a given ecosystem, only one of two similar species will occupy a particular niche. Kangaroo rats and jerboas that look alike do not live side by side in the same neighborhood. In human social organizations only one person typically occupies the niche of governor of a state and cognitive systems may be tuned to this type of exclusivity constraint. Thus, participant observers may confuse similar but different organisms that appear in the same place.

In short, the equivalence of Tom Dewey and my father is not simply a matter of perceived similarity that can be attributed to subjectively chosen common

---

[3]A niche is a slot in an ecosystem with purchase on particular resources.

features; their similarity is a matter of lawful physical, ecological, and genetic relationships that necessarily produce such similarity. Thus, "mistaken identity" may not be a matter of cognitive bias due to internal schemas (Bartlett, 1932; Taylor & Crocker, 1981); it may be based on perception of certain persistent properties connected across time and space by the constraints of the conditions of existence—gravitational constraints on structural properties, structural constraints on how "parts" can combine, constraints on possible "parts" due to shared genetic heritage, and constraints on possible niches in a shared ecosystem. The cognitive benefit is that identity and equivalence classes are efficiently and simultaneously specified in the same pattern (as we see in the section on flow patterns).

Yet there are compelling reasons why cognitive theories often are based on assumptions requiring mental mediation. Schematic processing, for example, can account for the subjective variability in different people's perception of the same event; it can also account for the fact that, on occasion, people seem to see illusions that are not accurate, have hallucinations of things that are not there, and jump to the wrong cognitive conclusions (Ben-Zeev, 1984).

THE QUESTION OF MENTAL MEDIATION

Theories come and go, the frog remains.

—Rostand

The concept of mental mediators such as schemas has impressive origins. In 1739, when David Hume published the first section of his "Treatise on Human Nature," he brought the British Empiricist philosophy of John Locke and Bishop Berkeley to its inevitable conclusion: Knowledge acquired through induction from empirical experience must pass through our senses and therefore is not necessarily reliable. It may not specify the world as it is. Such skepticism undermined the belief in knowable causes and consequently in scientific evidence. In a heroic attempt to refute Hume (although he agreed with him about the impoverished nature of immediate experience) and save science (especially the timeless universe of Newtonian mechanics), Immanuel Kant endowed the human mind with ordering properties—innate intuitions of space and time and a dozen categories of the understanding; he proposed that such internal mechanisms operated to schematize intrinsically incomprehensible raw experience into organized and meaningful phenomena—"We are constrained a priori to perceive objects of empirical intuition according to the laws of geometry: Empirical intuition is possible only by means of the pure intuition of space and of time" (Kant, 1781, p. 206).

Kant's reliance on mental mediation has several more recent versions: (a) The empirical world appears to us as a "buzzing, blooming confusion" that requires cognitive filtering, translation, or coding (Anderson, 1975; Lindsay & Norman, 1977), (b) the empirical world appears as an infinite number of unique and diverse items that requires reduction to generic categories (Smith & Medin, 1981), (c) the empirical world appears partially organized but because much of it is hidden inside other things or in the past, it requires augmentation from mental sources (Neisser, in press). Theories with both an empiricist and a Kantian heritage consider empirical information either unstructured, overwhelming, or hidden thus requiring some form of organization or extension by the mind. Kant (along with several contemporary theorists) does not explain how, if immediate experience is incomprehensible, we might choose what to schematize; even if we might in some way know what to choose, why we should schematize or organize our choices as we do and not otherwise (Russell, 1945)?

Kant's assumption that information specific to the objects and events of the world is intrinsically unknowable (and therefore must be made assimilable by mental processes) founders on the fact that it is hard to know a world that is unknowable; his explanation implies either that we invent the world, which gives no assurance of accuracy, or that the world is in some way built in, which makes it difficult to know new things or things that change. From a Kantian view we are detached observers (rather than participants) whose contact with the world comes primarily through our minds.

One way around these restrictions is to assume that information is available to us in a form that is both *specific* to the items at hand and *comprehensible* to us as it is (rather than that it is not). If we evolved with the world around us, it seems reasonable to assume that our cognitive system evolved in coordination with that world (rather than detached from it). From this view, we should be tuned to perceive the structural forms of the world in which we live. The one requirement is that we pay attention to the world around us. But the catch is, and Kant understood this when he introduced the intuitions of time and space, that objects and events may be extended in space and time in ways beyond our perceptual range or even the span of our lives. The question then becomes how do people whose cognitive transactions with their world appear to have temporal and spatial limitations (they cannot see around corners or backwards into history) overcome these restrictions? How do we know "here goes with there" (Tom Dewey's front and back), "then goes with now" (Tom Dewey in 1910 and again in 1948)? How do we know "here coheres with there" (Tom's hair and moustache) and "here (my father) is equivalent to there" (Tom Dewey) without the mental mediation of abstraction, comparison, and construction? Classical answers to such dilemmas are typically cast in a Kantian mold.

The Gestalt psychologists suggest that our brain organization's natural preference for "good form" accounts for understanding the relationship between here and there (Koffka, 1935; Wertheimer, 1923/1938). Gestalt theorists do not explain why the brain should be so organized. Theories about natural categories suggest that the world has a "correlational structure" wherein "information-rich bundles of perceptual and functional attributes occur that form natural category discontinuities" (Rosch, 1978, p. 31). Categorization theorists do not indicate how these attributes come to be bundled or correlated; their explanation implies that our knowledge depends on our perception of particular attributes (those with high cue validity) that by their particularity require some form of further organization (Barsalou, 1984; Reed, 1972; Rosch, 1978; Rosch, & Mervis, 1975; Rosch, Mervis, Gray, Johnson, & Boyes-Braem, 1976). Models of memory and pattern recognition based on mental comparisons of various versions of then and now (templates, schemas, scripts) also attribute the order perceived in the world primarily to mental processes (Foster, 1984; Neisser, 1967, 1976, in press; Reed, 1978; Shank & Abelson, 1977).

It is unclear how these mental mechanisms might deliver on their promises to (a) aggregate separate features into integral wholes (association theories and networks beg the question) (b) compare present aggregations to past ones (what features of these aggregations are compared?), (c) augment present perceptions with past knowledge (on what basis is past knowledge selected?), (d) specify when one aggregation ends and another begins (impute meaning), or (e) even select when the past ends and the present begins (Capek, 1971; Gibson, 1966) without taking leaps of faith. As long as we explain cognition as relying on internal schemas, we must cope with unsolved puzzles: How can impoverished input be turned into meaningful and practical representations of that input? How can a world under constant transformation and change be represented by cognitive structures whose a priori nature can only be adjusted in saltatory leaps from static state to static state (but see Neisser, in press)?

Russell (1945) questioned Kant and his followers by pointing out that if we come to know the world by projecting schemes such as an internal temporal order on a timeless universe, it is odd that we typically do so in ways that appear congruent with the properties of that universe. Given the capable way people function in their everyday lives, it would seem that the world itself must have some influence on our knowledge of it. For example, Russell asks why we consistently perceive phenomena such as lightning before phenomena such as thunder? Might there not be actual properties inherent in the sequence of lightning and thunder that do not originate in the sequencing capacities of our minds yet are knowable to us? As it turns out, there are. Lightning involves electric current surges that heat the surrounding air and produce a local climate of heat and pressure. Gases are produced that expand as a shock wave that travels a bit and then decays into the acoustic wave we hear as thunder. Clearly, lightning is thunder's source and thus its temporal predessor. But the properties of the lightning pattern *persist* and can be perceived in the complex waveform of the subsequent thunder signature (Few, 1975).

Because the lightning pattern is the source of the thunder pattern and continues to persist in the thunder pattern, lightning and thunder are clearly parts of one event. Even though the lightning itself is no longer visible, the information that specifies it continues to exist. *Information does not disappear into history or memory; it persists as long as the event it specifies continues.* The information that specifies the lightning/thunder event has three properties: First, it persists over the event's duration; second, it is invariant across the event's spatial and temporal period; and third, it is invariant or amodal across receptor systems (auditory and visual) and thus cannot be reduced to receptor-specific sensations. A key point is that the information that specifies the lightning is neither a point by point duplication or an abstract representation. It is a geometric summary (similar to the one that specifies swimming kicks) that includes all the attributes and relationships of the lightning/thunder event in one integral pattern. Knowing lightning by perceiving the information that specifies it in the thunder signature contrasts with the notion that people construct generic conceptualizations through a process of abstraction and reduction and then store those concepts in memory.

FLOW EVENTS AS SUMMARY PATTERNS

> *You must express and visualize a pattern as a kind of fluid image, a morphological feeling, a swirling intuition about form, which captures the invariant field which is the pattern.*
> —Christopher Alexander

Perhaps more light can be shed on this idea by considering the informative properties of "flow events." Flow events characterize the necessary transformations of all material structures (people, trees, mountains, rivers, lightning) that develop to conform to the everyday stresses inherent in the compression, tension, and shear of our gravitational atmosphere (Shuring, 1978; Williams, 1978).

Over time, everything flows under the relentless pull of gravity—tree trunks twist under torque[4] the Appenine strata undulate across Switzerland, glacial moraines meander down arctic valleys, growing bones remodel along the wave-like paths of electromagnetic fields, and after-dinner walkers move in angular oscillations leaving sinusoidal trails (see Fig. I.3). The characteristic specifications of flow events are variations on the meander and spiral patterns that are the path of kinetic energy (Grillo, 1960; Inman, Ralston, & Todd, 1981; Stevens, 1976). Quine (1973) states:

> Thus we might seek a . . . root notion of causality in terms of the flow of energy . . . this thermodynamical image requires us to picture energy, like matter, as

---

[4]Spiral growth in trees increases resistence to mechanical stress because such growth resists compression and stretching more than linear growth. Even with this basic law of form individual identity is preserved. Horse chestnuts spiral to the right and poplars spiral to the left (Gordon, 1978).

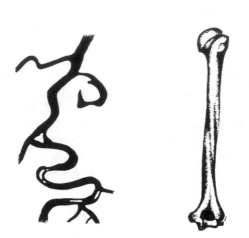

FIG. I.3. The similar flow patterns of mountain strata, a Mississippi river backwater, and a growing human humerus, from Theodor Schwenk, (1960), Sensitive Chaos, Stuttgart: Germany Verlag Freies Geistesleben, pp. 18, 24, 42. Reprinted with permission of the publisher.

traceable from point to point through time. Thus let us picture an event simply as any fragment of space–time, or the material and energetic content thereof. Given an event e, then imagine all its energy traced backward through time. Any earlier event that intercepts all of these energetic world lines qualifies as a cause of e.

The most noticeable flow patterns involve liquid events—the movement of water around boat hulls, twisting out of water hoses, oscillating between river banks, or spiraling down the bathtub drain. "The striking geometric regularity of a winding river is no accident. Meanders appear to be the form in which a river does the least work in turning; hence they are the most probable form a river can take" (Leopold & Langbein, 1966, p. 30). The defining (and measurable) attributes of most liquid flow events—viscosity, inertial force, size, and speed— disappear into the total pattern of flow. Yet, these criterial attributes continue to persist; their nonvisible but individual participation in the pattern as a whole allows us to distinguish one flow event from another (by their contributions to the degree of turbulence), predict what each event means (how much drag it specifies), and how it might affect other things (the waves that form its wake).

Even more important, *equivalent* flow events can be produced with *different* criterial attributes. For example, the flow pattern of honey flowing around a small obstacle can be duplicated by substituting wine flowing around a large one.

Thus, you can produce equivalence of both structure (pattern) and function (flow) with different "criterial" attributes. Such similarity cannot also be a function of the abstraction and construction processes subserving schemas that use the same criterial attributes. How we might "abstract" integrated attributes from such perceivable flow patterns, or why we would need to "construct" schemas to represent them, is not clear. The flow patterns specify all the pertinent information about both the whole event and its parts without presenting the parts as separate (or abstractable). This does not mean that in other flow events attributes cannot be discerned. They can, as we shall now see.

What is important is in this example is that perceiving and abstracting separate attributes is unnecessary to acquiring and using flow pattern information. And over time, everything flows. In cases where different attributes can be distinguished, it is still unnecessary to consider them separately. The flow event is itself comprehensively specific. Consider, for example, the flow event of human locomotion; its separate attributes, such as stride length and step frequency, can be distinguished from one another but such distinctions are unnecessary because those attributes combine to form an integrated pattern that provides comprehensive and specific information for any number of properties.

The Summary Flow Pattern for Human Walking

In forward locomotion, a person's center of mass (the belly button area around which the whole body rotates) describes a smooth sinusoidal curve (both vertically and laterally) that depends on coordinated angular displacements of the various limb segments as they rotate about their joints. The rotation flattens the arc of the center of mass by elevating its ends (and producing the continuous sinusoidal pattern), which in turn reduces ground impact and requires less energy to proceed forward (Inman et al., 1981).

Although the human body is like a linked lever system and each of its segments are discernable, each segment's specific motions combine to form the sinusoidal pattern that specifies the bipedal forward stride (see Fig. I.4). From the frontal plane this pattern with its vertical and lateral displacements produces a pattern resembling a figure eight (see Fig. I.5) (Inman et al., 1981).

The Perception of Natural Categories from the Pattern of Flow

Each person's unique body proportions produces a different variation of the figure eight pattern. Because the pattern systematically varies from person to person, it can specify identity (Broer & Zernicke, 1979; Inman et al., 1981). The figure eight pattern is also gender-and age-specific because it oscillates around a person's center of mass that is higher on the average in men then in women and in adults then in children [Related research indicates that people perceive both

FIG. I.4.   Sinusoidal patterns produced by oscillations of the joints around the center of mass in the sagittal plane, from Sven Carlsoo, How Man Moves, London: England, Heinemann, p. 96. Reprinted with permission of Swedish Management Group, Lindingo, Sweden.

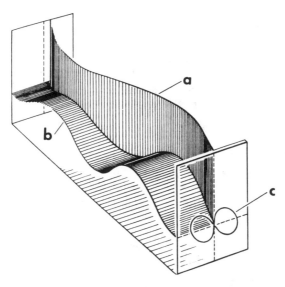

FIG. I.5.   Production of the figure eight pattern by displacements of center of mass in three planes of space during a single stride: (a) lateral displacement, (b) vertical displacement, (c) a and b combined displacements onto the plane perpendicular to the plane of progression, from Verne T. Inman, Henry J. Ralston, & Frank Todd, (1983) Human Walking, Baltimore: Maryland, Williams & Wilkins, p. 4. Reprinted with permission from the publisher.

identity and gender from the dynamic patterns of point–light displays (Barclay, Cutting, & Kozlowski, 1978; Cutting & Kozlowski, 1977; Frykholm, 1983; Runeson & Frykholm, Chapter 13)]. The figure eight also varies with speed, intention, and mood (all of which are also perceivable from point–light displays; Inman et al., 1981; Runeson & Frykholm, 1981).

From a simple oscillating pattern produced by the motion of human walking and etched out in a space–time manifold, we can perceive nested information that specifies (a) the human species (the figure eight is specific to the bipedal, upright stride characteristic of human beings), (b) individual identity (it summarizes each person's unique morphological proportions), (c) gender (it summarizes gender-specific proportions, (d) age (it reveals age specific proportions), (e) intention, mood, and activity (from the pattern of the action displayed).

The flow pattern for human locomotion was first recorded in 1890, by the French physiologist Marey. He photographed a light placed at the base of a man's spine as he moved away from the camera. Marey described the pattern he recorded as both particular and generic ''a luminous trail, an image without end, at once manifold and individual'' (Gideon, 1948, p. 24). Marey concluded from this work and other motion recordings such as the flight of birds that the patterns produced by moving events could be considered the ''language of phenomena'' (Gideon, 1942, p. 20).

The Language of Phenomena

In line with Marey's insight, I suggest that the dynamic patterns that are produced by and specify both fast and slow events are the ''language'' by which we know such phenomena. This gives us an incarnate, specific, and efficient alternative to the mediated information of information processing, the matched patterns of pattern recognition, and the traditional schemas, categories, and concepts of cognition.

For example, schemas need not be considered constructions of abstracted attributes that reduce and represent phenomena. Schemas could be incarnate summary patterns of persistence and change that specify events as integral wholes. Such patterns would not ''annihilate the particularity'' of phenomena (Cassirer, 1953) (see Chapter 5), or subject observers to the cognitive overload or mental chaos assumed to accompany an unreduced and unconstructed world of unique diversity (Smith & Medin, 1981). They would have the advantage of the world's natural redundancy and could specify many diverse things with variations on a few basic forms such as meanders and spirals. Flow patterns also avoid the dilemmas inherent in the ''holistic'' patterns of template theories (Reed, 1978). Templates both require some form of pattern matching (Neisser, 1967) and offer little in return except their obvious contours. In contrast, flow patterns not only specify integral events, they can also be analyzed at the level of their contributing attributes or dimensions. From this view, *cognition is the process of detecting and selecting the flowing specifications of events, those specifications that persist and those that change.*

SUMMARY

In the present chapter, I suggest that the priority unit for cognition (whether it refers to objects, organisms, or activities) is the event as it occurs over space and time (rather than a schematic representation); second, I suggest that the information that specifies such events is perceptible as dynamic geometric patterns that persist over the duration of the event; these patterns are produced by the conditions of existence that structure the world around us and follow the natural laws of form (rather than a set of criterial features); third, I suggest that this type of information is incarnate and comprehensive rather than constructed and abstract, thus isomorphic to whatever entity it specifies. Fourth, I suggest that we can perceive these patterns without mediation because our cognitive system has evolved under the same lawful conditions and is adapted to do so.

The chapter proceeds from a comparison of similarity within a particular event (identity) and between equivalent events (generic classes) to a review of the physical, biological, and ecological *conditions of existence* that constrain the forms that underlie all similarity. Next, I discuss the issue of schemas and mental mediation and contrast this theoretical perspective with several examples of incarnate patterns that specify the ongoing events of lightning and thunder, flowing rivers, and walking people. I then outline how the information for several natural categories (identity, gender, age, intention, and mood) is perceivable directly from the summary pattern produced by the dynamic event of human walking. In the last section I briefly describe how each of the following chapters exemplifies event cognition.

PREVIEWS

The first five chapters discuss universals, schemas, formal generators, symbols, and concepts. Chapter 1 describes *universals* as incarnate specifications for events (rather than as abstract mental forms) that are perceivable as patterns of geometric proportions. Chapter 2 takes cognition to be the interface between perception and action and sees *schemas* as the mechanisms that modulate this relationship over the span of the event at hand. Chapter 3 addresses the question of information overload by showing how a limited number of *generator* patterns produce the specifications for a whole event. Chapter 4 suggests that *symbols* are the mechanisms through which communicative events occur in organism/environment relationships and shows that people behave similarly toward symbols and stimuli. Chapter 5 critiques the concept of *concept* and indicates how concepts as epistemic entities are better characterized as events.

Chapters 6 and 7 describe *pictorial events*. Chapter 6 expands on the subject introduced in Chapter 3 and addresses how we perceive pictures of an event by using generators. Chapter 7 describes how we modulate an action event (walking a path) differently if we participate actively or observe passively. Chapters 8 and 9 are about *language events*. Chapter 8 relates language to action by describing research on the gestural patterns of American Sign. Chapter 9 shows how memory for language, like perception, is transparent to the real world and is modulated by significance more than mere typicality. Chapters 10 and 11 discuss *musical events*. Chapter 10 describes the similarities between musical events and events in general and Chapter 11 describes how musical events are unique. Chapters 12 and 13 are about *social events*. Chapter 12 shows how the perception of infantile specifications supports decisions about protecting primate infants and Chapter 13 shows how information available from moving point–light displays specifies gender and deceptive intention. An Epilogue concludes this volume on a more sober note. It addresses the relationship between *cognition* and *ethics* and suggests that the cognitive mechanisms we often use to know our world are rooted in unexamined theoretical assumptions that have ethical consequences.

Each section is introduced by tracing the lineage of the ideas presented to some of their historical origins in psychology. It is our way of paying our respect to some (there are many more) of the creative people who contributed to what is now called the ecological view, James J. Gibson, Kurt Koffka, Jacob von Uexkull, Karl Lashley, Gunnar Johannson, Ernst Cassirer, and more recently John Bransford and Jeffery Franks.

REFERENCES

Anderson, B. F. (1975). *Cognitive psychology,* New York: Academic Press.

Barclay, C. D., Cutting, J. E., & Kozlowski, L. T. (1978). Temporal and spatial factors in gait perception that influence gender recognition. *Perception and Psychophysics, 23,* 145–152.

Barsalou, L. W. (1984). Determinants of graded structure in categories. *Emory Cognition Project* (Report No. 4).

Bartlett, F. A. (1932). *Remembering,* Cambridge, England: Cambridge University Press.

Bem, S. L. (1981). Gender schema theory: A cognitive account of sex typing. *Psychological Review, 88,* 354–364.

Ben-Zeev, A. (1984). What is a perceptual mistake? *Journal of Mind and Behavior, 5,* 261–278.

Bertenthal, B. I., & Proffitt, D. R. (1984). Infant sensitivity to figural coherence in biomechanical motions. *Journal of Experimental Child Psychology, 37,* 213–230.

Broer, M. R., & Zernicke, R. F. (1979). *Efficiency of human movement.* Philadelphia: Saunders.

Bruner, J. S., Goodnow, J. J., & Austin, G. A. (1962). *A study of thinking.* New York: Basic Books.

Campbell, B. (1985). *Human evolution*. New York: Aldine.

Capek, M. (1971). The fiction of instants. *Studium Generale 24*, 31–43.

Carey, S. (1983). Constraints on word meaning. In B. Seiler & W. Wannenmacher (Eds.), *Concept development and the development of word meaning* (126–143). New York: Springer–Verlag.

Cassirer, E. (1953). *Substance and function*, New York: Dover.

Cutting, J. E., & Kozlowski, L. T. (1977). Recognizing friends by their walk: Gait perception without familiarity cues. *Bulletin of the Psychonomic Society, 9*, 353–356.

Cutting, J. E., Proffitt, D. R., & Kozlowski, L. T. (1978). A biomechanical invariant for gait perception. *Journal of Experimental Psychology: Human Perception and Performance, 4*, 357–372.

Cuvier, G. L. (1812). *Recherches sur les ossemens fossiles* (p. 60) (quoted in E. S. Russell, 1916/1982, *Form and function*). Chicago: University of Chicago Press.

Cuvier, G. L. (1817). *Le regne animal* (quoted in E. S. Russell, 1916–1982, *Form and function*. Chicago: University of Chicago press.

Darwin, C. (1859). *The origin of species*. London: John Murray.

Du Brul, L. E. (1969). Design for living. In D. Bootzin & H. C. Muffley (Eds.), *Biomechanics* (pp. 5–13). New York: Plenum.

Few, A. A. (1975). Thunder. In *The physics of every day phenomena: Readings from Scientific American* (pp. 39–49). San Francisco: W. H. Freeman.

Foster, D. H. (1984). Local and global computational factors in visual pattern recognition. In P. C. Dodwell & T. Caelli (Eds.), *Figural synthesis* (pp. 83–115) Hillsdale, NJ: Lawrence Erlbaum Associates.

Frykholm, G. (1983). *Action, intention, gender, and identity, perceived from body movement*. Uppsala, Sweden: Uppsala Universitet.

Futuymo, D. J., & Slatkin, M. (1983). *Coevolution*. Sunderland, MA: Sinauer Associates.

Ghiselin, M. T. (1981). Categories, life, and thinking. *The Behavioral and Brain Sciences 4*, 269–311.

Gibson, E. J., Owsley, C. J., & Johnston, J. (1978). Perception of invariants by five month old infants: Two different kinds of motion. *Developmental Psychology, 14*, 407–415.

Gibson, J. J. (1966). The problem of temporal order in stimulation and perception. *The Journal of Psychology, 62*, 141–149.

Gibson, J. J. (1975). Events are perceivable but time is not. In J. T. Fraser & N. Lawrence (Eds.), *The study of time* (295–301). New York: Springer–Verlag.

Gibson, J. J. (1979). *The ecological approach to visual perception*. Boston: Houghton–Mifflin.

Gideon, S. (1948). *Mechanization takes command*. New York: Oxford University Press.

Gordon, L. (1978). *Structures: Or why things don't fall down*. London: Dacapo.

Grillo, P. J. (1960). *Form, function, and design*. New York: Dover.

Hildebrandt, M. (1982). *Analysis of vertebrate structure*. New York: Wiley.

Hume, D. (1748/1936). *An enquiry concerning the human understanding and an enquiry concerning the principle of morals*. (Edited by L. A. Selby-Bigge). Oxford: The Clarendon Press.

Inman, V. T., Ralston, H. J., & Todd, F. (1981). *Human walking*. Baltimore: Williams & Wilkins.

Jacob, F. (1982). *The possible and the actual*. New York: Pantheon.

Johansson, G. (1964). Perception of motion and changing form. *Scandinavian Journal of Psychology, 5*, 181–208.

Johansson, G. (1973). Visual perception of biological motion and a model for its analysis. *Perception and Psychophysics, 14*, 201–211.

Kant, I. (1781/1966). *The critique of pure reason* (2nd ed., F. Max Muller, Trans.). New York: Anchor Books.

Keil, F. C. (1981). Constraints on knowledge and conceptual development *Psychological Review, 88*, 197–227.

Keil, F. C. (1983). Semantic inferences and the acquisition of word meaning. In B. Seiler & W. Wannenmacher (Eds.), *Concept development and the development of word meaning* (pp. 103–124) New York: Springer–Verlag.

Koffka, K. (1935). *Principles of Gestalt psychology.* New York: Harcourt, Brace, & World.

Krogman, W. M. (1972). *Child growth.* Ann Arbor: University of Michigan Press.

Kummer, B. K. F. (1972). Biomechanics of bone: Mechanical properties, functional structure, functional adaptation. In Y. C. Fung, N. Perrone, & M. Anliker (Eds.), *Biomechanics* (pp. 237–252). Englewood Cliffs, NJ: Prentice–Hall.

Lappin, J. S., Doner, J. F., & Kottas, B. L. (1980). Minimal conditions for the perception of structure and motion in three dimensions. *Science, 209,* 717–719.

Lindsay, P. H., & Norman, D. A. (1977). *Human information processing.* New York: Academic Press.

Leopold, L. B., & Langbein, W. B., River meanders. (1966/1979). In *The physics of everyday life, readings from Scientific American* (pp. 28–38), San Francisco: W. H. Freeman.

Luria, S. E., Gould, S. J., & Singer, S. (1981). *A view of life.* Menlo Park, CA: Benjamin/Cummings.

Mace, W. M., & Shaw, R. E. (1974). Simple kinetic information for transparent depth. *Perception and Psychophysics, 15,* 201–209.

Mark, L. S., Todd, J. T., & Shaw, R. E. (1981). The perception of growth: How different styles of change are distinguished. *Journal of Experimental Psychology: Human Perception and Performance, 7,* 355–368.

McCabe, V. (1984). A comparison of three ways of knowing: Categorical, structural, and affirmative. *Journal of Mind and Behavior, 5,* 433–448.

Neisser, U. (1967). *Cognitive psychology.* New York: Appleton-Century-Crofts.

Neisser, U. (1976). *Cognition and reality.* San Francisco: W. H. Freeman.

Neisser, U. (in press). From direct perception to conceptual structure. In U. Neisser (Ed.), *Concepts reconsidered: The ecological and intellectual basis of categorization.* New York: Cambridge University Press.

Pantin, C. F. A. (1969). Organism and environment. In M. Grene (Ed.), *The anatomy of knowledge.* (pp. 103–118) Amherst: University of Massachusetts Press.

Pittenger, J. B., Shaw, R. E., & Mark, L. S. (1979). Perceptual information for the age-level of faces as a higher order invariant for growth. *Journal of Experimental Psychology: Human Perception and Performance, 5,* 478–493.

Quine, W. V. (1973). *The roots of reference.* La Salle, IL: Open Court.

Reed, S. K. (1972). Pattern recognition and categorization. *Cognitive Psychology, 3,* 382–487.

Reed, S. K. (1978). Schemes and theories of pattern recognition. In E. C. Carterette & M. P. Friedman (Eds.), *Handbook of perception* (Vol. IX, pp. 137–162) New York: Academic Press.

Riddock, G. (1917). Dissociation of visual perception due to occipital injury with special reference to the appreciation of movement. *Brain, 40,* 15–57.

Rosch, E. (1978). Principles of categorization. In E. Rosch & B. B. Lloyd (Eds.), *Cognition and categorization* (pp. 27–48). Hillsdale, NJ: Lawrence Erlbaum Associates.

Rosch, E., & Mervis, C. B. (1975). Family resemblences: Studies in the internal structure of categories. *Cognitive Psychology, 7,* 573–605.

Rosch, E., Mervis, C. B., Gray, W. D., Johnston, D. M., & Boyes-Braem, P. (1976). Basic objects in natural categories. *Cognitive Psychology, 8,* 382–439.

Runeson, S., & Frykholm, G. (1981). Visual perception of lifted weight. *Journal of Experimental Psychology: Human Perception and Performance, 7,* 733–740.

Runeson, S., & Frykholm, G.Ven(1982). *Kinematic specification of dynamics as an informational basis for person and action perception: Expectation gender recognition, and deceptive intention.* Sweden: University of Uppsala Psychological Reports (no. 324).

Russell, B. (1945). *A history of western philosophy.* New York: Simon & Shuster.

Russell, E. S. (1916/1982). *Form and function.* Chicago: University of Chicago Press.

Saha, S., & Lakes, R. S. (1979). A new non-invasive device for monitoring the pizoelectric character of bone. In C. T. Brighton, J. Black, & S. R. Pollack (Eds.), *Electric properties of bone and cartilage.* Philadelphia: Grune & Stratton.

Sekuler, R. (1975). Visual motion perception. In E. C. Carterette & M. P. Friedman (Eds.), *Seeing: Handbook of perception* (Vol. V). New York: Academic Press.

Shank, R., & Abelson, R. (1977). *Scripts, plans, goals, and understanding.* Hillsdale, NJ: Lawrence Erlbaum Associates.

Shaw, R. E., & Pittenger, J. (1977). On perceiving change. In H. Pick & E. Saltzman (Eds.), *Modes of perceiving and processing information.* Hillsdale, NJ: Lawrence Erlbaum Associates.

Shepard, R. (1984). Ecological constraints on internal representation: Resonant kinematics of perceiving, imagining, thinking, and dreaming. *Psychological Review, 91,* 417–447.

Shuring, D. J. (1978). *Scale models in engineering.* New York: Pergamon Press.

Smith, E. E., & Medin, D. L. (1981). *Categories and concepts.* Cambridge, MA: Harvard University Press.

Stevens, P. (1976). *Patterns in nature.* Boston: Little, Brown.

Taylor, S. L., & Crocker, J. (1981). Schematic basis of social information processing. In E. T. Higgins, C. P. Herman, & M. P. Zanna (Eds.), *The Ontario symposium on personality and social psychology* (Vol. I). Hillsdale, NJ: Lawrence Erlbaum Associates.

Thompson, D. A. (1917/1962). *On growth and form.* London: Cambridge University Press.

Todd, J. T., & Mark, L. C. (1981). Issues related to the prediction of craniofacial growth. *American Journal of Orthodontics, 79,* 63–80.

Warren, W. H., & Shaw, R. E. (1985). Events and encounter as units of analysis for ecological psychology. In W. H. Warren & R. E. Shaw, (Eds.), *Persistence and change: Proceedings of the first international conference on event perception.* Hillsdale, NJ: Lawrence Erlbaum Associates.

Werthheimer, M. (1923/1938). Principles of perceptual organization. Reprinted in W. D. Ellis (Ed.), *Sourcebook of Gestalt psychology.* London: Harcourt, Brace.

Williams, C. (1981). *Origins of form.* New York: Architectural Book.

Wittgenstein, L. (1953). *Philosophical investigations* New York: Macmillan.

II ORDER IN BEHAVIOR AND EVENTS

Received doctrine characterizes real-world phenomena as aggregates of combinable parts, perception as the process whereby people internalize these parts, and cognition as the method by which the parts are constructed into meaningful representations. People are thought, for example, to manipulate bundles of features or dimensions and then match a concatenated aggregate to a prior, mentally constructed generic schema or concept. How such mental constructions work and what criteria are used to select the appropriate combinations of parts remains obscure (see Introduction and chapter 5, this volume). Cognitive theories tend to bypass the actual structural order in the world and, with little explanation, assign the generation of order to mental processes.

In general, problems of order in psychology have been neglected in two related ways: on the one hand by the tendencies of those interested in perception to entertain static models, and on the other by the tendencies of those interested in learning and thinking to entertain models treating temporal order as an instance of mere succession or concatenation of responses. For K. S. Lashley, it was the latter set of issues that was of primary concern. In his classic paper on serial order in behavior, Lashley (1951) suggested that faith in reductive and associationistic accounts of temporal order was misplaced. Lashley observed that such accounts were devised under the assumption of a quiescent system excited by an input, and that if this assumption were false, the whole edifice of associationistic theory might crumble with it. For if the system is always in a (variable) state of excitation, any given pattern of input will always be arriving in an essentially novel context. "Context sensitivity" is the bane of all associationistic models. But, Lashley argued, context sensitivity in this sense is intrinsic not only to the physiological functioning of the nervous system, but also to the structure of virtually all coordinated actions, from leg movements in insects to speech in humans.

Whenever a relatively small number of basic movements—more generally, elements—can be organized or ordered in flexible yet constrained ways, associative models are generally mute on both the flexibility and the constraint. If different temporal permutations of elements can occur, but not every possible permutation, the order(s) must arise from some source other than direct associative connection, which would provide no basis for selecting one ordering over another. Nor are things so different today that we avoid these problems despite the sophistication of modern cognitive theories. Whenever we account for a serially ordered behavior with a computer program, we are still begging all questions of how the temporal organization might arise—the origin of the "program"—or why it should take one form rather than another. This style of explanation accounts for the ordering of actions by the ordering of program steps, a level at which it has again become a "mere succession." Those who would employ programs as theories are thus just as vulnerable to Lashley's critique as their associationistic predecessors.

An alternative source for the generation of order lies in the intrinsic coordinative properties of the phenomena to be explained. To give these any serious consideration, as Gunnar Johansson has said, we can no longer seriously entertain static models of perception. Let us consider one of Johansson's classic demonstrations. If a stationary man with reflectant tape wrapped around his joints is videotaped with bright lights shining on him and presented on a monitor with the contrast turned all the way up and the brightness turned nearly all the way down, an observer sees what looks like a random array of light points on a dark background. Let the man begin to walk, however, and the lights begin to move and the observer sees a constantly transforming yet coherent and compelling pattern that reveals a man walking.

At a stroke, this demonstration shows that information specifying the event "man walking" has none of the features we might think of associating when we think of a man (skin, hair) or walking (legs, ground). It is not enough to say that the moving points exhibit "common fate"—strictly speaking, they do not, for the points do not translate at the same speed in the same direction, far from it. It is rather that the points exhibit precisely the style of "common fatehood" that is unique and specific to a sample of points on a walking man, and not a woman or a rolling wheel. The wheel and the woman too can be conveyed by the information in a point-light display; in fact, *two* points in motion are apparently sufficient to specify either event for human perceivers. Johansson and his colleagues, in work pioneered in 1950, have given us point-light demonstrations and experiments on a wide variety of rigid and nonrigid motion events.

Johansson's (1950) demonstrations of human apprehension of generic categories such as "man" or "walking" solely from the intrinsic coordinative properties of a walking man have several implications. The first is that generic classification does not depend on a concatenation of features. The second implication is that event cognition need not depend on the concatenation of static retinal "images." The third implication, one that is particularly germane to this book, is that there may be no limit to how "cognitive" a judgment can be and still have a firm perceptual basis. When such disparate events as the comprehension of language (Chapter 8, this volume) and the perception of gender (Chapter 13, this volume) may be occasioned by the "same" point-light displays that allow us to perceive rolling and bending events, we must pause and ask: How, using just an abstract syntax of points and lights, could we ever distinguish between the "higher" (cognitive) and "lower" (perceptual) categories of events they make available, or the "higher" and "lower" mental processes to which they putatively correspond?

From an ecological view, order is considered embodied in and intrinsic to the phenomena that we come to know in the world. Chapters 1 through 5 offer theoretical variations on the theme of how the order inherent in the world can be characterized and revealed. In Chapter 1 on universals, **McCabe** argues that, contrary to widely-held views, universals are not mental entities through which people identify the objects and events of the world. Rather, universals are manifest in the perceivable embodied structure of those objects and events. From this view, organisms perceive informative relationships that specify an object rather than separable components of an object that must be cognitively assembled.

Chapter 2 redefines the concept of schema. Traditionally, schemas are considered mental isomorphs for the plan or organization of an object or event. From this view, one can pass impoverished percepts through this mental mesh and find suitable schematic matches. **Shaw and Hazelett** offer an alternative conception of schemas as universals perceived interactively in terms of compatibility relationships or affordances that are specific to organism and occasion. The chapter also suggests how perceptions can be schematized over actions to yield internalized knowledge of the environment.

In Chapter 3, **Shaw, Wilson, and Wellman** introduce the principle of generative specification. According to the principle, a limited but essential set of instances of an event may have the capability to specify or *generate* a much larger set, possibly even the entire event. The essential generator set of instances exhibits a principle of connection that both links the presented instances and specifies the remainder.

von Foerster opens Chapter 4 with the familiar suggestion that stimuli are apprehended as a function of organism-environment compatibility relations. In his essay, von Foerster also addresses the differences between the ways stimuli and symbols specify their sources, and how the requirements of communication shape symbols in a manner rather similar to the way the laws of nature constrain the forms of stimulus specification.

In Chapter 5 it is the *concept* that comes under close scrutiny. In their examination of this mainstay of cognitive theory, **Balzano and McCabe** look at both psychological research and philosophical writings on concepts. Certain traditional views of concepts are found to lead to problems in both of these areas of concern. The authors propose an ecological reformulation of the issues that avoids these difficulties.

REFERENCES

Johansson, G. (1950). *Configurations in event perception*. Uppsala: Almqvist & Wiksell.
Lashley, K. S. (1951). The problem of serial order in behavior. In L. A. Jeffress (Ed.), *Cerebral mechanisms in behavior*. New York: Hafner.

1 The Direct Perception of Universals: A Theory of Knowledge Acquisition*

Viki McCabe
University of California, Los Angeles

CONTENTS

When we acquire knowledge, where does it come from and what is its nature? Mutually exclusive theoretical answers to this question are abundant. At one extreme, empirical realists assert that our observations produce raw sense data from which we abstract essential components. Empiricists then propose that we use the process of association to wed these abstracted components so that they sum to a comprehensible object. At the other extreme, rationalist idealists argue that our minds use innately given processes to keep us informed about the world. These ''processes'' yield knowledge such as Plato's ideal forms (Cornford,

---

*Portions of this chapter were previously published in *Synthese, 52*, 1982, 495–513. Copyright © by D. Reidel Publishing Company, Dordrecht, Holland.

1935) and Kant's schemas (1781/1966) that is hypothesized to mirror the structure of real-world things.

Association theory presupposes components as the basic units of knowledge in contrast to schema theory that presupposes systemic structure. Although both the basic unit of knowledge and its source differ for empiricism and rationalism, both views agree that because the person and the world are separate, some form of mental construction (association, innate ideas, schematizing) is crucial for knowledge acquisition. Arguing against the necessity for mental construction, Turvey and Shaw (1979) point out that the belief in an animal/environment dualism gives rise to the notion that when we acquire knowledge, the environment provides the signs (raw material) and the animal provides the significance (meaning). They suggest that it is unclear how animals acquire significance. Further, the possibility for error implicit in the interpretation of "brute matter" by "enlightened mind" makes our survival an admirable feat. There must be a better way to know what is going on.

I propose that we do not use mental mediation to construct perceptual information but apprehend it *directly* from the schematic structure inherent in the objects of our visual, auditory, and tactile experiences. These schemas are composed of essential invariant relationships that specify the systemic rather than the componential properties of objects and events in light of an observer's needs and intentions. Contrary to customary explanations, *we perceive the schemas of the idealists directly from the external world of the realists rather than the components of the realists in the internal world of idealists.*

This is not the common view. Ask someone, for example, how they know a face is a face and they will start listing components such as noses, mouths, and eyes. Is our knowledge of faces a function of salient components that we associate to one another in our minds? Or is it a function of the relationships between those components that are available in the face presented to us? A simple demonstration may answer this question. If you maintain the necessary relational invariance of a face and change its features, it will still be recognized as a face (Fig. 1.1A). If, however, you change the relational invariances and maintain the features, the face collapses into a partially random aggregate (Fig. 1.1B).

In effect, we tend to recognize a face in spite of componential changes such as those that accrue with aging (thinning lips, greying hair) or applications of cosmetics (reshaped lips, dyed hair). To maintain knowledge of a face with changing components we cannot simply sum an aggregate of those components, we need to calibrate the relationships between those components that stay constant over changes. Because these systemic relationships are directly available in the visual display as mathematical ratios (Gibson, 1979), it seems unnecessary to conclude that we abstract and mentally reconstruct them. In short, I am proposing that knowledge acquisition involves the direct perception of an informational structure composed of systemic relationships; this informational structure is isomorphic to the actual invariant structure of whatever entity we are apprehending.

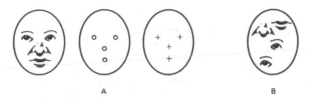

FIG. 1.1. Comparison between changing the components and changing the schema of a face.

Knowledge acquisition is then a matter of calibrating structures rather than associating components. A distinction must be made, however, between simply being aware of something and acquiring knowledge of that thing. It is possible to be conscious of seeing the nose, eyes, and mouth (as in Fig. 1.1B) without acquiring knowledge of a facial structure. It is also possible to acquire a facial structure from any one of the examples in Fig. 1.1A without being conscious of doing so. This point is argued later.

Although many cognitive theorists rely on the necessity of mental constructions, their work is pertinent to this point of view; concepts such as schema (Norman, 1979), structure (Piaget, 1971), script (Shank & Abelson, 1977), frame (Minsky, 1975), and prototype (Rosch, 1978) have a family resemblance. They all depict systemic relationships and address the same classic question; are there universals, and if so, what are they and how can we know them?

THE CONCEPT OF UNIVERSALS

A universal is an invariant across particulars (Russell, 1912). It could be a structural invariant that specifies the necessary relationships for a face to be a face and not something else; or it could be a transformational invariant that specifies the lawfully changing relationships within a face due to age (cranial proportions) or expression (anger, sadness, disdain) (see Chapter 3, this volume). Conceptions such as schema, structure, and plan often refer to universals.

Universals as Relationships not Components

Although universals can take other forms (attributes such as redness or resemblances such as "as big as"), this chapter is concerned with the universal of relationships such as "between" or "in," that specify the structural and transformational invariances of real-world entities. I argue that invariants are equivalent to information and components are equivalent to representation. Components, such as Nixon's nose, can come to stand for him in cartoons because his nose is salient. If, however, we attempted to identify Nixon using only his nose or even all his features lined up in a row, it is doubtful that we would have much success. If we come to know (rather than simply be aware of) Nixon's nose, it would be because we perceived its particular invariant structure, not its status as a facial component.

When we acquire knowledge, we acquire relational invariances. Although it is possible to experience something without apprehending its invariant structure, acquiring knowledge requires acquiring structure. Cassirer (1923/1953) addressed this issue when he said, "It is, as it were, the fundamental principle of cognition that the universal can be perceived only in the particular, while the particular can be thought only in reference to the universal" (p. 86). Components act as placeholders for structure, representational paraphrases if you will, for the many transformations that are possible for any particular real-world thing. For example, a gothic novel remains a gothic novel across different characters or a tree remains a tree even when, in autumn, its leaves fall off. Components, of course, can be structures in their own right. That, however, is a question of the hierarchical nesting of structures rather than the comparison of the informational value of components versus structure.

Cognitive Concepts as Universals

Schemas, scripts, structures, frames, and prototypes can be considered universals because they preserve essential structure. The script for an event such as a wedding remains invariant across changes of brides, grooms, churches, or types of wedding cake. A cognitive structure for seriation is the same whether marbles, pebbles, or numbers are manipulated, and we can distinguish a novel from a play or short story regardless of who wrote it (except perhaps J. Joyce or G. Stein!) or what it says, because its schematic organization remains constant. Mandler, Scribner, Cole, and DeForest (1980) argue that folk tales also have an invariant structure across cultures. By combining data from an American sample (Mandler & Johnson, 1977) with a Liberian population, they showed that folktales are recalled in a similar fashion across literate, illiterate, urban, rural, African, and American subjects.

When invariant structure is violated, people rarely know what is going on. Picasso's cubist paintings are a good example of both the violation of normal structure and the display of metastructure. Picasso realigned the normal invariant structure of the objects he painted by using devices such as transparency and overlap to present simultaneously different perspectives that are normally seen over time. When he eliminated time he increased the complexity and density of the image. This disrupted conventional structure and obscured the structural information that specifies the objects he painted. People often complain that they cannot understand Picasso's paintings. What they are really saying is that they cannot recognize the everyday world in his work. If one learns the new system of invariance he depicted, a new world can be seen, a world of metauniversals that specify not only structural invariance but combinations of transformations possible for that structure over different perspectives. The metauniversal quality of Picasso's work is responsible for its power.

The Uncertain Status of Universals

It was suggested (but not yet argued) that structural relationships may be acquired nonconsciously. This may be why universals have traditionally been shrouded in mystery. Acknowledging their existence, but hard put to locate them, Plato and Kant relegated universals to the soul. According to Arendt (1979), Plato explained his view by proposing that "the soul is invisible because it is made for the cognition of the invisible in a world of visible things" (p. 73) Kant extended this view (Arendt, 1979) by proposing that "This schematization of our intellect is an act concealed in the depths of the human soul whose real modes of activity nature is hardly even likely to allow us to discover, and have open to our gaze" (p. 100). Both philosophers, being idealists, were not able to conceptualize universals as part of the real perceivable world. More important, however, is that they were attempting to characterize the nonconscious aspect of the apprehension of universals.

In general, philosophers could not decide if universals were separate from the particulars they accompanied and if they really existed or were products of the mind. Bertrand Russell (1912) put it this way. "Suppose for instance that I am in my room. I exist and my room exists; but does 'in' exist? (p. 90). Russell asserts that "in" does not exist in the same way as his room and he exist. In contrast to theorists such as Plato and Kant, Russell is not willing to relegate "in" to a product of the soul or of the mind. He points out that if an earwig was in his room, this fact could not be attributed to mental construction because he may or may not know about it (and neither would the earwig). Russell concludes that the universal of relations "must be placed in a world which is neither mental or physical" (p. 90). That may not have been a bad idea. Perhaps our traditional emphasis on mind or matter has obscured some other possibilities. In any case, it may be a contradiction in terms to conclude that a universal is a mental construct. Each person's idiosyncratic experience, heredity, and isolated mental functions mandate against their ability to construct consensual universals. Clearly, to be a universal, relationships such as "in," "between," or "north of" must be invariant across both circumstances and people. In effect, Edinburgh must be north of London and mouths must be below noses on all occasions for everyone. Thus, universals seem to be a property of real-world things in contrast to a property of ideas we may entertain about those things.

Universals as Information

Universals seem to be a better candidate than either sensations or innate processes as providers of reliable information (information is used here to mean organized data as distinct from pure experience that apprehends presentness).

Our innate processes would probably be inadequate when faced with a laser beam, a black hole, or a hula hoop. On the sensate level, we may look at a friend across the room and confidently conclude that the person is Mary Brown. On closer inspection, however, we find that Mary looks different from different perspectives. She also changes her hairstyle daily, wears sunglasses, and is variously tan or pale depending on the season. How can we be sure that this changeable person is Mary? In fact, Mary is constituted of a unique invariant structure, which maintains its proportional ratios over most componential changes. If she loses a limb or becomes pregnant, she is still recognizable because her structurally invariant properties are available under a set of acceptable transformations (Shaw & Pittenger, 1977).

Similarly, a table may appear different to different people and from different perspectives (tables can look like trapezoids when viewed head on), but it is consistently a function of the ratio of the four corner angles that specify its rectangularity (Gibson, 1966). In addition, although no two snowflakes are exactly alike, we know that each one is a snowflake because of its structure (see also Chapter 4, this volume).

Universals as Properties of the Real World

I would like to suggest that if we relax our metaphysical assumptions about the nature of real entities as palpable matter or spiritual mind, and our epistemological assumptions about the contents of knowledge as sensation-based mental constructions or innate processes, it becomes possible to entertain the following proposals: Universals such as relations actually exist and are directly perceivable in the structural invariants that specify the objects and events of the world.

Our habits of thought may obscure this view. Western tradition tends to focus on material objects such as noses and mouths rather than the space between them. Further, the English language can be both ambiguous and inadequate to the task of describing relationships; "to the left of," for example, changes with the direction one is facing, and words such as "north of," "beside," or "between" lack the conceptual salience of nouns such as nose or mouth. (Try thinking about "beside" and compare that experience to thinking about "nose.") Last, we may not be as fully aware of our acquisition of relational knowledge as we are of salient components. Thus, we can mistake the contents of our consciousness (salient components) for the actual information we acquire (structural invariances).

In order to help put these proposals in perspective, I briefly (through exemplar philosophers) review a few pertinent points made by classic philosophical positions on knowledge acquisition. I acknowledge that many finer distinctions can be made, and that the philosophers mentioned may have at some time claimed to hold a somewhat different position.

THEORIES OF KNOWLEDGE

Two dichotomous concepts underlie many theories of knowledge. The first is empiricism/rationalism, which addresses beliefs about the source of knowledge. Empiricists believe that knowledge comes from the world and rationalists believe it comes from the mind. A related dichotomy exists between realism and idealism. Realists believe that the furniture of the world is materially extended in space and idealists believe that it is a function of ideas. The assumption of some form of mental intervention forces each combination of these dichotomous concepts into serious flaws.

Empirical Realism

Philosophers such as Locke (1690/1894) believe that the "where" of our knowledge is the external world and the "what" of our knowledge is our sensate experience. In order to know that a robin is a bird, for example, we must abstract the essential features of the general category of bird from the concrete experience we have of a particular robin; we must then reassemble those features to comply with what we know is a bird. The empirical realist position suffers from at least two unexplained gaps. How do we know what features to abstract if we do not already know what a bird is, and second, how do we assemble individual features (wing, feather, etc.) into an intelligible whole bird?

In contrast, if we do not abstract and reassemble features but rather directly perceive invariant structure, we are perceiving the essential relationships (information) that specify what a bird is. Because our perception is already organized (schematic), there is no need to assemble it.

Empirical Idealism

On the other hand, philosophers such as Hume believe that although knowledge is of the world, we can only experience our own mental states; the "where" and "what" of knowledge coalesce in the contents of the mind (Hume, 1748/1936). Critics of empirical idealism insist that there is an intentional relationship that holds between the knowing subject and the comprehensible object. People actively select what they want to learn. This implies that something more is at work than internal mental states or there would be nothing to seek (Ajdukiewicz, 1973).

J. J. Gibson's (1979) idea of affordance is useful here. An affordance coordinates a species' intentions with the world's "offers" to fill those intentions. In Gibson's terms, for a human, a chair affords sitting so the structural invariance or affordance that we perceive is its form as specified by its "sit-on-ability." Other species would perceive a different structural invariance that matched their particular intentions. Each species perceives that part of any real-world entity that meets its needs. There are many world structures that humans can not perceive such as certain tones dogs can hear or odors rats can smell.

Although we might not be able to perceive or possibly conceive of another species' perceptual experience, it is unwarranted to conclude that their experience is constructed in their heads. If their receptor capacities (not their epistemology) are different from ours, the world should remain constant and each species would simply apprehend a portion (not a translation) of it.

There seems little reason to separate the information that specifies chairs from the real properties of those chairs. If structural invariants can be directly seen, heard, or touched, why should we amalgamate them in our heads from the components of sensation or retrieve them from a storehouse of memory? Spelke (1976) has demonstrated this point. She showed that 4-month-old infants detect informational invariants across modalities. The infants were offered two simultaneous movies to watch. Centered between the two movie screens and directly opposite the infant's midline was a speaker playing the soundtrack from one of the films. Although they had never seen a movie before or heard a soundtrack, the infants spent more time watching the film that matched the soundtrack. Because no specific components were involved, and no prior memories laid down, it must be that the amodal invariants specifying both the visual and auditory stimuli were directly available to the infant. It seems unlikely, as empirical idealism would propose, that the infants experienced solely the contents of their own minds. It seems more likely that the same mathematical properties are available in both types of stimulation and that the infant directly perceives those properties.

Rationalist Idealism

Rationalism asserts that knowledge does not come from the world but from innate mental sources. Rationalist idealists such as Plato believe that the connection to true knowledge is innate and that knowledge takes the form of pure ideas or universal truths, which we "remember" as we mature (Cornford, 1935). Plato believed that the changeable nature of sensate experience disqualified it as a source of real knowledge. Because we navigate in and adapt to a changing environment, and new forms appear daily, critics of rationalist idealism insist that we cannot be limited to innate ideas or our survival would be at peril (Ajdukiewicz, 1973).

The theory offered in this chapter bears some similarity to Plato's in that the "what" of knowledge is invariant forms; it differs in that the "where" of knowledge is not restricted to an otherwordly connection between mathematics and the mind but is directly available in the structures of the world.

The Kantian Synthesis

Kant (1781/1966) attempted to resolve these philosophical differences by proposing that there were indeed real objects—noumena—but we could not know them directly. We could only know phenomena, objects as organized by Kant's hypothesized categories of the mind—time, space, and causality. These categories of the mind had an interesting property. They allowed synthetic a priori judgments. In Kant's terms, these judgments came from innate schemas or universal concepts that matched the world in such a way as to make the judgments true.

In effect, Kant proposed that our minds can schematize a world we cannot perceive. In contrast, I am proposing that we actually perceive the schematic relationships of the world but are typically unaware of doing so. Kant, however, also asserted that we intuit the regularities (universals) of the world using these synthetic a priori capacities. There seems to be a contradiction between Kant's ideas about schematizing and his ideas about intuiting. The first is clearly a mental construction, the second, by definition, is direct unmediated apprehension. Although Kant is commonly considered a constructivist, his ideas on intuition may cross the border into the theory of direct perception (Gibson, 1979).

Phenomenology

Intuition is also asserted in Husserl's phenomenological philosophy. Husserl (1913/1962) proposes that we not only perceive sensately but we have immediate (direct) experience of the essence of things. These essences are neither mental nor physical phenomena but rather the universal in the particular, which we intuit (Wesensschew). Husserl proposes that if we deliberately bracket out the sensate world and also set aside all our preconceived notions of that world (reminiscent of Zen techniques), we can directly intuit the essences of things by contemplating the contents of our consciousness.

Husserl believes that consciousness is intentionally related to the essential structure of the world, which in turn provides the basis for our perception and knowledge of natural phenomena. He asserts that intentionality allows direct awareness of entities as they are (cf. Gibson, 1979). In his terms, however, entities are not mental constructs of physical objects caused by sensations or ideas but rather, the fundamental givens at the core of experience. For Husserl, entities are not constructed by consciousness, they give themselves to consciousness as part of the latter's constitution. Essences, the basic structure of entities, are directly given to intuition, which has the capacity to be directly aware of the universal structures of the world.

In a sense, Husserl is proposing that we have a capacity called intuition that allows us to examine the interaction between our consciousness and the furniture of the world; this capacity leads to awareness of the structural invariances (essences) mirrored in that interaction. Husserl based his theory on the belief that all reality, whether internal or external, was similarly constructed and that a pure consciousness (created by bracketing out sensate experience) has the same ideal structure as the basic structure of the world.

Phenomenology actually comes the closest to the position of this chapter in that the "what" of knowledge is conceptualized as invariant structure and the "where" of knowledge, although seen as located in consciousness, is conceived as an interaction between an observer and the observed.

One last step remains to complete this chapter's theory. I propose that what Plato calls "forms", Husserl calls "essences," Shaw and Gibson call "invariances," and Russell calls "universals" exist independently as the relationships that constitute the essential structure of real-world entities. Although all possible invariants may not be perceptually available to all species, it does not follow that invariants are mental constructs; even though the information available in structural invariants may be isomorphic to the information we seek, it is still independently available in the set of specifications for that object. In other words, information is not abstract and mental or physical and opaque; it is embodied in the invariant relationships that reflect the essential structure of a real-world entity in light of a species' intentions and needs.

INVARIANTS AND DECISIONS PERTINENT TO SURVIVAL

The apprehension of structural and transformational invariants has biological value. For example, flight or fight decisions are predicated on this type of information. Portielje (1921) showed that the European bittern locates and pecks at a predator's head by distinguishing the structural relationship between the predator's head and body. When Portielje first approached the bird, it tried to attack his head. He then obscured his head/body distinction by hunching up his shoulders and covering his head with his coat. The bird accepted his approach. Next he crouched down with his coat still over his head and raised a head-shaped disc above his own covered head in the normal position of a head. The Bittern attacked the disc. Portielje stated in Tinbergen (1961) that "a very schematic imitation of a head on top of a body is sufficient to elicit defense reactions and that any detail in a head, eyes for instance, does not play an important part" (p. 215).

A related study with geese by Tinbergen and Lorenz (reported in Tinbergen, 1961) tested the head/neck relationship as an informational basis for spotting predators. They devised a silhouette of a bird that when sailed overhead facing one way had a short neck and a long tail (predator) but when sailed overhead facing the other way, had a long neck and a short tail (goose). The short-neck version elicited alarm responses from Lorenz's flock of geese but the long-neck version did not. On a more subtle level, systematic postural displays (such as "facing away" or "oblique" postures in Herring gulls) that signify deference, aggression, or invitations to mate appear to be composed of transformational invariants (see pp. 33–54 in Tinbergen, 1972 for excellent pictures).

Tinbergen also compared adult and infant heads as eliciters of parental responses. He concluded that "the ideal baby face must have a small facial part and a large brain part" (p. 222). McCabe (1984) tested this hypothesis and found that the craniofacial complex is indeed implicated in caregiving (see also Chapter 12, this volume). In any case it is the spatial relationships of the head, rather than its features, which are responsible for the response. Also related to these findings are Shaw and Pittenger's studies on head growth reported in Chapter 3, this volume.

These experiments are of special interest here, because it appears they can obtain the same effects with a Volkswagen Beetle as with a human head! It would seem that the transformational invariant necessary to judge growth is content-free, qualifying it as a universal. It is doubtful, however, that subjects could explain how they were making these judgments. The information appears to be processed in some manner that is nonconscious. One possible account for the nonconscious acquisition of relational knowledge is that this type of spatial information is generally processed in the right hemisphere of the brain. The right hemisphere lacks strong verbal skills. Although we can experience the "presentness" of spatial information it may not be possible to keep the knowledge of complex spatial relationships in consciousness without adequate linguistic representation. It is doubtful that the right hemisphere has the linguistic capacities adequate to this task.

A LATERALIZATION HYPOTHESIS

Although highly speculative, it may be that the mystery surrounding universals and the reliance on constructionism in otherwise mutually exclusive epistemological theories can be attributed to the differential functions of the two hemispheres of the brain. The brain's two cortices are organized to process different types of information. The left hemisphere generally contains the language center and is dominant for verbal functions and the right hemisphere appears to be specialized for the complex visuo-spatial information available in patterns such as faces. A growing body of evidence supports this specialization-of-function hypothesis. For example, right-hemisphere lesions are more likely to disrupt spatial functions whereas left-hemisphere lesions are more likely to disrupt language functions (Levy, 1979; Moscovitch, 1979). Further, spatial stimuli presented to the left visual field (with more direct right-hemisphere connections) are processed faster than the same stimuli presented to the right visual field (with more direct left-hemisphere connections). The reverse is true for verbal stimuli (Levy, 1979; Moscovitch, 1979). Evidence also shows visual dominance for spatial problem solving (Scagnelli, 1969). In fact, a good case can be made that visual processes are better integrated within each hemisphere than between the hemispheres (Geshwind, 1965; Myers, 1962; Sperry, 1962) and that the right hemisphere has executive functions over the visual systems of both hemispheres because the right temporal cortex has stronger connections to both left and right striate areas whereas left temporal cortex is strongly connected only to the left striate area (Dorff, Mirsky, & Mishkin, 1965; Kimura, 1963; Milner, 1958). In support of the argument presented here, evidence clearly shows that faces are apprehended better by the right hemisphere than by the left (Benton & van Allen, 1968; Geffen, Bradshaw, & Wallace, 1971; Hecaen, 1962; de Renzi, Faglioni, & Spinnler, 1968; Rizzolati, Umilta, & Berlucchi, 1971). If facial and spatial information is processed in the right hemisphere and there is little linguistic representation available, then the information must cross the corpus callosum to the left hemisphere to be verbally coded and expressed. This compounds the problem of knowing about how we process spatial information. If you examine the structure of our language, it becomes clear that it is far easier to talk about components such as eyes and noses than to describe relationships such as "in front of," "between," or "next to." There are simple salient nouns to represent individual components but more complicated and ambiguous verbal forms to talk about many relationships. It is difficult to maintain consciousness of something that is hard to express. If you have ever struggled to explain what was to the left of something else this needs no further argument. It is proposed that the inadequacies of the English language and/or the verbal choices of the left hemisphere produce misleading representations of spatial information. The relational structure of information is obscured while salient components are emphasized.

A lateralization account of the direct perception of structural invariants sheds light on a number of previously unanswered questions. It explains why we may have focused on components rather than relationships (available language and left-hemisphere dominance for expression) and why Western philosophy has hypothesized mental construction rather than direct perception of information (lack of awareness of right-hemisphere capacities). For Plato and Kant, perhaps it might even specify the location of the soul.

CONCLUDING REMARKS

I have suggested that the partial muteness of the right hemisphere, plus a paucity of good verbal representations of spatial relationships, coupled with a lack of focus on relationships (it was argued that we focus on material components) combine to obscure the nature of our acquisition of knowledge. Further, because our verbal left hemisphere triggers so much thought and talk about the components of the world, we conclude that we are processing information about components rather than relationships.

I propose that our lack of awareness of our right-hemisphere activity has led us to believe that we schematize, summarize, or abstract features from the world using higher mental processes. The human brain can probably do all those things, but in addition, the right hemisphere can apprehend that which we call schematic or universal information in the perceptually available information offered by real-world entities. Because we are not fully conscious of these perceptions, it is easy to see how otherwise widely divergent philosophical positions agree that mental construction rather than direct apprehension is necessary for the perception of universals.

This analysis is speculative and limited. It does not in its present form account for such things as fantasies, complex events occurring over substantial amounts of time, or social phenomena such as conversations, which are mutually constructed between two people. Nor does it account for the perceptual and conceptual distortions that occur when cultural norms conflict with actual circumstances (Allport & Postman, 1949; Bruner, Postman, & Rodriguez, 1951; McCabe, 1980). Nevertheless, I feel that the position taken in this chapter can be extended to include these more complex phenomena. In spite of the added complexity, we would still be apprehending the relationships that specify the structure of events.

REFERENCES

Ajdukiewicz, K. (1973). *Problems and theories of philosophy.* (H. Skolimowski and A. Quinton, Trans.) Cambridge, England: Cambridge University Press.

Allport, G., & Postman, L. J. (1949). The basic psychology of rumour. *Transactions of the New York Academy of Sciences,* Series II, *VIII,* 61–81.

Arendt, H. (1979). *The life of the mind: Vol. I.* Thinking. New York: Harcourt Brace Jovanovich.

Benton, A. L., & Van Allen, M. W. (1968). Impairment in facial recognition in patients with cerebral disease. *Cortex, 4,* 344–358.

Bruner, J. S., Postman, L., & Rodriguez, J. (1951). Expectation and the perception of color. *American Journal of Psychology, 64,* 216–227.

Cassirer, E. (1953). *The philosophy of symbolic forms: Vol. 2. Language.* (R. Manheim, trans.). New Haven: Yale University Press. (Original work published 1923).

Cornford, F. M. (1935). *Plato's theory of knowledge.* London: Kegan Paul.

Dorff, J. E., Mirsky, A. F., & Mishkin, M. (1965). Effects of unilateral temporal lobe removals in man on tachistoiscopic recognition in the left and right visual fields. *Neuropsychologia, 3,* 39–51.

Geffen, G., Bradshaw, J. L., & Wallace, G. (1971). Interhemispheric effects on reaction time to verbal and nonverbal stimuli. *Journal of Experimental Psychology, 87,* 415–422.

Geshwind, N. (1965). Disconnection syndromes in man part I and II. *Brain, 88,* 237–294, 585–644.

Gibson, J. J. (1966). *The senses considered as perceptual systems.* Boston: Houghton–Mifflin.

Gibson, J. J. (1979). *The ecological approach to visual perception.* Boston: Houghton–Mifflin.

Hecaen, H. (1962). Clinical symptomology in right and left hemispheric lesions. In V. B. Mountcastle (Ed.), *Interhemispheric relations and cerebral dominance.* Baltimore: Johns Hopkins University Press.

Hume, D. (1798/1936). *An Enquiry concerning the human understanding and an enquiry concerning the principles of morals.* (L. A. Selby-Bigge, Ed.). Oxford: The Clarendon Press.

Husserl, E. (1931/1962). *Ideas: General introduction to pure phenomenology.* (W. R. Boyce Gibon Trans.). New York: Collier Books.

Kant, I. (1781/1966). *Critique of pure reason* (F. Max Muller Trans.). New York: Anchor Books (Original work published 1781).

Kimura, D. (1963). Right temporal lobe damage: Perception of unfamiliar stimuli. *Archives of Neurology, 8,* 264–271.

Levy, G. (1979). Cerebral assymetry and the psychology of man. In M. Wittrock (Ed.), *The brain and psychology.* New York: Academic Press.

Locke, J. (1894). *An essay concerning human understanding.* (A. C. Fraser, Ed.). Oxford: The Clarendon Press. (Original work published in 1690).

Mandler, J. M., & Johnson, N. S. (1977). Remembrance of things parsed: Story structure and recall. *Cognitive Psychology, 9,* 111–151.

Mandler, J. M., Scribner, S., Cole, M., & DeForest, M. (1980). Cross-cultural invariance in story recall. *Child Development, 51,* 19–26.

McCabe, V. (1980). *Memory for meaning: The effect of implicit belief systems on recognition.* Unpublished doctoral dissertation, University of California, Los Angeles.

McCabe, V. (1984). Abstract perceptual information for age-level: A risk factor for maltreatment? *Child Development, 55,* 267–276.

Milner, B. (1958). Psychological defects produced by temporal lobe excision. *Proceedings of the Association of Nervous Disease, 36,* 244–257.

Minsky, M. (1975). A framework for representing knowledge. In P. H. Winston (Ed.), *The psychology of computer vision.* Boston: MIT Press.

Moscovitch, M. (1979). Information processing and the cerebral hemispheres. In M. S. Gazzaniga (Ed.), *Handbook of behavioral neurobiology.* New York: Plenum.

Myers, R. E. (1962). Transmission of visual information within and between hemispheres: A behavior study. In V. B. Mountcastle (Ed.)., *Interhemispheric relations and cerebral dominance.* Baltimore: Johns Hopkins University Press.

Norman, D. (1979). Perception, memory and mental processes. In L. Nilsson (Ed.), *Perspectives on memory research: Essays in honor of Uppsala University's 500th anniversary.* Hillsdale, NJ: Lawrence Erlbaum Associates.

Piaget, J. (1971). *Structuralism.* New York: Harper Colphon Books.

Portielje, A. F. J. (1921). Zur Ethologie bzw. psychologie von Botaurus Stellaris. *Ardea, 15,* 1–15.

de Renzi, E., Faglioni, P., & Spinnler, H. (1968). The performance of patients with uni-lateral brain damage on face recognition tasks. *Cortex, 4,* 17–33.

Rizzolati, G., Umilta, C., & Berlucchi, G. (1971). Opposite superiorities of the right and left cerebral hemispheres in discriminative reaction time to physiognomical and alphabetical material. *Brain, 94,* 431–442.

Rosch, E. (1978). Principles of categorization. In E. Rosch & B. B. Lloyd (Eds.), *Cognition and categorization.* Hillsdale, NJ: Lawrence Erlbaum Associates.

Russell, B. (1912). *The problems of philosophy.* New York: Oxford University Press.

Scagnelli, P. (1969). *Relationships among visual imagery, language, and haptics in spatial perception.* Unpublished doctoral dissertation, Duke University.

Shank, R., & Abelson, R. (1977). *Scripts, plans, goals, and understanding.* Hillsdale, NJ: Lawrence Erlbaum Associates.

Shaw, R. E., & Pittinger, J. (1977). On perceiving the face of change in changing faces: Implications for a theory of object perception. In R. Shaw & J. Bransford (Eds.), *Perceiving, acting and knowing*. Hillsdale, NJ: Lawrence Erlbaum Associates.

Spelke, E. (1976). Infants intermodal perception of events. *Cognitive Psychology, 8,* 553–560.

Sperry, R. W. (1962). Some general aspects of interhemispheric integration. In V. B. Nountcastle (Ed.), *Interhemispheric relations and cerebral dominance*. Baltimore: Johns Hopkins University Press.

Tinbergen, N. (1961). *The Herring Gull's world*. New York: Basic Books.

Tinbergen, N. (1972). *The animal in its world*. Cambridge MA: Harvard University Press.

Turvey, M. T., & Shaw, R. E. (1979). The primacy of perceiving: An ecological reformulation of perception for understanding memory. In L. Nilsson (Ed.), *Perspectives on memory research: Essays in honor of Uppsala University's 500th anniversary*. Hillsdale, NJ: Lawrence Erlbaum Associates.

2 Schemas in Cognition

Robert E. Shaw
University of Connecticut

William M. Hazelett
Hampshire College

CONTENTS

The Role of Action and Perception in the Schematization of Knowledge
The Event Perception Hypothesis
The Concept of Schema Revisited
    Affordance Structure as a Modulatory Invariance
    Affordances as Amodal Information
Thought as Schematization

The purpose of this chapter is to sketch the outlines of an ecological theory of the growth of knowledge. The working hypothesis that guides us here is that there is a fundamental cognitive function that is invariant across all the various forms and levels of knowledge acquisition. In short, we are proposing that the principles that account for the *ontogenesis* of knowledge (cognitive development) are the very same as those that explain the *epigenesis* of knowledge (learning), and perhaps even the *phylogenesis* (evolution) of mind as well. Let us begin by posing our central theoretical question in a way that presupposes our working hypothesis: *What is the nature of the general cognitive capacity that underlies all knowledge acquisition?*

Piaget has introduced us to the notion of *functional invariance*. In his theory, the complementary processes of assimilation and accommodation provide the basis for all intellectual functioning, as well as a fixed point around which cognitive development proceeds (Flavell, 1963). Moreover, because these processes are found to operate at all levels of phylogenetic and ontogenetic development, they can be said to constitute *functional invariants* of all adaptive pro-

45

cesses. We adopt Piaget's notion of functional invariance as the starting point for our theory. In these terms, the working hypothesis just introduced is stated as the claim that the functional invariant responsible for the growth of knowledge is also a functional invariant for the acquisition of knowledge. A second hypothesis we would like to introduce concerns the role of perception in the development of knowledge, but here we depart somewhat from Piaget.

THE ROLE OF ACTION AND PERCEPTION IN THE SCHEMATIZATION OF KNOWLEDGE

According to Piaget, the young infant begins life equipped with certain native endowments called *elementary schemas*. These include action sequences like sucking, grasping, and searching. Originally there is no real distinction for the child between sensory-motor schemas and sensory-motor concepts. Objects and activities constitute for the infant a single indivisible experience (Piaget, 1936/1954). Through development, as these schemas are elaborated and differentiated through repeated application to objects and events, they become progressively internalized as concepts. This is just the barest outline of the process, of course, and it is not our purpose here to provide a general critique of Piaget. But we do wish to state that we feel Piaget shortchanges the role of perception in the development of conceptual schemas. It is our contention that perception is as much an epigenetic source of conceptual knowledge as action. By making perception merely figurative instead of operational, Piaget fails to do justice to this aspect of knowledge acquisition (Piaget, 1961/1969).

The concept of "cognitive schema" has been a problematic one. Even scholars of Piaget, like Flavell (1963), express frustration at trying to pin down precisely what he means by it. Bartlett (1932), perhaps equally responsible as Piaget for its current use, expressed his chagrin at the need to borrow such a vague concept from Sir Henry Head (1920). Nevertheless, we are adopting the term here, and would like at least to try for a more precise rendition of it. Let us first disavow some connotations that have become attached to the term. A schema, in our view, is not definable simply in terms of organismic variables but necessarily refers to environmental ones as well. Neither does it refer to an overt pattern of responses, nor to an implicit "mental" or motor-synergistic program for sequencing responses. Nor do schemas refer solely to the dynamic control process governing actions, nor are they derived solely from actions as Piaget, Head, and Bartlett argue. Rather there exist perceptual schemas as well as action schemas, and the two play a reciprocal role in the epigenesis of conceptual knowledge.

Kantian theory is relevant to our discussion here, because for Kant, a schema is the principle by which similar objects of experience can be assigned to the same abstract equivalence class. It is the rule by which perceptual experiences become cognitively structured. Kant's theory emphasizes the operational aspects of perceptual schemas much as Piaget's theory emphasizes the operational aspects of action schemas. The common thrust of the Kantian and Piagetian positions and the conclusion we wish to explore and clarify amount to the general hypothesis that the structure of knowledge is a function of the type of cognitive schemas that interface action and perception. We believe that the use of such schemas is what is meant by thought itself.

Let us examine this hypothesis in relation to the interdependence of *knowing how* and *knowing that*. A distinction has been made between knowing *how* to do something and knowing *that* something is the case. Knowing how to relate to or interact appropriately with our environments in order to achieve a desired end, say, knowing how to eat, is a different form of knowledge than knowing that what we intend to eat is an apple rather than a pear. Knowing how to do x necessarily presupposes the ability to act in a certain way or the existence of cognitive structures we have previously referred to as *action schemas*. On the other hand, knowing that x is a y rather than a z presupposes the ability to perceive in a certain way or the existence of what we have called *perceptual schemas*.

Because the two forms of knowledge are distinctive the schemas underlying each cannot be identical. However, because knowing how to act involves knowledge of that which affords being acted upon, we should expect a close relationship to exist between knowing how and knowing that, between action schemas and perceptual schemas.

Indeed, there exists a reciprocal interaction between the two types of schemas so that we say an organism behaves adaptively when one schema becomes calibrated in terms of the other. Put differently, the control processes for the execution of action schemas are perceptual schemas whereas the control processes for the pickup of perceptual information are action schemas. Every action, like every perception, is the achievement of a mission in the service of adaptation rather than a random behavior or a casual pickup of information. This is not to deny that the systems responsible for action and perception may also engage in capricious or whimsical activities possessing no obvious survival value, but to emphasize that such random meanderings of the cognitive systems are not the primary functions for which millenia of evolution has designed them.

It goes without saying that, like all sciences, psychology has the task of explaining the significant aspects of natural phenomena rather than those that are accidental spin-offs of deeper governing principles. Thus, as psychologists, we must at last come to grips with the problem of the meaning and purpose of behavior in the contexts for which the organism has been designed to function adaptively. We should not content ourselves with the study of contrived behaviors in artificial situations where success or failure, even in principle, is of little consequence for the subject. Every action.should be viewed as a product of a cognitive system that has been tuned by evolution to produce purposive behaviors that possess intrinsic survival value. Likewise, every perception should be considered a function of the same cognitive system whose primary mission is to detect meaningful information that can be used in the service of needs. From this ecological viewpoint the need for mutual calibration of the action and perception systems vis-à-vis their schemas provides what we feel to be the most useful interpretation to the statement that *cognition consists of all those psychological processes by which an organism adapts to its environment*. Thus, perception and action are modes of cognition just as thought and communication are.

This view of the reciprocal relation between acting and perceiving may also help shed light on two other difficult concepts, meaning and intent. From the ecological viewpoint, cognitive psychology is the study of how significant meanings (i.e., perceptual information with adaptive significance) are conveyed and how intents (i.e., purposive behaviors with adaptive significance) are satisifed. Perception, in the broadest sense, is a process by which an organism evaluates the significance of relations among structures in its world—relations that often change over time—for acts it may perform. Actions are the means by which an organism modifies those structures in the service of its needs. Thus, *meaning* refers to the structural significance objects or events possess for helping organisms adapt over time to their environments, whereas *intent* refers to the functional or utilitarian significance such structures may possess.

From this point of view, every event available to an organism simultaneously possesses structural as well as functional significance. Traditionally, however, this point has often been missed by theorists, giving rise to the classic distinction between *structuralism* and *functionalism*. Structuralists attempt to reduce all knowledge to structural concepts by arguing that the perceived meaning of events (actions being one type of event) is completely determined by the structural properties of the objects, their relations, and configural changes over time. Hence they subjugate action to perception and intents to meanings. Functionalists, on the other hand, attempt to make the contrary case by arguing that structural properties of events may only be defined by reference to the actions they spawn. Thus the perceived meaning of events is subjugated to the action intended. For instance, a structuralist might argue that the concept of "wheel" refers to an object with a particular shape (circular) and a particular composition (rigid), whereas a functionalist might argue that by an object that is circular and rigid we mean nothing more than one that can be rolled.

The ecological approach to cognitive psychology differs from either of these one-sided views by offering a common ground by which the pairwise interaction of structure and function, meaning and intent, and perception and action may be properly balanced. Following Gibson (1966, 1979) we call this organizing principle the *affordance structure of events*. A proper understanding of this principle is crucial to a full appreciation of how action schemas and perceptual schemas may be reciprocally calibrated, and how knowledge can somehow be neutral in spite of its epigenetic roots in one of these.

Gibson (1966, 1979) argues that what we perceive are the *affordances* of objects and events, the invariant perceptual information made available by objects and events that can be picked up by an active, investigative organism, and that is sufficient to specify how the organism might adaptively interact with its environment. He illustrates the concept of affordance by referring to the case of Köhler's (1925) ape perceiving the "rake-character" of a stick, by virtue of which a banana may be retrieved.

Like "schema," the notion of "affordance" may invite certain potential misunderstandings that we would like to clarify. As realists, we maintain with Gibson that affordance properties are objectively determined rather than subjectively constructed by the mind. This is not to argue, however, that perceiving organisms are merely passive recipients of energy structures impressed upon them by the physical environment. It is an egregious error to interpret Gibson's view, or our own, as somehow denying that organisms are active, investigative creatures whose perceptual interests in their world are guided by their intents.

Thus, Gibson's claim that perceptual information is independent of the *particular* organism who processes it should not be taken to imply that perceptual information is, in general, organism-independent. Gibson stresses the physical basis of information specifying affordances, but he also clearly asserts that such properties belong to ecological science rather than to physics proper. Logically speaking, an affordance, by Gibson's own usage, refers to just those properties of objects or events that possess ecological significance for some organism. Such information is always *about* the world but also *for* some perceiving organism. Clearly, the ecological significance of perceptual information specifying affordance properties (e.g., "jump-across-ability," "step-over-ability," "edibility," "mate-ability," etc.) depends as much on the structure of the organism involved as on that of the object. We use the affordance concept, then, only to refer to invariant perceptual information that specifies how organisms may potentially interact with environmental settings to further their own adaptation.

When the main source of control for this interaction emanates from the environment we call the relationship *perception*. When it emanates from the organism, we call it *action*. The concept of affordance thus provides a rubric under which actions and perceptions are seen to commute, that is, they stand to one another as different sides of the same coin, as dual aspects of any ecologically significant event. The joint role they play with affordances in the structuralization of knowledge can now be considered.

THE EVENT PERCEPTION HYPOTHESIS

The central theoretical claim we have been working toward through the aforementioned considerations may now be stated: *All conceptual knowledge ultimately has its origins in the perceived affordance structure of events.* This means that all concepts, even the most abstract ones, ultimately refer to events. For instance, the concepts of running, smiling, or eating may be exemplified by events involving running, smiling, and eating. But what of more abstract concepts such as love, justice, or truth? We also assume that these concepts ultimately derive from the perceived affordance structure of events, namely, that the concept of *love* is derived from perceived instances of loving, *justice* from perceived instances where justice has been properly administered, and *truth* from perceived instances where something believed to be the case was in fact shown to be the case. This is not to argue, however, that each concept understood by a particular individual must be learned by him from experience with actual events, for surely we often learn vicariously from verbal descriptions or surrogate forms (e.g., movies, pictures, etc.) of other people's experiences, as well as from descriptions or representations of fictitious or inferred entities (e.g., stories, plays, models, or proofs).

This hypothesis should not be interpreted merely as a dressed-up version of the empiricists' claim that all knowledge is passively received through the senses, for ecologically relevant knowledge requires ongoing active accommodation of organisms to their world. Rather, the hypothesis is meant to underscore the claim that whether instances of concepts are perceived by us or described to us, neither procedure possesses efficacy for promulgating concepts unless the affordance structure of the relevant event is sufficiently well specified by the information conveyed so as to be recognized and properly acted upon. If the affordance structure of an event is poorly specified by the available information or by words or example, then the concept will itself be vague. The entailed concept is not truly understood until we are able to specify clearly the actions afforded by the invariant information common to all events in the class denoted by the concept.

So, for instance, if a child could recognize, say, an eggbeater by its form alone, yet have no idea of its use, we would simply say the child had a less than full understanding of the concept. Nor is any problem for the event perception hypothesis posed by the fact that we may know that particular events fit the same concept—say that two paintings are rendered in the style of the cubists—although we are unable to articulate precisely the relevant criteria. Rather, such phenomena are of considerable interest to any theory of cognition, because they testify to the need for a better understanding of tacit knowledge mechanisms (Polanyi, 1966). At any rate, our hypothesis is intended to bear on the functional invariant of cognition underlying all knowledge acquisition—tacit or otherwise. The justification of this hypothesis will of course ultimately hinge on whether it can be shown that the meaning of events for an observer is indeed determined by their perceived affordance structure, and, most importantly, on whether the affordance structure can itself be precisely characterized (cf. Shaw, McIntyre, & Mace, 1974). Let us further explore that question and attempt a more precise formulation of the concept of cognitive schemas in light of what has been said about affordances.

THE CONCEPT OF SCHEMA REVISITED

Henri Bergson (1911) suggested that perception measures our possible action upon things, and thereby, inversely, the possible actions of things upon us. Thus, as we modulate the structure of the world by acting upon it, so the world modulates our cognitive structures by our perceiving it. The verb to *modulate* is quite aptly chosen in this regard because it literally means to regulate or adjust to a certain measure or proportion and to alter or adapt according to circumstances. Furthermore, the modulation concept not only seems suitable for capturing the desired ecological implications but also offers a common term for relating action to perception. By considering action and perception to be modulatory schemas, we may now ask if they share any *modulatory invariance,* that is, does there exist a common factor, some reciprocal calibration, by which perception is scaled to action and action to perception? Let us explore this possibility for a moment.

The so-called "distal senses" (seeing, hearing, smell) constitute an "early-warning" system that provides information for anticipating events and preparing oneself accordingly. In his lyrical idiom, Bergson puts it this way: The perceived distance between our bodies and an object is a measure of the greater or lesser imminence of danger, the nearer or more remote fulfillment of a promise. However, because an interval of distance separates our bodies from the object perceived, incipient actions exist only as plans for behavior (i.e., intents). The intent that is to be actualized in behavior must be scaled to the information about the object that is picked up by the perceptual systems.

To illustrate this notion, consider what is involved when an infant coordinates action schemas with perceptual schemas in order to grasp a desired object. To orient correctly to the object the infant must perceive the direction and distance of the object and use this information to scale appropriately the movements of her body and arm or she will not make contact with the object. The infant must also select the correct posture of her hand at the proper moment in accord with the perceived size, shape, and material composition of the object.

Now we come to the main point: The perceptual information that is needed for calibrating the action schema for grasping is none other than that information that specifies the affordance of the object, its "graspability." This is not a mere play on words; nor is it merely analytic (i.e., true by definition), although it is so obviously true one might take it as such. Rather this claim constitutes an empirical hypothesis, one whose fruitfulness can be tested. Stated tersely, the hypothesis asserts that *perception is virtual action.*

The aforementioned statement is to be taken literally, rather than figuratively. The word "virtual" literally means having the power to produce similar effects but requiring a different mode of actualization. Clearly, perception and action are different modes of cognition. One is an incoming process, the other an outgoing one; one has its primary seat of modulatory control in the environment, the other in the organism itself. Perception requires the orientation of active receptor systems that differentiate information picked up from the environment, whereas action requires the orientation of the body parts in accordance with a complex orchestration of highly differentiated muscular synergisms. Thus, a fundamental component of every action schema is a motor system, just as a fundamental component of every perceptual schema is a receptor system. However, there is still another component that is common to each type of schema. Indeed, it is that component that makes them truly cognitive rather than merely "physiological."

The second component of every cognitive schema is the affordance structure of the event that determines the perception and renders it a virtual or incipient action (see Jenkins, Jiminez-Pabon, Shaw, & Sefer, 1974). Because this is admittedly an unusual if not radical claim, some clarification is called for.

Affordance Structure as a Modulatory Invariance

Grasping, running, smiling, hitting, jumping, and other activities can be identified even though they are defined with respect to distinct environmental structures. One can grasp forks, spoons, toys, rocks, limbs, steering wheels, radio knobs, and sundry other objects that share the *structural invariants* affording prehensile seizure. Similarly, other activities may be actualized with respect to a plethora of distinct objects whose structures are suitable. The activity, although it must be accommodated differently for each context, is still recognizable for what it is, the functional or transformational invariant for an equivalence class of events.

The same is true for our ability to perceive the equivalence of events not directly caused by an organism. In short, we perceive distinct instances of either animate or inanimate events precisely because they share the same affordance structure (Shaw et al., 1974). Perceiving the affordance structure of a class of events as the same involves (1) perceiving that the transformational (or functional) invariant of the activity is the same in each case, as well as (2) perceiving the material structures involved as invariant in just those ways required to support the same actions. There are, therefore, no events, actions, or otherwise, that do not involve both structural and transformational invariants. Consequently, all we mean by the affordance structure of an event is a precise (formal if possible) characterization of both the transformational *and* structural invariants over which the event is defined.

Hence events are by their very nature abstract in the sense that the information needed to specify them (i.e., their concept) involves abstract principles for the definition of the equivalence class of instances that exemplify the event concept. These abstract principles are none other than a specification of the relevant transformational and structural invariants that determine the affordance structure of the event.

What remains to be shown is how both forms of modulation defined by events, e.g., actions and perceptions, necessarily depend on the same information that defines the affordance structure of the events for which they are schematized. It is this information that constitutes the modulatory invariance of action schemas and perceptual schemas and that allows for, indeed is essential to, their reciprocal calibration.

Another way of stating the proposed hypothesis is to say that cognitive schemas are event schemas, that is, ways in which organisms schematize physical structures vis-à-vis the energy distributions made available so as to make the event, as far as possible, relevant to their adaptive efforts to succeed in life. Hence cognition is a schematizing process that "ecologizes" the stuff of the world (events) either to render it more assimilable by the organism or to accommodate the organism to it, a process of harmonization denoted elsewhere as the postulate of cognitive symmetry (Shaw & McIntyre, 1974; Shaw et al., 1974).

The insight required to appreciate this concept of cognitive schema is to see that it is defined over ecological events (i.e., events encompassing organism-environment interactions) rather than just physical events on the one hand, or organismic events (e.g., physiological processes or body movements) on the other hand. To confuse the notion of cognitive schema with either the environmental or organismic components of an ecological event is to confuse the longitudinal aspect of an information flow with one of its cross sections. The reciprocal modulation of information from organism to the world (actions) and from the world to the organism (perceptions), however, is not perfectly commutative because each direction involves distinct organismic variables. When the affordance structure of an event is transduced through the effector systems of the organism's body we call it an action; when it is transduced through the receptor systems we call it a perception. Logically speaking, if we ignore the organismic variables altogether and abstract from the cognitive schema of an event just the modulatory invariance, its affordance structure, then actions collapse upon perceptions and meanings become synonymous with intents. An illustration may help clarify why this is so.

Consider a paper cup. Such an object, due to its thin shell, can be easily crushed if sufficient force is brought to bear upon it, that is to say, it *affords* crushing. Whether a human hand or a stray rock from a landslide inaugurates the cup-crushing event, the same invariant information is liberated and specifies the identical affordance property in either case, namely, the cup's "crushability."

Moreover, whether one initiates the cup-crushing event or merely witnesses it, the information perceived is abstractly equivalent to the information needed to calibrate the action schema for crushing that particular cup. Why this is so may be elusive unless one understands that affordance properties entail action just as they do perception, that is to say, because affordance properties of objects are event-dependent properties, they are as relevant to what actions may be performed as to what perceptions may arise. Perceptions specify the events into which objects may enter (e.g., they appear crushable, graspable, edible, lovable, etc.), whereas actions, because they are themselves events, determine what perceptual information may arise.

Hence, information specifying the affordance atructure of events must be considered *amodal,* because this information is common to both acting and perceiving modes of cognition. Again, this is not to imply that action schemas and perceptual schemas are identical, but that events may be schematized in two ways. However, both forms of schematization possess a common factor that provides a basis for their mutual compatibility. This hypothesis is important because it suggests that action and perceptual schemas become reciprocally calibrated when they come to share identical affordance components. Only if information specifying affordances is amodal over all levels of cognitive processing can that information be a modulatory invariance and, thus, provide the common basis necessary for the reciprocal calibration of action and perceptual schemas. Without reciprocal calibration such schemas could not be mutually constrained by events so as to permit cognitive adaptation.

Affordances as Amodal Information

Information specifying affordance properties is amodal at the sensory level as well as at the cognitive level. That this is so is crucial to understanding how perceptual information can be the epigenetic basis of abstract knowledge.

One of Gibson's main theses (1966, 1979) is that the stimulus information conveyed by each sense is amodal because it specifies the same affordance properties of objects or events. His argument, of course, is not that stimuli are equivalent when they are in fact different. Seeing a piano is not hearing a piano. Rather, it is that stimulus information can be identical although its sensory qualities differ. The senses work as systems for detecting amodal, higher-order invariants of stimulation. This view is elegantly summed up by Hornbostel (1927/1938) in his remark, "it matters little through which sense I realize that in the dark I have blundered into a pigsty" (p. 83).

Another example of how information conveyed to different senses can be abstract is the fact that the gradient of projected sizes of a passing object, say a train, is proportional, over a wide range of values, to the corresponding amplitude and frequency gradients of sounds reaching the ear (the Doppler effect). Both eye and ear are equally capable of detecting information specifying the "passing train" event. Similarly, an analysis of the general cases of auditory and optical looming indicates an abstract equivalence at the level of the variables for rate of change. (We thank J. Pittenger for this example.) Furthermore, there exists additional evidence from other classes of events—"felt" textures versus optical textures, Dallenbach's "facial" vision in the blind, "seeing" with the skin (White, Saunders, Scadden, & Bach-Y-Rita, & Collins, 1970)—to suggest that affordances of events constitute amodal information. As such, affordances qualify as the functionally invariant bases by which the various senses can become calibrated as a system. But can this same argument be made at a higher level with respect to action and perception?

One may accept the aforementioned argument and still balk at the claim that the information involved in the calibration of action and perceptual schemas is also amodal. Difficulty may arise due to the traditional distinction between information picked up about the world, so-called "sensory" information, and information about the orientation of one's moving body in the world, so-called "action-produced" or proprioceptive information (Gibson, 1966). Where the former kind of perceptual information is *efferent,* the latter is *reafferent* in that it involves a feedback control of afferent processes by efferent ones.

This distinction, though perhaps well motivated from a neurological viewpoint, is nevertheless misleading from a cognitive one, for it suggests no way in which proprioception and perception can be adaptively coordinated. An alternative hypothesis is that proprioceptive stimulation, which provides feedback to the motor system, is useful for evaluating the progress of an intended action precisely because it conveys amodal information about the affordance properties of the objects.

Consider again the action of crushing a cup with the hand. When one presses down on an inverted paper cup with the palm of the hand, the resistance of the cup to being crushed is felt due to the stimulation of cutaneous receptors sensitive to mechanical deformation of the skin. This proprioceptive stimulation is directly related to the mechanical pressure exerted on the bottom of the cup. At the maximum point of pressure, just prior to the collapse of the walls of the cup, the "felt" resistance of the cup provides a measure of its structural rigidity. (A dynamometer can be used to check this fact.)

But one need not actually press on a cup to the point of collapse in order to perceive its relative rigidity; Information about the structural properties can also be picked up visually. The fact that it is seen to stand upright, with a fairly opaque rather than an excessively translucent shell, to have a fairly low height to width ratio, to be composed of stiff waxed paper rather than some more flimsy material, and so forth, all attest to the cup's structural rigidity. Thus, rigidity is an affordance property of objects that can be apprehended with considerable accuracy by vision as well as by proprioception. (A similar argument can be made for audition if a blindfolded person is allowed to hear the object being tapped, scraped, dropped, sawed through, etc.)

The information for the relative rigidity of the cup that can be visually perceived, therefore, provides a basis for parametrizing the control variables in an action schema for crushing. Thus, the action schema for producing a cup-crushing event shares an affordance component with the perceptual schema required for differentiating the information propagated by the event. For this reason, the two modes of cognition (action and perception), when transducing the same event, share a modulatory invariance (symmetry) by which they might be mutually calibrated. Consequently, the event-perception hypothesis provides a plausible account for why action and perceptual schemas may be considered to function as a single system.

THOUGHT AS SCHEMATIZATION

Let us now attempt to sum up this theory of the epigenesis of abstract knowledge and examine what ramifications it has for the concept of thought in general.

Organisms are naturally endowed with elementary schemas that guide their initial interactions with their environments. They are also endowed with the cognitive capacity for adaptation to a complex, changing environment by processes of elaborating and amending those elementary schemas into a system of more and more general reciprocally calibrated schemas. It is this creative aspect of intelligence that we believe is a functional invariant of both learning and development, as well as evolution. In the earliest stages, elementary schemas are combined into more complex schemas by a process of *coordination*. Although coordination implies more than mere concatenation—schemas must be reciprocally assimilated to each other—the schemas formed by this process, although more complex, are no more abstract than the elementary ones from which they are formed.

A second cognitive mechanism is responsible for the development of more abstract kinds of knowledge. This is *schematization*—the process of recursively applying schemas to other schemas. To see what we mean by this, recall that a schema is an abstract description consisting of two types of variables, structural and functional ones. The structural component is the affordance structure of an event, and the functional component is either the motor or sensory system required to modulate or be modulated by that event. A schema, therefore, effects a *schematization* by assimilating one set of structures to a system of operations defined over another set of structures. In this way, the first set of structures come to be treated in the same systematic fashion as the second. For example, we might say that linguistic utterances are schematized over abstract syntactic variables under the rules of grammar; or displacements of objects are schematized over variables of mathematical groups.

Consider the concrete illustration of a young child in bed discovering how to make her fingers "walk" up her blanket-covered knees like a miniature man climbing a hill. Here the action schema for controlling finger postures becomes schematized over the action schema controlling leg postures involved in walking. Now because the motor states for walking the fingers are not the same as those involved for walking the legs, and the perceptual information for how the arm moves the hand up the covers is not the same as that for how the legs carry the body up a slope, the two schemas involved cannot be identical. But the schema for walking the fingers is surely an action analogue of the schema for walking the legs. The two are abstractly equivalent in that they share the same modulatory invariance, the same affordance structure. The concept of "walking" developed by this process of schematization is thus more general than any particular instance of walking.

We can see how this process of schematization can yield even more abstract concepts of various types. For example, the modulatory invariance shared by the action schemas for walking and for sliding an object may underlie the even more abstract concept of, say, translation in general. The just mentioned examples of *functional* concepts arise from the schematization of one action schema over another. When a perceptual schema is schematized over another perceptual schema, *structural* concepts arise. For example, the perceptual schemas required to perceive different people of different age levels share a modulatory invariance underlying the abstract structural concept of "age level." And when a perceptual schema is schematized over an action schema, or vice versa, we have the mechanism for explaining the reciprocal calibration of action and perception schemas discussed earlier.

A more complete discussion of all the implications and possibilities suggested by this concept of schematization must be deferred to another time. For now, let us simply state in conclusion what we claim to be the explanatory relevance of this notion to our original problem, namely the nature of the underlying cognitive capacity that is the functional invariant of knowledge acquisition. We propose that schematization is what we mean by thought *per se*. It is the process by which abstract concepts both arise and are marshalled to support the actions intended to service needs in accordance with the perceived meaning of events. The recursive schematization of action and perceptual schemas create what Cassirer (1923/1953) has called *relational structures*. The schematization process provides an account of the epigenesis of concepts at any level of abstraction, without committing the fallacy of progressive deletion of content with increasing abstraction, as in concept theories based upon the operation of class intersection (cf. Chapter 5, this volume; Bransford, 1971). Hence, because it is by the schematization process that all concepts arise, the totality of all cognitive schemas appropriated for experiencing events constitutes the total extent of a person's conceptual knowledge of the world.

REFERENCES

Bartlett, F. C. (1932). *Remembering*. Cambridge, England: Cambridge University Press.
Bergson, H. (1911). *Matter and memory*. London: George Allen and Unwin Ltd.
Bransford, J. D. (1970/1971). Temporal integration and the acquisition of linguistic ideas (Doctoral dissertation, University of Minnesota, 1970). *Dissertation Abstracts International, 1971, 31,* 6277-B. (University Microfilm No 71-8129).
Cassirer, E. (1953). *Substance and function*. New York: Dover. (Original work published 1923)
Flavell, J. (1963). *The developmental psychology of Jean Piaget*. New York: Van Nostrand.
Gibson, J. J. (1966). *The senses considered as perceptual systems*. Boston: Houghton Mifflin.
Gibson, J. J. (1979). *The ecological approach to visual perception*. Boston: Houghton Mifflin.
Head, H. (1920). *Studies in neurology*. Oxford, England: Oxford University Press.

Hornbostel, E. M. von. (1938). The unit of the senses. *Psyche,* 1927, *7,* 83–89. Reprinted in W. D. Ellis, *A source book of Gestalt psychology.* Harcourt Brace.

Jenkins, J., Jiminez-Pabon, E., Shaw, R., & Sefer, J. (1974). *Schuell's aphasia in adults.* New York: Harper & Row.

Köhler, W. (1925). *The mentality of apes.* (E. Winter Trans.). London: Routledge & Kegan Paul.

Piaget, J. (1954). *The construction of reality in the child* (M. Cook, Trans.). New York: Basic Books. (Original work published 1936)

Piaget, J. (1969). *The mechanisms of percpetion* (G. N. Seagrim, Trans.). New York: Basic Books. (Original work published 1961).

Polanyi, M. (1966). *The tacit dimension.* Garden City, New York: Doubleday.

Shaw, R., & McIntyre, M. (1974). Algoristic foundations for cognitive psychology. In D. Palermo & W. Weimer (Eds.), *Cognition and the symbolic process.* Hillsdale, NJ: Lawrence Erlbaum Associates.

Shaw, R. E., McIntyre, M., & Mace, W. (1974). The role of symmetry in event perception. In R. B. MacLeod & H. Pick (Eds.), *Studies in perception: Essays in honor of J. J. Gibson.* New York: Cornell University Press.

White, B. W., Saunders, F. A., Scadden, L., Bach-y-Rita, P., & Collins, C. C. (1970). Seeing with the skin. *Perception and Psychophysics, 7,* 23–27.

3

Abstract Conceptual Knowledge: How We Know What We Know*

Robert E. Shaw
University of Connecticut

Buford E. Wilson
Governors State University

Henry Wellman
University of Michigan

CONTENTS

THE ABSTRACT NATURE OF CONCEPTS

A basic characteristic of human intelligence is the ability to formulate abstract conceptual knowledge about objects and events. Abstract conceptual knowledge is exemplified when we can deal appropriately with novel instances of a concept, that is, when our knowledge goes beyond just those instances experienced.

---

*Portions of this chapter were originally published in D. Klahr (Ed.), *Cognition and Instruction*. Hillsdale, NJ: Lawrence Erlbaum Associates, 1976, 197–221.

There is abundant evidence that our knowledge of language must be abstract given the novelty that must be dealt with. Indeed, the role of novel events in language has long been recognized by linguists. Sentences are usually novel events. To verify this fact you need only pick at random a sentence in a book and then continue through the book until the sentence is repeated. Unless you have picked a cliché or a thematic sentence, it is unlikely that the sentence will reoccur. We readily admit that many sentences are novel, but what about the elements from which sentences are constructed? These elements must be the same in order for us to understand sentences. Further examination, however, shows that words too are typically novel events. The apparent physical sameness of words is an illusion supported by the use of printing presses. If we consider handwriting, we find a great deal of variation in the construction of letters and words. The novelty of words becomes even more clear when we think of the same word spoken by different speakers, male and female, child and adult, or by the same speaker when he is shouting or whispering. Words, like sentences, are typically novel events. To say that words are thoroughly novel events may be incorrect in some instances. We have heard our friends use the same words many times, our own name being a case in point. The importance of the argument for novelty is to illustrate that this repetition is not necessary for our understanding of words; thus our ability to recognize words is not a function of having experienced that particular *physical event* before.

Greenberg and Jenkins (1964) demonstrate an even more striking example of the capacity to deal with novel instances of a class. They found that English speakers could deal appropriately with novel sequences of English phonemes. Sequences of phonemes in English are subject to powerful constraints described by rule structures for syllable and word formation. If we randomly sample strings of English phonemes we produce three types of strings: strings that are actual English syllables or words; strings that violate the rules for English syllables and word construction and are therefore not English syllables or words; and finally, strings that are in accord with English rule structure but are not found in English. Given only consonant-vowel-consonant (CVC) strings we all recognize *cat* as an actual English word and *cah* as clearly not an English word. However, what about the strings *dib* and *lutt*? Both of these CVC's respect English rules of syllable construction. *Dib* is in fact an English word. What Greenberg and Jenkins did was to construct a measure of distance from English, based upon the rules of English syllable construction, which accurately predicted subjects' judgments of novel strings of phonemes. The subjects' judgments about novel strings of phonemes were consistent and predictable on the basis of linguistic rules for syllable construction in English.

This research clearly demonstrates that the knowledge by which English speakers recognize and construct English words is abstract in the sense that it is not knowledge of particular physical events but knowledge about systems of abstract relationships. One's ability to recognize novel sequences of phonemes as acceptable or unacceptable English strings demonstrates knowledge of rules of phoneme sequencing, that is, abstract conceptual knowledge that allows us to recognize and produce novel events.

But phonemes too are abstract classes of events that cannot be specified in terms of common physical elements. Research in the perception of speech has shown that the same phonemes are specified by different physical events in different contexts and that the same physical event can specify different phonemes in different contexts (Fant, 1964; Liberman, Cooper, Shankweiler, & Studdert-Kennedy, 1967). So, with phonemes too, the basis of recognition is knowledge of a system of relationships, not knowledge of particular physical elements. As we have seen, breaking language events into smaller and smaller elements does not result in a level of analysis based upon particular physical elements. Rather, at each level we find still another system of abstract relations specifying the nature or meaning of particular physical events.

Similarly, we are able to recognize a melody played on a piano even though we have only experienced instances of that melody played on other instruments. To do so, therefore, we must have an abstract concept of the melody that specifies the isomorphisms among the various instances. Often we are able to recognize that a painting is executed in the style of impressionism or by a particular artist, say Cézanne, even though we have never seen that particular work before. To do so we must have an abstract concept that specifies the style of the school or artist such that the instances, novel ones included, are seen as similar. Thus, there seems to be ample reason to conclude that concepts are not necessarily based upon knowledge of particular physical events, nor upon physical units, elements, or features. Instances of many concepts are only abstractly related.

GENERATIVE CONCEPTS

Due to their generality, abstract concepts apply to a potentially infinite equivalence class of instances. This fact poses a serious problem for a cognitive theory of how they are acquired. Because one's experience is with but a sample of the entire set of instances to which such concepts refer, several puzzling questions arise: First, how can experience with a subset of objects or events lead to knowledge of the whole set to which it belongs? There is a problem of explaining how *some* part of a structure can be equal to the whole structure. Indeed, the claim that *some* can, under certain circumstances, be equivalent to *all* seems to involve a logical contradiction. That it does not, fortunately for cognitive theory, can be amply illustrated in many different areas of conceptual knowledge. In a moment, we illustrate this fact with examples drawn from three distinct fields— mathematics, linguistics, and perceptual psychology.

A second crucial question that must be answered, given a precise answer to the first, concerns the nature of the subset that can provide the knowledge necessary to deal with the entire set. Will just any subset of instances do, or must the subset be a certain size or quality? In other words, how do instances of a concept (collectively) qualify as exemplary cases of the concept? A precise answer to this last question is of some theoretical importance, and it has obvious implications as well for the selection of effective instructional material for teaching concepts.

Generative Concepts in Mathematics

In mathematics the concept of an infinite set provides a structure for which it is literally true that a proper subset is equal to the total set. Cantor proposed this definition of the infinite when he discovered that a subset of all natural numbers, such as the even integers, can be placed into a one-to-one relationship with the total set of integers. But more relevant for our purposes is the problem of providing a precise description for an infinite class of objects. By a precise description we mean a finite specification for all instances of the infinite class.

A moment's reflection reveals that so-called *nominal* concepts are quite inadequate for this purpose because it is impossible to define an infinite class ostensively, say by pointing to each element. Hence the label "infinity" could not be consistently applied, because finite enumeration would not discriminate between classes just a little larger than the ostensive count and ones infinitely larger.

For similar reasons so-called *attributive* concepts of infinite classes are not possible, because the attempt to abstract common features from all members of such classes fails. If only a sample of members of an infinite class is considered by a process of finite abstraction, a potentially infinite number of cases may exist that fail to exhibit the attribute common to the finite subset actually experienced. Thus, the learning of concepts that refer to classes with a potentially infinite number of members, such as trees, people, and red stars, cannot be adequately explained by a cognitive process involving finite abstraction. The process of abstraction postulated to explain the acquisition of abstract concepts must work in some other way. As a mill for abstract knowledge, it must take a finite set of exemplars as grist for producing concepts of potentially infinite extension.

This problem has perplexed philosophers for many centuries, leading some empiricists and nominalists to propose that in fact no concept of an infinite class is really possible. Their argument was that if finite abstraction is the means by which all concepts are formed, then the concept of the infinite must be a negative concept referring only to our ignorance regarding the exact size of a very large class indeterminately surveyed by the senses. This argument fails to recognize the creative capacity of human intelligence. It led the empiricists to a theory of knowledge founded upon associative principles defining knowledge as nothing more than the association of memoranda of past sense impressions—what Dewey (1939) rightfully called "dead" ideas because they cannot grow.

Infinite structures can be represented by finite means only if the finite means are creative, in the sense that a "schema" exists by which the totality of the structure can be specified by some appropriate finite part of the structure. A schema by which a whole can be realized from an appropriate part can be called a *generative* principle, whereas the appropriate part can be called a generating substructure or just *generator* for short. That a structural totality can be specified by a generator *plus* a set of generative principles can usually be verified by the principle of mathematical induction.

Consider the problem of how one comes to know the concept of natural numbers. Two stages seem to be involved: One must first learn the set of numerals 0, 1, 2, . . . , 9, and a system of syntactic rules for concatenating them to form ordered pairs (e.g., 10, 11, . . ., 99), triples (e.g., 100, 101, . . ., 999), etc. The number of potential numerical strings is, of course, infinite. Hence the numeral set 0, 1, 2, . . ., 9 constitutes the generator that yields all possible numerical strings when the appropriate generative rules of the grammar are applied.

The second stage in acquiring the concept of natural numbers entails, *inter alia,* knowledge of the *closure* of arithmetic operations by which (a) any number can be shown to be a logical product of an arithmetic operation applied to a pair of numbers e.g., $1 + 0 = 1, 1 + 1 = 2, 1 + 2 = 3, . . .$, and (b) any logical product of numbers always yields numbers.

Indeed, it does not take children long to realize that any combination or permutation of the members of the generator set (0, 1, 2, . . ., 9) yields a valid number. For example, is 9701 an instance of the concept of natural number? Of course, you will recognize it as a valid instance. But how do you know? Have you ever seen this number before? Does it matter? Unless it is part of an old phone number, address, or some serial number that you have frequently dealt with, then you probably have no idea whether it is a familiar or a novel instance of natural number. Nevertheless, one knows immediately that it *is* an instance, presumably because one's knowledge of strings of numerals is as abstract as that for English sentences.

Generative Linguistic Knowledge

A similar line of argument can be developed with respect to the best way to characterize a speaker's knowledge of his native language. The problem is: "How do we acquire the linguistic competence to comprehend sentences that have never before been experienced?" For instance, it is unlikely that you have ever experienced the following sentence: *The impish monkey climbed upon the crystal chandelier, gingerly peeled the crepes from the ceiling, and threw them at the furious chef.*

This fact, however, in no way diminishes your ability either to recognize it as a grammatical (if novel) sentence or to understand the sentence.

Whatever the precise details, it seems clear that the child acquires generative knowledge of his language from limited experience with a part of the whole corpus that is potentially available. Furthermore, on the basis of this limited experience, he is able to extrapolate knowledge about sentences never before experienced by him, as well as knowledge about those never before experienced by anyone.

Presumably, the child's immediate linguistic environment, consisting of his or her family and local aspects of his culture, provides him with a generator set of exemplary structures from which he educes the generative principles by which all other sentences are known. Chomsky (1965) has argued that a transformational grammar provides the operations defining the mapping of the generator set of clear-case utterances onto the corpus of all utterances; other theorists disagree. However, no one disputes that the acquisition of language requires cognitive schemata that are truly generative in nature.

It is also worth noting that during acquisition specific memory for sentences experienced seems to play no necessary role in the process. Several lines of research support this contention. Sachs (1967) demonstrated that subjects were unable to recognize syntactic changes in sentences that did not change the meaning as readily as they were able to detect changes in meaning. This suggests that people often do not remember the explicit form of sentences experienced. Other researchers (e.g., Blumenthal, 1967; Mehler, 1963; Miller, 1962; Rohrman, 1968) have argued that rather than the surface structure of sentences being remembered, it is the deep structural relations (say, assumed by transformational grammars) that characterize the abstract conceptual knowledge retained.

One important insight that emerges from a study of such cases is that for generative concepts there are no truly novel instances. There are only those instances that are actual, because they belong to a generator set, and those that are potential, because they lie dormant among the remaining totality of instances. Consequently, the only difference between actual *versus* potential instances is whether the instance has been made manifest by application of the generative principle. Once this is done, a newborn instance bears no marks of its recent birth to denote that it is new rather than old.

On the basis of the aforementioned reasoning, we can formulate our first empirical hypothesis: *Acquiring an abstract concept does not necessarily entail the ability to recognize novel instances of the concept as being novel; that is, instances in the generator set of a concept (i.e., clear-case exemplars) will not always be distinguishable from instances never before experienced.*

In the next section we review some research that lends plausibility to the hypothesis that generative systems provide a precise description of the function of the cognitive capacity by which we obtain abstract concepts.

EXPERIMENTS ON GENERATIVE CONCEPTUAL SYSTEMS

The problem of how people learn abstract conceptual systems is by no means new to psychology. Sir Fredric Bartlett (1932), in his classic book *Remembering*, realized that what people learn must be some kind of an abstract system or schema rather than a discursive list of simple instances. Clearly, concepts can be learned from a small set of very special instances, which might be called *prototypes* or exemplars of the concept. Considerable research has shown this to be the case but has also uncovered some curious results. Furthermore, the attempt to characterize the nature of prototypic instances sufficient for learning a given concept has proven more elusive than expected.

Attneave (1957) demonstrated that experience with a prototype facilitated paired-associate learning of other instances of the concept. In related research, Posner and Keele (1968) found that subjects were able to classify correctly novel dot patterns as a result of experience with classes of patterns that were abstractly related to the novel instances by statistical rules. Later, Posner and Keele (1970) isolated the following properties of the conceptual systems that enabled subjects to classify novel instances of the classes of dot patterns: (a) The conceptual system was abstracted during initial experience with the classes of patterns, and (b) although derived from experience with patterns, it was not based upon stored copies of the patterns. One week after the original exposure to the patterns, the subjects' ability to classify the patterns actually seen earlier had decreased, although their ability to classify "new" prototypic patterns surprisingly had not. This result supports Bartlett's view by strongly suggesting that these "new" instances were classified in terms of a highly integrated system of abstract relations (a conceptual system) rather than being mediated at the time of classification by memory of individual patterns.

The question then is: "How can a subset of instances of a class be used to generate the entire class?" One avenue that we pursue here is to see what insight the concept of group generator may give into the generative nature of conceptual systems.

The notion of a group generator can be understood intuitively by careful study of the illustrations of the generator and nongenerator sets of card stimuli used in the experiment reported later (Figs. 3.1 and 3.2). The *generator* set consists of cards whose relations define the displacements that figures undergo when orbiting around the center of the card, that is, when the ordered sequence of cards specifies orbiting. On the other hand, the *nongenerator* set of stimuli consists of cards that are physically similar to those in the generator set, differing, however, in that no sequence of these cards is sufficient to specify the orbiting concept. At most they specify a displacement of four figures over the diagonal path running from the upper left to the lower right hand corners of the card.

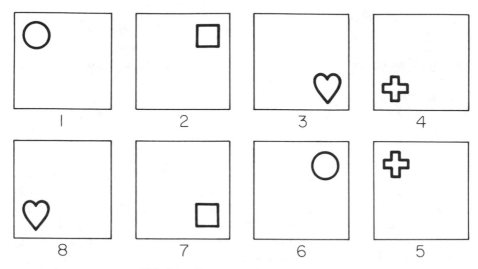

FIG. 3.1.   Group generator acquisition set.

In the next section a more formal account of the group generator notion is presented.

The Concept of Group Generator

Many examples of the generative property of mathematical groups exist. For instance, for each integer n, it is possible to construct a group having exactly n

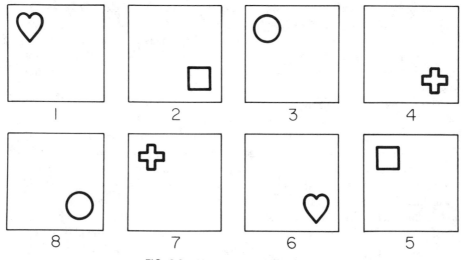

FIG. 3.2.   Nongenerator acquisition set.

elements (a group of order n) by considering $1, a, a^2, a^3, \ldots, a^{n-1}, a^n$, where $a^0 = a^n = 1$ and the operation is ordinary algebraic multiplication. Such a group is called *cyclic* because the initial element (a^0) is identical to the terminal element (a^n); the symbol a is called a *generator* of the group, because every group element is a power of a, that is, $a \times a = a^2, a \times a^2 = a^3, \ldots, a \times a^{n-1} = a^n = a^0$.

The (integer) representation of the concept of a group with a generator is but one application of this abstract system. As another example, consider the rational (cyclical) symmetry of a square.

There are four different (clockwise) angles through which one can rotate a square about its center that leave its appearance unchanged. These angles are $0°$, $90°$, $180°$, and $270°$, and together they form a group. Designate the transformations corresponding to these rotations with the symbols I, II, III, IV, respectively. Then the following table summarizes how the different transformations combine ($\times$).

$\times$	I	II	III	IV
I	I	II	III	IV
II	II	III	IV	I
III	III	IV	I	II
IV	IV	I	II	III

For example, a $180°$ rotation combined with a $270°$ rotation yields the same total effect as a single $90°$ rotation, III $\times$ IV = II in the table. From inspection of the table it should also be clear that I is the identity element and that every element has an inverse, e.g., II $\times$ IV = I, III $\times$ III = I, etc.

The most important observation for our purposes is that the group of rotations for the square has two generators, namely II and IV. Either of these, if combined iteratively with itself, yields all elements of the group. Thus, $II^2 = III$, $II^3 = IV$, $II^4 = I$, $II^5 = II$ and similarly, IV^n yields III, II, I, IV, respectively. This generative property is not trivial because neither I nor III are generators of the group; $I^n = I$ because it is the identity and III^n alternates between I and III, never producing II or IV because III is its own inverse. A most important group is that of perspectives of solid objects. The fact that, for many objects, a few perspectives provide sufficient information to specify shape suggests a way in which perceptual systems, like conceptual ones, may be generative (Shaw, McIntyre, & Mace, 1974).

The basic strategy for testing the applicability of the group-generator description in explaining generative conceptual systems is to construct acquisition sets that either are or are not generators specifying the total class of instances referred to by the concept. This suggests the following hypothesis:

> If the information specified in a group generator acquisition set is sufficient to allow subjects to generate the entire class, subjects should then treat novel instances of the class in a fashion similar to the way they treat experienced instances of the class. In contrast, subjects who are given a nongenerator acquisition set should treat experienced and new instances of the class differently.

A Generative Concept Experiment

To investigate the hypothesis, we constructed a system consisting of four simple geometric figures (a *cross,* a *heart,* a *circle,* and a *square*) orbiting through the four corner positions of a square card. This leads to 16 distinct stimuli (i.e., four figures × four positions = 16 cards). These 16 cards provide the underlying set over which the concept of *orbiting* can be defined by appropriate orderings of the cards. Moreover, the system of relationships among the cards determined by the discrete orbiting of the figures specifies a group of transformations (displacements) that is isomorphic with the group of rotations of the square just discussed. By definition, two specific groups (e.g., the *orbiting* and *rotation* groups denoted earlier) are abstractly equivalent if some third group can be found to represent each. The transformations I—IV with the operation "×" constitute such a group.

A sample generator set of eight cards used in the acquisition phase of the experiment is shown in Fig. 3.1. The cards for a nongenerator acquisition set are shown in Fig. 3.2. Each set was seen by a different group of subjects.

During recognition, both subject groups were shown the eight cards they had experienced during acquisition *plus* the eight novel instances of the system. Additionally, both groups were shown nine cards that did not fit the system. These "noncases" were constructed by using inappropriately colored geometric forms, forms occurring in the center of the card, and forms that were oriented differently on the card than those in the system. The recognition set, therefore, consisted of 25 cards, 8 "old" cards, 8 "new" but appropriate cards and 9 "noncases." Subjects were shown each of the 25 cards one at a time and asked to judge each card as "old" or "new," depending on whether it had been seen during acquisition or not.

As might be expected, both groups consistently rated the old items as old and identified the noncases as new cards. The generator set subjects identified old cards as old on 80% of the cases and the noncases as new on 99% of the cases.

The two groups were strikingly different, however, in their judgments of the new but appropriate cards. The nongenerator-set subjects correctly identified these new instances as new on more than 90% of the cases. In marked contrast, the generator-set subjects judged the new cards to be old 50% of the time; that is, their judgments of the new but appropriate instances were at a chance level; on 50% of their judgments, they identified novel instances of the system as cards they had experienced during acquisition. This group could clearly discriminate system from nonsystem cards, as shown by their rejection of the noncases, but they could not consistently discriminate experienced instances of the system from novel ones.

Two conclusions can be drawn from these results:

1. During acquisition, subjects are acquiring information about the abstract relations existing among items in the acquisition set; that is, they are gaining more information than can be characterized by copies of the individual cards experienced.

2. The information specified by the group generator is sufficient to allow subjects to generate the entire system. This supports the claim that these subjects' knowledge of the system of orbiting cards is indeed generative.

The fact that generator-set subjects could not consistently discriminate between previously experienced and novel instances of the system strongly suggests that subjects are acquiring an abstract relational concept that defines a class of events, not simply information about the specific instances they had experienced. Furthermore, this result suggests that these subjects acquired a knowledge of an event (the orbiting of cards) that is truly generative. (More about this type of event conception is said in the next section.)

Assuming that subjects are acquiring abstract relational systems from experience with the generator acquisition set rather than specific memory of experienced instances, the question arises of what effect more experience with the acquisition set would have. Conceptions of memory based on the abstraction of static features, or copies of the experienced events, would predict that more experience with the acquisition set should facilitate subjects' recognition of new instances as new. If, instead of storing copies of the experienced instances or abstracting the common attributes of the instances, subjects are acquiring information about the abstract relations among these instances in the system, more experience with the acquisition set would not necessarily result in an increased ability to recognize new instances of the system as being novel. As subjects better acquire the abstract relational system they should be more able to discriminate instances of the concept from noncases. However, the novel instances of the system may be more difficult to discriminate as new precisely because they are instances of an abstract relational system.

To investigate this possibility, four additional groups were run, two with each of the two types of acquisition sets. One group experienced the generator acquisition set twice, and a second group three times. Similarly, a third experienced the nongenerator acquisition set twice and a fourth group experienced it three times. Following the acquisition phase, all groups were tested for recognition.

For the nongenerator-set subjects, the greater amount of experience with the acquisition set resulted in an increased ability to recognize new instances of the system as new. The subjects who experienced the acquisition set three times were able to recognize the new instances as new on 100% of the cases. However, the results obtained with subjects who experienced the group-generator acquisition set were quite different. Not only were these subjects generally unable to identify novel instances of the system as new, but additional experience with the acquisition set *decreased* the subjects' ability to recognize new instances as new. As mentioned earlier, subjects who experienced the acquisition set once accepted the new instances as old 50% of the time. Subjects who experienced the acquisition set twice before recognition misidentified the new instances as old on 75% of their judgments, and subjects who experienced the generator acquisition set three times misidentified the new but appropriate instances of the system as old on over 80% of their judgments. All these subjects continued to perform well on the old instances and the noncases.

These results provide strong evidence that subjects are acquiring information about an abstract system of relations and not simply information about static properties or attributes of experienced instances. If subjects' judgments were based solely upon the attributes or static features of the experienced instances, subjects should be able to recognize new but appropriate instances as new, and increased experience should enhance this recognition. As we have seen, these results were not obtained. On the other hand, if subjects are acquiring a generative conceptual system, then instances appropriate to the system should be recognized as familiar. As the abstract conceptual system is better learned, the subjects should be more likely to recognize novel but appropriate instances as belonging to the system and therefore, identify them as old.

These results provide strong support for our hypothesis that knowledge of a subset of the instances of a concept is in fact tantamount to knowledge of all instances of the concept. When the system was well learned, subjects could not distinguish old from novel instances. Clearly, experience with the group-generator acquisition set was in this case tantamount to experience with the entire system.

Finally, it should be noted that in these experiments subjects were *not* instructed to find relations between individual instances; nor were they told that they would be tested for recognition. Rather, subjects were told that we were studying short-term memory of geometric forms. Their task was to reproduce (draw) each card in the acquisition set after performing an interfering task. In this case, abstraction of systematic relations among instances of the system was apparently automatic in that it was not intentional.

EVENT CONCEPTS AS GENERATIVE KNOWLEDGE

In this section we present evidence in support of the claim that event concepts are abstract and generative in nature.

We treat the structure of an event as consisting of two necessary components: the transformation over which the event is defined (the transformational invariant) and the structure(s) undergoing the change wrought by application of the transformation (the structural invariant). The transformational invariant must be perceptually specified in the acquisition set if the dynamic aspects of the event are to be identified (e.g., that the event is of x running, rolling, growing, smiling, etc.); the structural invariant must be perceptually specified if the subject of the event is to be identified (e.g., what x is: *John* runs, the *ball* rolls, the *flower* grows, *Mary* smiles, etc.).[1] A set of instances of an event cannot be an exemplary set (and, therefore, cannot constitute a generator set for the event) if it fails to specify both the transformational and the structural invariants.

In the experiment discussed in the previous section we showed that a certain subset of object configurations qualified both formally and psychologically as the generator set for an event concept, that of an "orbiting" event defined over geometric forms. The group-generator description does seem to offer a viable means of making explicit the manner in which abstract conceptual systems may be creative.

---

[1]Perhaps a better way to clarify the difference between structural and transformational invariants is as follows: Given that John runs, John walks, John smiles, and John loves, the subject of all these events is John; the subject's structure is what is common or invariant and, hence, is the *structural* invariant, of all the events denoted. On the other hand, given the following events: John runs, Bill runs, Mary runs, Jill runs, then there is no common subject. All we know is that some object with a minimal structure to support the operation *to run* is involved. The operation on the minimal structure x is the transformational invariant. But note that even here, defining that transformation presupposes some minimal structural invariant as its necessary support. A similar argument for the necessity of postulating minimal transformational invariants in order to define structures can also be given. (See also Shaw & Cutting, 1980.)

The abstract concept derived from perceiving the orbiting of the stimulus figures can be analyzed as follows: The generator set in the acquisition phase of the experiment consisted of stimulus configurations sufficient to specify a subgroup of a larger group of displacements, namely, the orbiting group. This set of stimuli constituted the structural invariant of the event. The subjects successfully acquired the concept of this event by detecting the two invariants that, taken together, constituted the structure of the event.

The orbiting group itself provides a description of the relevant aspects of the abstract concept of the event. Thus construed, the perceived meaning of the event *is* the orbiting group interpreted over the stimulus structures presented. Consequently, we see no way or reason to avoid the conclusion that through event perception, abstract concepts come into existence. Under this view, the generator for the abstract event concept is that set of instances that conveys sufficient perceptual information to specify both the transformational and structural invariants defining the event. The meaning of this invariant information for the human or animal perceiver is the structure of the event.

In our opinion, this analysis argues in favor of the hypothesis that perception is a direct apprehension of the meanings of events. Because abstract concepts are generatively specified by (i.e., abstractly equivalent to) their exemplary instances (generator set), their acquisition can also be considered direct, requiring no augmentation by voluntary inferential processes. Similarly, no constructive cognitive process need be postulated to explain how abstract concepts are built up from elementary constituents, as argued by the British Empiricists, if such elementary constituents need play no role in the definition of the concept.

Have we made too much of the apparent success of the generative systems approach in a single line of experiments? It is important to ask whether the same analysis can be applied to a variety of experimental phenomena. We explore this possibility next.

So far we have presented an example involving an event whose structure can be formally described by a very simple group structure. We would now like to discuss a complex event, the structure of which, although more elaborate, still seems amenable to a generative systems analysis.

The Shape of Nonrigid Objects

Theories of object perception usually attempt to explain the perception of objects and patterns that do not change their shape over time. However, a truly adequate theory must also explain the origin of concepts of events where object configurations or the shapes of objects undergo dynamic change. Shaw and his associates have conducted a series of experiments designed to explore this problem (Mark, Todd, & Shaw, 1981; Pittenger, Shaw, & Mark, 1979; Shaw & Pittenger, 1977).

The starting point for this work is that *shape* is considered an event-dependent concept rather than an absolute property of static objects. This is contrary to the traditional view that identifies shape with the metric-Euclidean property of *geo-*

metric rigidity under transformation, that is, the fact that under certain transformations (e.g., displacements) the distances between points on an object do not change. Unfortunately, this definition is too narrow, because it fails to apply to many natural objects that remain identifiable in spite of being remodeled to some extent by various nonrigid transformations (e.g., growth, erosion, plastic deformation under pressure).

Biomorphic forms, such as faces, plants, bodies of animals, leaves, and noses, inevitably undergo structural remodeling as they grow, although their transforms retain sufficient structural similarity to be identified. Such forms, like geological structures under plastic deformation or archaeological artifacts under erosion, are relatively nonrigid under their respective remodeling transformations. Because the property of geometric rigidity is not preserved, it cannot provide the invariant information for identification. Clearly, then, a new and more abstract definition of shape must be found upon which to develop a theory of object perception that is broad enough in scope to encompass nonrigid as well as rigid objects. We propose the following definition: *Shape, as an event-perception concept, is formally construed as the totality of invariant structural properties by which an object might be identified under a specified set of transformations.*

Notice that by this definition, the geometric rigidity of an object under displacement is but one of the many kinds of structural invariants possible. By a careful study of the perceptual information used to identify human faces at different stages of growth (i.e., age levels), we hoped that the generality and fruitfulness of the event perspective might be further tested.

Perceiving the Shape of Faces as a Growth Event

Faces, no less than squares or other shapes, are dynamic events; their shape is derived from a growth process (the transformational invariant) that preserves sufficient structure (structural invariant) to specify the identity of the face of the person undergoing the aging transformation. In a similar fashion, different people at the same stage of growth can be perceived as being at the same age level because growth produces similar effects over different structures (Pittenger & Shaw, 1975). These common effects constitute the information specifying the transformational invariant of the growth process. Thus, each transformation can be identified by the style of change wrought over various objects to which it is applied.

In addition to empirically discovering the invariant information specifying the identity of structures over which an event is defined, a problem of equal weight for event perception is to isolate the invariant information specifying the transformation by which the dynamic aspect of an event is defined. Both of these informational invariants must be found in every event-perception experiment if the structure of the event being studied is to be experimentally defined. Shaw and his colleagues conducted the following experiments in an attempt to discover the structure of the growth event defined over human faces. The biological literature suggests two classes of transformations for the specification of skull growth: strain and shear. A strain is a geometric transformation that, when applied to a two-dimensional coordinate space, changes the length of the units along one axis as a function of the units along the other axis. For instance, a strain transformation can take a square into a rectangle or vice versa. On the other hand, a *shear* is a geometric transformation that changes the angle of intersection of coordinate axes from a right angle to something else. Such a transformation might take a square into a rhombus. A set of stimuli was constructed by having a computer apply different degrees of these two transformations to a human facial profile, and then photographing the computer-plotted transforms of the given profile. A number of experiments were run to test the hypothesis that the perception of age level is derived from information made available by growth events.

To illustrate the application of these transformations to faces, we describe the production of stimuli for one of the experiments. The stimuli were produced by applying combinations of the transformations globally to a two-dimensional Cartesian space in which the profile of a 10-year-old boy had been placed such that the origin was at the ear hole, and the y axis was perpendicular to the Frankfurt horizontal (a line drawn tangent to the top orb of the ear hole and the bottom orb of the eye socket).

The formula used for the shear transformation in rectangular coordinates was $y^1 = y$, $x^1 = x + \tan \alpha y$, where α is the angle of shear and x^1, y^1 are new coordinates. The formula for the strain transformation, expressed for convenience in polar coordinates, was $\theta^1 = \theta$, $r^1 = r(1 - k)$, where r is the radial vector and θ is the angle specifying direction from the origin. Here k is a constant determining the parameter value of the strain. Thus, in producing the stimuli, α and k are the values to be manipulated for varying the amount of shear and strain, respectively. (For a detailed discussion of this approach see Shaw & Pittenger, 1977.) The calculations were performed by computer and the profiles drawn by a computer-driven plotter.

The initial outline profile was transformed by all 35 combinations of seven levels of strain ($k = -0.25, -0.10, 0, +0.10, +0.25, +0.35, +0.55$) and five levels shear ($\alpha = -15°, -5°, 0°, +5°, +15°$). These transformations are not commutative; shear was applied first.

These shape changes approximate those produced by growth. We hypothesized that the changes are relevant to perception in two ways; they are a sufficient stimulus for the perception of age while at the same time leaving information for the identity of the face invariant.

Experiment 1

To test the effects of the shape changes induced by shear and strain, profiles were presented to subjects in a task requiring magnitude estimates of age. Twenty subjects were instructed to rate the ages of the profiles by choosing an arbitrary number to represent the age of the first profile and assigning multiples of this number to represent the age of succeeding profiles relative to the age of the first. The results were straightforward. We found that 91% of the judgments agreed with the hypothesis that the strain transformation led to monotonic perceived age changes. On the other hand, using the shear transformation to predict judgments produced only 66% agreement. Because strain was by far the stronger variable of age change, we next tested the sensitivity of subjects to very small changes in profiles due to this transformation.

Experiment 2

Sensitivity to the shape changes produced by the strain transformation was assessed in a second experiment by presenting pairs of profiles produced by different levels of the transformation and requiring subjects to choose the older profile in each pair. A series of profiles was produced by applying strain transformations ranging from $k = -0.25$ to $+0.55$ to a single profile. Eighteen pairs of profiles were chosen; three for each of six levels of difference in degree of strain. The pairs were presented twice to four groups of ten subjects. Different random orders were used for each presentation and each group. Subjects were informed that the study was concerned with their ability to make fine discriminations of age, and that for each pai' they were to choose the profile that appeared to be older. During the experiment, subjects were not told whether or not their responses were correct. (By correct response we mean the choice of the profile with the larger degree of strain as the older.)

Several results were found. An analysis of variance on percentage of errors as a function of difference in strain showed a typical psychophysical result—a decline in accuracy with smaller physical differences and an increase in sensitivity with experience at the task. However, two other aspects of the results are more important for the question at hand. First, subjects do not merely discriminate the pairs consistently but, in addition, choose the profile with the larger strain as the older profile with greater than chance frequency; in the first presentation, the profile with larger strain was selected on 83.2% of the trials, and the second, on 89.2% of the trials. In each presentation, every subject selected the profile with the larger k as older on more than 50% of the trials. A sign test showed the chance probability of this to be far less than .001. Thus, the conclusion of the first experiment is confirmed in a different experimental task. Sensitivity to the strain variable proved to be surprisingly fine.

Experiment 3

A third experiment was designed to determine if a structural invariant existed by which individual identity might be perceived. We have all had the experience of recognizing someone we know as a child years later when he or she has grown to maturity. As a preliminary test of preservation of identity under the strain transformation, profile views of the external portions of the brain cases of six different skulls were traced from x-ray photographs and subjected to five levels of strain. Five pairs of transformed profiles were selected from each individual; the degree of strain for members of three pairs differed by 0.30 and those of the other two pairs by 0.45. A profile of a different skull with the same degree of strain as one of the members of the pair was added to each pair. Slides were constructed of the profile triples such that the two profiles from distinct skulls that had the same level of strain appeared at the bottom of the slide. Thirty subjects were presented the slides and asked to select which of the two profiles at the bottom of the slide appeared most similar to the profile at the top. The overall percentage of errors was low: The mean error rate was less than 17%, with no subject making more than 33% errors. Because no subject made 50% or more errors, a sign test on the hypothesis of chance responding by each subject yields a probability of far less than 0.001.

The results of these three studies provide support for two important hypotheses: The strain transformation, due presumably to growth, not only provides the major source of the relevant perceptual information for *age level* (transformational invariant) but also leaves invariant sufficient perceptual information for the specification of *individual identity* (structural invariant) from the shape of the head alone.

These experiments also support the notion that the perceived shape of an object is not simply the shape of a static, rigid object but is rather a higher-order structural invariant that remains relatively unchanged by the events (i.e., transformational invariants) into which such objects may enter. Further dramatic support for this claim is provided by the fact that the identity of human faces is preserved under elastic transformations as distinctive from growth as artistic characterization. The success of political caricaturists rests on their ability to satirize a political figure by exaggerating distinctive body or facial properties without obscuring the identity of the famous (or infamous) personage depicted. Indeed, there is evidence that artistic rendition of complex structures can facilitate their identification (Ryan & Schwartz, 1956). This could not occur unless the structural invariants specifying personal identity were somehow preserved under the caricaturing transformation.

GENERAL CONCLUSIONS

Each of the experiments discussed in this chapter is not only amenable to a generative systems explanation but seems to require it. The range of events surveyed, from simple events such as orbiting objects to more elaborate events involving growth of human faces, suggests that the ability to formulate abstract concepts is a basic cognitive capacity underlying knowledge acquisition. This characterization of knowledge acquisition has several important implications.

The most general implication concerns how we should conceptualize the nature of those situations in which we accrue useful knowledge about our natural, cultural, social, and professional environments. If the majority of our experiences in these areas involve encounters with either novel instances of old events or fresh instances of new events, then we must go beyond concern for how particulars may be learned. Rather, the primary goal should be to understand and to exploit more efficiently the cognitive capacity to assimilate knowledge that is abstract and, therefore, generative.

Moreover, if adaptive responding even to ordinary events like human faces entails generative knowledge of abstract relationships, then that is all the more true for dealing with higher forms of knowledge in such fields as science, philosophy, mathematics, art, history, or law. Acquisition of knowledge in all areas is a result of abstraction over well-chosen instances of events. What we have proposed is that the generative capacity to formulate abstract concepts may be naturally engaged when the learner experiences a very special subset of exemplars, namely, the generator.

Obviously, there is still much work to be accomplished before drawing any final conclusions about the proposed theory. It already exhibits, however, in our opinion, sufficient promise in both theoretical and practical areas to merit further development by cognitive psychologists.

ACKNOWLEDGMENTS

Preparation of this chapter was supported in part by a Career Development Award to Robert Shaw from the National Institute of Child Health and Human Development (1 KO4-HD24010), in part by a postdoctoral traineeship awarded to Buford Wilson by the same agency, and by grants to the University of Minnesota, Center for Research in Human Learning, from the National Science Foundation (GB-17590), the National Institute of Child Health and Human Development (HD-01136), and the Graduate School of the University of Minnesota. The chapter was completed while the senior author was a fellow at the Center for Advanced study in the Behavioral Sciences to whom our heartfelt thanks are given for its support.

REFERENCES

Attneave, F, (1957a). Physical determinants of the judged complexity of shapes. *Journal of Experimental Psychology, 53,* 221–227.

Bartlett, F. C. (1932). *Remembering: A study in experimental and social psychology.* Cambridge, England: Cambridge University Press.

Blumenthal, A. L. (1967). Prompted recall of sentences. *Journal of Verbal Learning and Verbal Behavior, 6,* 203–206.

Chomsky, N. (1965). *Aspects of the theory of syntax.* Cambridge: MIT Press.

Dewey, J. (1939). *Intelligence in the modern world* (J. Ratner, Ed.). New York: The Modern Library.

Fant, G. (1964). Auditory patterns of speech. In W. Wathen-Dunn (Ed.), *Models for the perception of speech and visual form.* Cambridge, MA: MIT Press.

Greenberg, J. H., & Jenkins, J. J. (1964). Studies in the psychological correlates of the sound system of American English, I. Measuring linguistic distance from English, II. Distinctive features and psychological space. *Word, 20,* 137–177.

Liberman, A. M., Cooper, F. S., Shankweiler, D. P., & Studdert-Kennedy, M. (1967). Perception of the speech code. *Psychological Review, 74,* 341–461.

Mark, L. S., Todd, J. T., & Shaw, R. E. (1981). The perception of growth: A geometric analysis of how different styles of change are distinguished. *Journal of Experimental Psychology: Human Perception and Performance, 1,* 355–368.

Mehler, J. (1963). Some effects of grammatical transformations on the recall of English sentences. *Journal of Verbal Learning and Verbal Behavior, 2,* 346–351.

Miller, G. A. (1962). Some psychological studies of grammar. *American Psychologist, 17,* 748–762.

Pittenger, J. B., & Shaw, R. E. (1975). Perceptions of relative and absolute age in facial photographs. *Perception & Psychophysics, 18*(2), 137–143.

Pittenger, J. B., Shaw, R. E., & Mark, L. S. (1979). Perceptual information for the age level of faces as a higher-order invariant of growth. *Journal of Experimental Psychology: Human Perception and Performance, 5,* 478–493.

Posner, M. I., & Keele, S. W. (1968). On the genesis of abstract ideas. *Journal of Experimental Psychology, 77,* 353–363.

Posner, M. I., & Keele, S. W. (1970). Retention of abstract ideas. *Journal of Experimental Psychology, 83,* 304–308.

Rohrman, N. L. (1968). The role of syntactic structure in the recall of English nominalizations. *Journal of Verbal Learning and Verbal Behavior, 7,* 904–912.

Ryan, T. A., & Schwartz, C. B. (1956). Speed of perception as a function of mode of representations. *American Journal of Psychology, 69,* 60–69.

sachs, J. (1967). Recognition memory for syntactic and semantic aspects of connected discourse. *Perception and Psychophysics, 2*(9), 437–442.

Shaw, R. E., & Cutting, J. E. (1980). Clues from an ecological theory of event perception. In U. Bellugi & M. Studdert-Kennedy (Eds.), *Signed and spoken language: Biological constraints on linguistic form.* Weinheim: Verlag Chemie.

Shaw, R. E., McIntyre, M., & Mace, W. (1974). The role of symmetry in event perception. In R. B. MacLeod & H. Pick (Eds.), *Studies in perception: Essays in honor of J. J. Gibson.* New York: Cornell University Press.

Shaw, R., & Pittenger, J. (1977). Perceiving the face of change in changing faces: Implications for a theory of object perception. In R. Shaw & J. Bransford (Eds.), *Perceiving, acting, and knowing.* Hillsdale, NJ: Lawrence Erlbaum Associates.

4 From Stimulus to Symbol*

Heinz von Foerster
Pescadero, CA

> **CONTENTS**
> Introduction
> Environment: An Analysis
> Symbolization: A Synthesis

Man's heritage is of two different kinds. One has been accumulated through perhaps 2 billion years of evolution and is encoded in the molecular structure of his genetic makeup. The other has been built up during approximately 1 million years of communication and is encoded in the symbolic structure of his knowledge.

Although man evolved as a result of interplay between genetic mutability and environmental selectivity, his self-made symbols evolved as a result of interplay between his flexibility in expressing and his sensitivity in distinguishing. This observation links these two evolutionary processes in a not-too-obvious way and gives rise to the formidable problem of demonstrating this link by tracing structure and function of the symbols he uses back to the cellular organization of his body. It is clear that we are today still far from a solution to this problem. First, we do not yet possess a consistent comprehension of structure and function of our symbols, to wit, the Cyclopean efforts by various linguistic schools to establish a concise language for dealing with language; second, our knowledge of the cellular organization of the body is still meager, despite the incredible amount of knowledge accumulated over the past decades. As a matter of fact, it is indeed doubtful whether with presently available conceptual tools this problem can be

*Portions of this chapter were originally published in G. Kepes (Ed.), *Sign Image Symbol*. New York: George Braziller, 1966, 42–61. Reprinted with permission of the publisher. George Braziller, Inc. New York, Copyright © 1966.

solved at all. These tools, however, will permit us to get an insight into the magnitude of this problem.

An approach that considers symbolization in the framework suggested by the formulation of this problem does have the advantage that it can tie together evidence accumulated in a variety of fields. Moreover, within the framework suggested here, it becomes impossible to talk about symbols in a static, ontological way and not consider the dynamic evolution of symbolic presentation. Likewise, it becomes impossible to separate a symbol from its symbolizer, his perceptual, motor, and cognitive capabilities and constraints. And further, it becomes impossible to separate symbol and symbolizer from the environment, which we have to populate with other symbolizers in order for symbolization to make any sense at all.

The following is an attempt to establish clues for the understanding of potentialities and limits of symbolization through the understanding of variety and constraints in the maker and user of symbols and in his environment.

ENVIRONMENT: AN ANALYSIS

Evolution, like memory, is an irreversible process. The man who once knew a datum but has forgotten it now, is different from the man who never knew it. Irreversibility in evolution permits one to picture this process in the form of a tree with divergent branch points only. Fig. 4.1 is such a representation of evolutionary differentiation in vertebrates over the last 500 million years. Time runs from bottom to top and the number of different species at any time within each branch is indicated by the width of that branch. A subspecies among mammals called *homo sapiens,* including its entire temporal extension, occupies in this graph but a tiny speck of space in the upper right corner of the mammalian branch, number 8.

It is perhaps easy to see that this graph represents paleontological estimates of only those species that were sufficiently stable to leave detectable traces. All unstable mutants escape detection and thus cannot be accounted for. In other words, the figure is essentially a picture of the success story of living forms. This observation permits us to look at this representation in a slightly different way, namely, to consider each point in a branch as being an instant at which a crucial problem is presented to a particular species. If the species solves this problem the point will be retained and moves upward an ever so slight amount. If not, the point will be removed, i.e., the species is eliminated. It is clear that the crucial problem referred to here is how to survive, and it is also clear that this crucial problem is posed by the properties of the particular environment, which is in interaction with elements of this species or its mutants.

From this viewpoint, "environment" is seen in a two-fold way: as a set of properties of the physical world that act upon an organism; and also as an

FIG. 4.1. Evolution of vertebrates over the last 500 million years. Time runs
from bottom to top. Width of branches corresponds to approximate abundance of
different species within the branch (class). 1. Jawless fishes. 2. Cartilage fishes. 3.
Placoderms. 4. Bony fishes. 5. Amphibians. 6. Birds. 7. Reptiles. 8. Mammals.

accumulation of successful solutions to the problem of selecting such conditions
in the physical world that are at least survivable. In this discussion "environment" will always carry this relative notion as "environment of . . .," where
environment and the organism associated with it will be duals to each other in the
sense a particular organism O implies its particular environment E(O), and vice
versa, that a particular environment E implies its appropriate organism O(E).

By carving out from the physical universe just that portion E(O) that is
"meaningful" for this organism O, one has carved out a portion that is necessarily of compatible complexity with that of the organism. An organism that

tolerates a variation of temperature of, say, 30° Fahrenheit around a certain mean, cannot move into places where temperatures vary beyond this tolerance.

This statement can be expressed differently. An organism that is matched to its environment possesses in some way or another a means for detecting the order and the regularities of this environment. Perhaps the most fundamental principle involved in this registration is the correspondence between the *neighborhood relationships* that determine environmental structures, and the *neighborhood logics* that are incorporated into neural connectivity, which determine the "whether" and "where" of certain environmental properties.

This suggests two levels of "computation." First, computation on the grand scale of evolutionary differentiation that incorporates the environmental constraints into the structure of neural networks that, on the second level, compute within the limits of their structure spatiotemporal quantities of useful universal parameters. The first level refers to the species, the second to the specimen. It is on the first level that the notion of "Platonic Ideas" arises.

At this point the concept of environmental "order" needs further clarification. Intuitively, one would associate order with the relation of parts in a whole. But what are parts? Again intuitively, parts emerge as "separabilia," because the relation among their components is of higher order than that of the parts of the whole. Although this definition is somewhat circular, it points in the right direction, for it relates order to the strength of constraints that control the interaction of elements comprising the whole. These constraints manifest themselves in the structure they produce: For example, a globular star cluster has simple spherical symmetry, because the weak gravitational forces that hold the approximately 100,000 elements of this system in statistical equilibrium have themselves radial symmetry. In a similar fashion, the growth mechanism of snow crystals is subject to a major constraint, namely the triangular shape of the water molecule H_2O that has two hydrogen atoms attached to the big oxygen atom at angles that are close to either 30° or 60°. This slight deviation from the condition that would produce equilateral shapes introduces a certain amount of "freedom" for the molecules to attach themselves to each other, which in turn allows for the large variability within this constraint. Note that in spite of the great difference in the individual shapes of these crystals, no difficulty arises in recognizing these forms at a glance as snow crystals. This suggests that what the perceptual-cognitive apparatus extracts ("computes") in answer to the question "What is this?" is the one thing that is common to all these shapes, and this is the constraint in their growth mechanism. The name we give to this constraint is simply "snow crystal."

In the temporal domain, environmental order is again generated by the constraints of the "Laws of Nature" that, on the macroscopic scale of direct observation, control the chain of events. Chaos would permit transitions from any state to any other state, mountains transforming themselves into flying pink elephants, pink elephants turning into yellow goo, etc. Not only are organisms impossible in this world, for there is no law that holds the organism together, but also this world is indescribable, for description requires names, and names refer to the "invariabilia"—the constraints—in the environment.

One clue of how to extract these constraints from the structure of the environment is suggested by the preceding examples. Structure in space was determined by a law in the growth mechanism that permitted attachment of new neighbor elements only at particular points; structure in time was determined by a law in the transition process that permitted only a particular event to be neighbor to an existing one. In other words, spatiotemporal order is generated by constraints that control spatiotemporal neighborhood relationships. Hence, if these can be "sized up," the constraints can be evaluated.

If chaos permits every event to appear with equal probability, order emerges from chaos only when certain transitions of events become more probable than others. Certainty of an event following another creates a perfect, deterministic universe, and the problem of how to survive in such a deterministic universe is reduced to finding the constraints that govern the transitions from one event to the next. Clearly, the simplest of all such deterministic universes is the one where no transitions take place, i.e., where everything is at motionless and uniform tranquility. Hence, it was the oceans, where temperature variations, changes in the concentration of chemicals, and destructive forces are kept at a minimum, that served as the cradle for life.

The dual interdependence of organism-environment permits a dual interpretation of the tree of evolution (Fig. 4.1). Instead of interpreting points on this graph as *species of organisms,* one may interpret them as *species of environments.* Thus viewed, this chart represents the evolution of environments that were successively carved out of the physical universe. These environments evolved from simple, almost deterministic ones, to extremely complex ones, where large numbers of constraints regulate the flow of events. An environmental subspecies among mammalian environments, called "E (*homo sapiens*)," occupies in this graph a small speck of space in the upper right corner of branch number 8. Hence, its dual, "*homo sapiens* (E)," sees "his universe" as a result of two billion years of environmental evolution, which step-by-step carved out from the physical universe an ever-increasing number of constraints of all those in this universe that are computable within the limits of the evolving organism.

Figure 4.2 sketches the circular flow of information in the environment-organism system. In the environment constraints generate structure. Structural information is received by the organism that, in turn, computes the constraints. These are finally tested against the environment by the actions of the organism.

With the emergence of self-reflection and consciousness in higher organisms a peculiar complication arises. A self-reflecting subject may insist that introspection does not permit him to decide whether the world as he sees it is "real," or just a phantasmagory, a dream, an illusion of his fancy. A decision in this dilemma is important in the present discussion, because, if the latter alternative

ENVIRONMENT

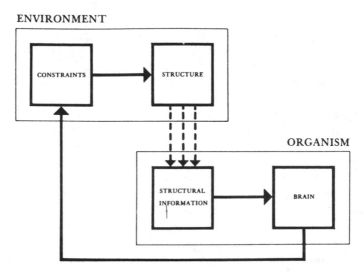

FIG. 4.2.   Information flow in the organism-environment (O–E) system.

should hold true, no problems of how organisms "represent internally" the features of their environment would arise, for all environmental features would be just internal affairs in the first place.

In which sense reality indeed exists for a self-reflecting organism becomes clear by an argument that defeats the solipsistic hypothesis (von Foerster, 1960). This argument proceeds by *reductio ad absurdum* of the thesis: "This world is only in my imagination; the only reality is the imagining 'I.'"

Assume for the moment that the gentleman in the bowler hat in Fig. 4.3 insists that he is the sole reality, and everything else appears only in his imagination. However, he cannot deny that his imaginary universe is populated with apparitions that are not unlike himself. Hence he has to grant them the privilege, that they themselves may insist that they are the sole reality and everything else is only a concoction of their imaginations. On the other hand, they cannot deny that their fantasies are populated by apparitions that are not unlike themselves, one of which may be *he,* the gentleman with the bowler hat. With this the circle of contradiction is closed, for if one assumes to be the sole reality, it turns out he is the imagination of someone else who, in turn, insists that *he* is the sole reality. The resolution of this paradox establishes "environment" through stipulating a second observer. Reality is what can be witnessed, hence, rests on "together-knowledge," that is, *conscientia:* Reality is conscience.

Can these notions be translated into the language of the neurophysiologist? Indeed, this can be done if one realizes that all sensory modalities translate stimuli into the universal "language" of electric pulse activity, so that invariants computed by different senses may be coordinated on higher levels of neural activity (cf. Pitts & McCulloch, 1947). Because it is on this level where we have to search for the origin of symbolization, this point may be illustrated by an example.

A hypothetical anthropologist visits a fictitious tribe whose members use (among others) two particular symbols, of which one is rounded and the other jagged. It is significant that no further information is needed for the anthropologist to identify which one of the two is called an "Oo boo," and which an "Itratzky." It may indeed be argued that in this case the pattern of neural activity

FIG. 4.3. *Reductio ad absurdum* of the solipsistic hypothesis. The hominid apparitions of the gentleman with the bowler hat have the gentleman with the bowler hat as apparition.

associated with the visual stimulus configuration is homologous to that generated by configurations of the auditory stimulus. This argument is going in the right direction, but it fails to cope with a strange situation, namely, that earlier experience and learning are not involved in this spontaneous identification process.

Because associations gained from experience are excluded, one must assume that this audio-visual correspondence rests upon the fabric without which experience cannot be gained. The structure of this fabric must permit some cross talk between the senses, not only in terms of associations, but also in terms of integration. If this structure permits the ear to witness what the eye sees and the eye to witness what the ear hears then there is again "together-knowledge," *conscientia,* but here we call it consciousness.

SYMBOLIZATION: A SYNTHESIS

To survive is to anticipate correctly environmental events. The logical canon of anticipation is inductive inference, that is, the method of finding, under given evidence E, the hypothesis H that is highly confirmed by E and is suitable for a certain purpose. This is computation of invariants within the limits of available information and follows the principles of invariant computations as before, only on a higher level. Knowledge is the totality of these hypotheses (invariants, laws, regulations) and is accumulated on three levels. First, on the molecular level in the genetic structure that tests the viability of its hypotheses, the mutations, through the vehicle of the developed organism; second, on the level of the individual organism, through adaptation and learning; and third, on the social level, through symbolic communication that cumulatively passes information on from generation to generation.

Because these are evolutionary processes, and hence irreversible, error would accumulate with knowledge, were it not for a preventative mechanism: death. With death, all registers are cleared and untaught offspring can freshly go on learning. This mechanism works on the first and second levels, but not on the third.

For cumulatively acquired knowledge to be passed on through generations, it must be communicated in symbols and not in signs. This separates man from beast. Communication among social insects is carried out through unalterable signs linked to the genetic make-up of the species. Whereas signs refer to objects and percepts and serve to modify actions and manipulations, symbols refer to concepts and ideas and serve to initiate and facilitate computation.

Because the ultimate relation between symbols and environmental entities is cascaded over the relations symbol/concept and concept/environment, it is in its logical structure very complicated indeed. This gives rise to breakdowns that manifest themselves on various levels of semantic morbidity.

Symbols share with concepts and ideas the property that they do not possess the properties of the entities they represent. The concept of roses "smells" as much, or as little, as the concept of jumping "jumps." The concept of a square is not quadratic. If this point is missed, a number would be just so many fingers and a square with area 2 would have nonexistent sides.

Because symbols refer to concepts and ideas, they too may not have the properties they represent. The symbol of a square may not be quadratic, as can be clearly seen by the string of peculiarly shaped little marks on this paper that have just been used to refer to this geometrical figure.

What, then, determines the form of a symbol; is it an arbitrary convention, or does it convey its meaning by its shape? Again, ontologically this question cannot be resolved. One has to look into the ontogenesis of symbolic representations.

Look again at Fig. 4.2, which represents the information flow between a single organism and its environment. Because symbolization requires at least two interacting subjects who are immersed in an environment that is common to both, we must extend this diagram to admit a second subject. This is done in Fig. 4.4a.

Subjects S_1 and S_2 are coupled to their common environment E. In contrast to Fig. 4.2, in which the organism is faced only with an environment with given constraints, now each of these subjects is confronted with the additional complication of seeing his environment populated with at least one other subject that also generates events in the environment E. Hence S_2 sees, in addition to the events generated by E, those generated by S_1, and because these take place in E, they shall be labeled E_1; conversely, subject S_1 sees in addition to events generated by E those generated by S_2, which will be called E_2. Thus, in spite of the fact that both S_1 and S_2 are immersed in the same environment E, each of these subjects sees a different environment, namely, S_1 has to cope with (E, E_2), and

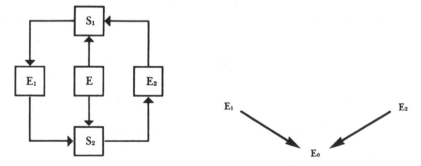

FIG. 4.4.   (a) Communication system including two subjects S_1 and S_2 generating (linguistic) events E_1 and E_2 in a common environment E. (b) The convergence process to a common "language" E_0 indicative of successful communication.

S_2 with (E, E_1). In other words, this situation is asymmetrical regarding the two subjects, with E being the only symmetrical part.

Assume that E_1 and E_2 are initial attempts by S_1 and S_2 to communicate environmental properties to each other. It is clear that these attempts will fail unless—and this is the decisive point—both subjects succeed in eventually converging to like representation for like universal features. This process may be expressed symbolically as in Fig. 4.4b. The arrows indicate the convergence process, and E_o stands for the final universal "language" spoken by both subjects. At this point the initial asymmetry ceases to exist and both subjects perceive the same environment (E,E_o).

As in all evolutionary systems, the outcome of this process cannot be predicted in the usual sense, because the goal that established equilibrium is not directly apparent in the final equilibrial state, which is a communicable symbol, whereas the goal is *communicability*.

Symbols must not necessarily have the shape of the objects they ultimately refer to, yet within that freedom there are constraints working in the evolution of symbolic representation that confine their (the symbols') development within reasonable limits. One of these constraints is dictated by the tools with which these symbols are generated, another is their syntactical structure.

An example of the first kind of constraint operating on the development of written symbols is given in Fig. 4.5, which shows the development of highly stylized symbolic forms from initially representational pictograms (Neugebauer, 1934). This transition is believed to have taken place in the two millennia of Sumerian cultural activity between 4000 and 2000 B.C. As one goes down the column it can be seen how the constraints imposed by the writing tools—a stylus with triangular cross section pressed into soft clay—strongly modify the early pictogram given at the top. It may be interesting to note that simultaneously with this departure from structural representation goes an increase in the possibility to add modifiers to the original meaning. Although the pictogram at the top of the column indeed says "foot," after 2000 years of stylization (bottom) it may stand for "walking," "running," "delivering a message," or other "foot-connected" actions if associated with appropriate modifiers. Nevertheless, in some instances it seems to be possible to see behind the form of later symbols the shape of earlier pictorial representations.

The other kind of constraint is a structural one and does not show itself in an obvious way, for symbols carry rules of connectivity and not so much rules of entity. Symbols may be compared to atoms that react to particular atoms to form the molecular compounds but are inert to all other atoms. Take, for instance, these "molecular" sentences:

"Socrates is identical."
"4 + 4 = purple."

FIG. 4.5. Formalization of pictograms through constraints imposed
by writing tools. This development is
estimated to have taken place in Mes-
opotamia during a period from the
fourth to the second millennium B.C.

The disturbing thing about these is that they are neither true nor false; they are
nonsensical. The connection rules of the symbols have been violated in these
examples. "Identical" sets up a relation between two entities. "Socrates is
identical with Plato" is a sentence that makes sense although it happens to be a
false proposition. The compound "4 + 4 =   " requires a number to
follow. Putting "6" at the end is a good guess, but "purple" is an operator with

an entirely different structure. This indicates that somehow structure is still preserved in symbolical discourse, but in a syntactical and not in a representational sense. The language of symbols has, so to speak, its own logical grammar (Wittgenstein, 1921/1961). Uniqueness in symbolic expressions is established in a way similar to that of a jigsaw puzzle in which pieces can be put together in one and only one way. It is the sometimes far-extending neighborhood relationship among the pieces—the symbols—that puts them into place.

It is clear that the constraints expressed in the neighborhood relationships of symbols reflect constraints in the environment. For instance, a sentence that refers to two particular persons must employ two proper names, that is, the connection rules among symbols mirror relations between objects.

However, symbols are by no means proxy for their objects (Langer, 1957). There are two morbid states of the mind, magical thinking and schizophrenia, in which this distinction is erased. In both cases, symbol and object become indistinguishable. In purpose-oriented Jou Jou and in Voodoo the identity of symbol with object is used to manipulate the world by manipulating the symbol. In schizophrenia, symbol and object are freely interchanged to produce peculiar hierarchies of identities. In order to comprehend in depth the modality of this affliction, a short passage of the extensive description of the case of a 6-year-old boy by the name of Walter (= water) is given here (from Meduna & McCulloch, 1945).

Late in November, 1936, presumably because he had heard a rumor about a child killed in an accident in an elevator there, he became terrified when taken to a department store. He trembled, cried, vomited, and remained "hysterical" for 2 days during which time he made little jerking movements of his body and shoulders and said scarcely a word. The following day, Dr. Hamill was for the first time able to make out that he failed to distinguish between himself (Walter) and water. Walter shifted to water, thence to Deanna Durbin who played in "Rainbow on the River" and so to water again. Being water, he felt he could not be drowned but might be imprisoned in the radiator. On hearing the knocking of water in the radiator, he said, "elevator just came up and gave a kid a knock" and again, "they are killing the kid," which terrified him because he was the kid. Then followed "the telephone burnt and got water after Suzy burnt."

(Dr.: "Where does water come from?") "I come from the show." (Dr.: "You thought water and Walter were the same thing.") "My father used to take me across the river." (Dr.: "And he called you Walter?") "And got drowned. I do not live on Springfield. Bad boys drink water. They do not drink milk. Good boys live on Springfield. I used to live on Springfield—Mississippi River."

It may be speculated that evolution did not weed out mental disorders that afflict proper use of symbols because the survival value of the ability to symbolize is so enormous that occasional deviations of this ability in individuals and in whole cultures could still be tolerated. The enormous advantage of organisms that are able to manipulate symbols over those who can only react to signs is that logical operations do not have to be acted out, they can be computed. It is obvious that this saves considerable amounts of energy. But the crucial point here is that errors in reasoning are not necessarily lethal.

The emergence of the ubiquitous computer, either as the giant number cruncher or as the small personal microprocessor, illustrates the immense advantage of operating within syntactic relational structures; these systems manipulate symbols only, they do not know objects. The laws of algebra and logic are incorporated in their structure. Hence, they cannot err by confusing modality as does a schizophrenic, nor can they err in syntax and generate nonsense. The only error they can make is confusing true with false and false with true.

ACKNOWLEDGMENTS

This chapter is in part based on work sponsred by the Air Force Office of Scientific Research under Grant 7–64 and by the National Institute of Health under Grant GM-10718.

REFERENCES

Langer, S. (1957). *Philosophy in a new key* (3rd ed.). New York: New American Library.

Meduna, L. J., & McCulloch, W. S. (1945). The modern concept of schizophrenia. In *Symposium on neuropsychiatric diseases*. Philadelphia: Saunders.

Neugebauer, O. (1934). *Vorgriechische mathematik*. Berlin: Springer.

Pitts, W., & McCulloch, W. S. (1947). How we know universals: The perception of auditory and visual form. *Bulletin of Mathematical Biophysics, 9,* 127–147.

von Foerster, H. (1960). On self-organizing systems and their environments. In M. C. Yovits & S. Cameron (Eds.), *Self-organizing systems*. New York: Pergamon.

Wittgenstein, L. (1961). *Tractatus logico-philosophicus* (D. F. Pears & B. F. McGuinness, Trans.). New York: Humanities Press. (Original work published 1921

5 An Ecological Perspective on Concepts and Cognition

Gerald J. Balzano
University of California, San Diego

Viki McCabe
University of California, Los Angeles

CONTENTS

FROM CONCEPTS TO COGNITION

When we talk about cognition we are fundamentally talking about what an organism *knows*. Traditionally knowing implies knowledge and knowledge implies acquisition and storage, presumably inside the organism (or even more localized, in the organism's mind). The assumptions of storage and mental location imply that knowledge of the world is somehow represented in the mind; this leads easily to the conclusion that the study of cognition is the study of internal representations and that knowledge is a kind of code (e.g., neural, computational) that abstracts, translates, and freezes the world into mental quanta that can be retrieved for future epistemic acts.

An alternative ecological view is to treat knowing as a process (rather than treating knowledge as a thing) and consider it a continuously ongoing transaction of participation and coordination between an organism and its environment. This transaction yokes intention, perception, and action in an open cognitive system that is scaled to the transforming structure of meaningful events—both fast events, such as fleeting facial expressions or honking horns, and slow events, such as the course of a symphony or a child growing up; it is largely concerned with the persistence and permanence of significant environmental information and involves the detection of how an event unfolds, which of its properties remain constant and which transform.

Focusing on internal representations tends to obscure the mechanism of coordination with the environment and the kind of information available from such coordination that is central to the ecological view. Indeed, because cognitive studies typically focus on internal representations, cognitive processes and the information they use have been considered largely invisible.

Representation theorists seem to have chosen to take the "invisibility" of cognitive processes as a mandate to assert invisible internal processes operating on invisible internal representations. One problem with this strategy is an overabundance of degrees of freedom; with theories coming in the form of representation-process pairs, there is an indefinite amount of fiddling you can do with the representations in your theory as long as you fiddle with the processes that operate on the representations in a compensatory way (Anderson, 1978). But the real irony of this position is that, despite a thoroughgoing commitment to the detailed study of (mental) *process*—processes to transform, access, and store knowledge in many forms—the representation theorist ultimately thinks of knowledge (we would say "knowing") itself as a thing. Knowledge is said to be represented in the mind, and the major questions are not about how and what we know, but rather take the form, how is knowledge organized, and in what form(s) is it represented? Although there has been considerable controversy over the latter question, the consensus on the former has been reasonably good that knowledge is organized into *concepts*. Accordingly, the nature of concepts has become a central issue in psychology. In the classic book *A Study of Thinking* by Bruner, Goodnow, and Austin (1956), the forming and using of concepts is viewed as "one of the . . . most ubiquitous phenomena in cognition" (p. ix).

A primary purpose of this chapter is to reexamine prevalent approaches to and theories about concepts and to suggest some alternative perspectives on these matters from an ecological point of view. In carrying out this aim, we are somewhat at a disadvantage, for we have already defined the terms of the discussion in a manner more conducive to talk about knowledge than talk about knowing; to some extent, we have no choice here if we wish to represent current thinking fairly. But as we go, we try to inject clues about how we would prefer to talk about the phenomena and ideas under discussion, and by the end we hope to have conveyed a general understanding of what it would mean to take an ecological turn in the area of "concept theories." Filling in some of the details of this understanding is, then, the job we leave to the individual chapters that follow.

SOME PAST AND PRESENT RESEARCH
ON CONCEPTS

At first blush, the concept of a concept is quite modest. Some examples: In the words of Bruner et al. (1956), "from a common response to an array of objects we infer that [someone] 'has' an equivalence or identity category" (p. 2). It has not even been uncommon to think of "concept behavior . . . in terms of a common mediating response" (Adams, 1967, p. 201). And of the traditional doctrine of the concept, Cassirer (1923/1953) states, "Nothing is presupposed save the existence of things in their inexhaustible multiplicity, and the power of the mind to select from this wealth of particular existences those features that are *common* to several of them" (p. 4).

Early empirical work on concepts was also of a modest sort, dealing with what appeared to be the simplest sort of concepts, like "blue," or "triangle," or "blue triangle." The stimulus was generally viewed—and constructed in the laboratory—as a collection of cues or attributes, one or more of which would be chosen by an experimenter as "relevant" to the concept to be acquired. In the simplest case, an experimental subject would have two responses available, say 'C' and 'D,' and the experimenter would give two kinds of feedback, "right" and "wrong." In this simple associationist framework, one might talk about the attributes of the concept C getting associated to the response 'C' under the control of feedback or other reinforcement. But the lineage of theorists initiated more or less by Bruner et al. (1956) had a more *cognitive* approach, according to which the concept learner was thought of as one who tested hypotheses against the stimuli (Bower & Trabasso, 1963; Levine, 1969). It is this cognitive perspective that enjoys greater popularity today. Interestingly enough, for all the apparent differences in connotation between cognitive and associative views, it has frequently been suggested that the main prediction upon which they differ is whether concept attainment proceeds in an incremental or all-or-none fashion (Bourne, 1968). This evidence generally favors the all-or-none models and therefore tends to confirm the more "cognitive" hypothesis-testing theories, although staunch associationists are not necessarily persuaded by such evidence. For example, Bourne (1968) has suggested that hypothesis-testing advocates have cleverly manipulated task variables that are not systematically represented in either kind of theory in such a way as to favor the hypothesis-testing view. This is not an unfamiliar story in the history of psychology. According to Bourne, in order to maximize the chances of obtaining evidence favorable to all-or-none hypothesis-testing theories, one should use (a) stimuli that are well spaced along familiar dimensions, (b) responses that are "primitive and highly integrated" (Bourne, 1968, p. 244), and (c) concepts that are simple, involving only one or two relevant dimensions.

Such examples of concepts seem both biased toward a particular theoretical view and hardly representative of the kinds of concepts that help us understand the world. The latter variety, certainly, are at least more complex in that they are characterized by a greater number of "features" or "dimensions." Another difference that has been suggested, most notably by Brunswik (1949), is that many real concepts are not deterministic but only *probabilistic* functions of their stimulus attributes. This notion, in particular, has received strong support in recent psychological theorizing about concepts, to the point where it is unusual to believe in a strict set of singly-necessary-and-jointly-sufficient stimulus attributes for most concepts (Smith & Medin, 1981). Yet under the (apparently) more "ecological" Brunswikian rubric, one could still do experiments with artificial concepts, except that the features or dimensional values of a stimulus in the experiment would be only probabilistically related to their category membership.

It wasn't until the work of E. Rosch in the early 1970's that psychologists became more interested in natural concepts, or "natural categories," as Rosch called them. Instead of looking at blue triangles, Rosch looked at things like birds, fruit, tools, and furniture (Rosch, Mervis, Gray, Johnson, & Boyes-Braem, 1976). With this change in focus came also a change in the kind of questions asked. Most adults already *knew* these concepts, so the issues of acquisition were put aside. Instead, Rosch asked how these categories were related to one another, and what their "internal structure" was. We refer to these issues as ones of intercategory and intracategory structure, respectively.

On the question of *inter*category structure, Rosch has found, not surprisingly by most accounts, that concepts are related to one another in a hierarchical manner, with the larger more inclusive concepts at the "top" of the hierarchy defined by features common to lower–level concepts. For example, "bird" would be a high-level concept constituted by features common to the lower-level concepts "robin," "bluejay," and "eagle." This might give us properties like "has wings," "can fly," "is warm-blooded," and "has a beak" as examples of bird features, although the feature "warm-blooded" is more general and could be considered a feature of the still higher–order concept "mammal." Rosch did introduce an important qualification to the hierarchical picture: that not all levels of the hierarchy are created equal. The supporting data go something like this: When subjects are asked to list features characteristic of a particular concept, they tend, perhaps not surprisingly, to list more features for concepts situated lower on the hierarchy. But if one looks more closely at the increasing number of features for any particular series of nested concepts, following a path down the hierarchy, one will nearly always find a particular level at which there is a *substantial* increase in number of features listed, and only small increases at levels lower than that. Rosch described the level so distinguished as the "basic level." A number of other properties seem to characterize the basic level: It is the most inclusive level "to have motor sequences in common" (Rosch, 1978, p. 33) and "for which it [is] possible to form a mental image" (p. 34). In other words, the basic level is a level of object description at which objects share many shape properties and, relatedly, share ways in which persons interact with them.

Most researchers take the hierarchical nature of concepts for granted, and the basic level idea itself has generated only a small amount of research. The dominating issue that has guided research in this area for the past 10 or so years has been the second issue, that of *intra*category structure or the "internal structure" of concepts. One particular phenomenon has risen to the status of a veritable *sine qua non* of human concepts: as with levels in the hierarchy, all instances of a concept (we also, after Rosch, use the locution 'members of a category') are not created equal. Some are more *prototypical* than others, are somehow better instances of the concept than others. The initial evidence for this claim about human categorization came from reaction-time studies in a "semantic memory" framework (e.g., Collins & Quillian, 1969; Meyer, 1970; Rips, Shoben, & Smith, 1973) where subjects were timed as they verified (or rejected) statements of the form "An S is a P," e.g., "An axe is a tool." The basic finding is that, for a given P, there is significant variation in the time it takes to verify the category membership of different S terms. Those that lead to the speediest acceptance are called the most prototypical. If subjects are asked directly to judge how "good" various instances of a concept are, or how well they exemplify that concept, the variation in the judgments correlates well with the reaction times, viz. the "best" instances are those that are verified most rapidly. These sorts of experiments have been done both with words denoting the objects and with pictures of the objects (e.g., Smith, Balzano, & Walker, 1978) with similar results.

Smith and Medin (1981) have proposed a useful taxonomy of current theories of concepts. The "classical view" in their taxonomy is the (discredited) view that concepts are given by necessary and sufficient features. Given that prototypicality effects are taken to infirm this theory, researchers have come up with two alternatives, which Smith and Medin call the "probabilistic view" and the "exemplar view." All three views start from the general perspective that a concept is represented in the mind by some kind of information that is used to "match" against incoming stimulation, differing only in what they take the nature of that (internal) information to be. According to the classical and probabilistic views, the internal representation of a concept contains summarizing information about the concept that is abstract and that corresponds to no specific example of the concept, the difference being that in the probabilistic case the summarizing information need not be true of all of the instances of the concept. The most successful models of this type of theory take a leaf out of Wittgenstein and talk of "family resemblances" (Rosch, 1978; Rosch & Mervis, 1975). What is stored amounts to a list of features (or dimensions with values or value ranges) together with conditional probabilities specifying the likelihood that something is concept C, given that it has feature f. A computation is performed on these probabilities over the various features detected, and if/when the value exceeds some threshold, the person responds that the (picture of, word denoting) object in the world is indeed an instance of C. According to the "exemplar view," on the other hand, there is no abstraction as such, no summarizing information, merely a storing of something like literal copies of (features of, dimension–values of) instances encountered. When presented with an object to classify, stored exemplars that are similar to the presented object are accessed, and the decision about category membership is made on the basis of category membership of the accessed exemplars, e.g., the three best matches are accessed and a "yes" decision is made if two out of three belong to C. Although there has been some controversy generated about the virtues of probabilistic versus exemplar views, Smith and Medin (1981) suggest that the major differences between them concern issues of "storage" and "computation," and little if anything in terms of empirical consequences.

Not only are the so-called probablistic and exemplar views of concepts difficult to distinguish experimentally; some recent evidence suggests new problems for distinguishing even the probabilistic and "classical" views. In a simple but telling experiment by Armstrong, Gleitman and Gleitman (1983), subjects were given the standard sorts of classification and goodness-rating tasks for instances (and noninstances) of concepts like *odd number, female, and plane geometry figure*. These concepts are different from the kind usually studied in the literature in that they are unusually well-defined. Concepts like "tool" and "furniture" are fuzzy in the sense that their boundaries are not sharply given; is a radio a piece of furniture, a telephone, a tool? It depends both on the particular example we have in mind (or at hand) and how we choose to use the word (is a word a tool?). On the other hand, a number is either odd, or it is not; there is no fuzziness here. But in the studies of Armstrong et al. the very same phenomena that characterize the fuzzier concepts emerge for nonfuzzy concepts like odd number, viz. subjects give graded typicality or goodness judgments upon request, and said judgments are reasonably good predictors of classification latency in a speeded task. The dire consequences can be summed up simply: "Tool" and "odd number" would seem to be an excellent pair of examples of categories with different *structures* as that term is used in current cognitive psychology. Yet the experimental methodologies chiefly used to elucidate putative internal structure of categories—the goodness rating and the categorization latency tasks—give the same results for both categories and would therefore not appear to be measuring "category structure" at all but something rather different. Whatever these subjects did in the tasks, we can be reasonably sure they did not *really believe* that being an odd number is a property that can be possessed to varying degree. Indeed, even concepts like "bird," which seem fuzzier than "odd number," are not really objectively graded in the way the experimental data would suggest either: as Rey (1983) asks, does anyone think a penguin "is a bird only to a relatively small degree"? If not, then there is a serious question whether the results of the most popular tasks in the current concept literature have anything to do with the way we actually use and reason with concepts. (p.248)

On top of the large questions about the empirical adequacy of current research on concepts, there are a number of theoretical conundra to which the ideas behind this research lead. In the next section we look at two of these, and are prompted to examine the kinds of models proposed for categorization more closely than we have so far. The final section of the chapter provides antidotes to at least some of the problems we encounter.

SOME CONCEPTUAL DIFFICULTIES WITH CURRENT NOTIONS ABOUT "CONCEPT"

Cassirer's Critique

That objects are bundles of features and that concepts are sets of objects sharing common features certainly seem like innocuous enough notions. Yet they lead, as Cassirer (1923/1953) noticed, to a most curious theory of concepts in a number of ways. One is that the concept is constructed in a fundamentally *negative* manner: "we ascend from the species to the higher genus by abandoning a certain characteristic" (p. 5). The more abstract concepts apply to more things in the world but are characterized by a smaller number of properties. In general, intension decreases as extension increases. Consider "chair" versus "furniture"; the latter applies to more objects (greater extension) but is said to have fewer features (smaller intension). But this has the further curious consequence that the most general all-embracing concepts "no longer possess any definite content" (p. 6). Such a formulation seems strangely inappropriate for what we would consider sophisticated or scientific concepts of great generality and power. Such concepts, one would think, ought to sharpen formerly ambiguous ideas, but on the contrary, "the sharp lines of distinction seem the more effaced, the further we pursue the logical process" (p. 6). Under the present concept-schema, the height of our conceptual pyramid is simply an indeterminate "something" or "thing" category to which all things (!) may claim membership but which is correspondingly devoid of any specific meaning.

This negative view of concepts also has undesirable psychological consequences. In particular, the process of "concept formation" becomes difficult to distinguish from "stimulus generalization" and "ignorance of detail." Recall that, for all of the cognitive processing we insert into the picture, the methodology for studying concepts outlined by Bruner and still essentially followed today is barely distinguishable from classical associationistic/behavioristic experimentation. We present stimulus ("category," "concept") C to the subject ("concept learner," "animal") and measure and/or shape the response. Then we present D and note the response. If it is different, we can say the subject has "discriminated" C and D; if it is the same, we can say the subject has "formed the concept" defined by the common features of C and D. Of course, the subject *could* be responding similarly to D as to C because he has simply not remembered properties of C that distinguish it from D; alternatively, he may simply not notice novel properties of D. Cassirer observes that under this view, "What enables the mind to form concepts is just its fortunate gift of forgetfulness" (p. 6). Nor is this position any mere caricature. Cases like Luria's (1965/1969) mnemonist are frequently interpreted along these very lines—the man couldn't form abstract concepts *because* he remembered too much. But Cassirer (1953) relentlessly exposes the poverty of the idea: "all the logical labor which we apply to a given sensuous intuition serves only to separate us more and more from it. Instead of reaching a deeper comprehension of its import and structure, we reach only a superficial schema from which all peculiar traits of the particular case have vanished" (p. 19).

The difficulty just outlined is related to a second, and in some ways more fundamental, difficulty. The idea that concepts are mere conjunctions of properties selected by the mind leaves us with no account of why certain concepts arise rather than others, nothing to guarantee that useful concepts will evolve. There is nothing to prevent, for example, the grouping of cherries and meat together to form the "concept" of *frubidinousness,* which roughly translates as "red, juicy, and edible." Some researchers in the field have tried to parlay this problem into a virtue by talking about our "wondrous ability" to form arbitrary, nonsensical concepts like "meloncat," which refers to an object "just in case it is a watermelon about to be squashed by a giant pussycat, or a pussycat about to be squashed by a giant watermelon" (Osherson, 1978, p. 264). Somewhat tamer concepts formed along similar lines, like "square tomato," are honorifically dubbed "products of conceptual combination" (Osherson & Smith, 1982), and treated as one of the primary things "an adequate theory of concepts must account for" (p. 299). But it seems to us that an adequate theory of concepts must explain how we know the real world from a mentally constructed world and must therefore instead keep hold of the fact that "meloncat" *is* a nonsensical concept. In a fragmented description of the world where objects are considered bundles of features and the totality of possible concepts is enumerated by all possible conjunctions of features, there simply is no notion of what actually specifies an object or what gets one set of concepts selected over another, save the caprice of the mind doing the selecting. And if a mind is capricous enough, it can even construct truly devilish concepts like Nelson Goodman's "grue," which functions mainly to plague philosophers (Goodman, 1973). It can also construct ethically questionable concepts such as Vietnamization or cultural deprivation. These last two concepts, used to obscure dreadful events in the first case and to cast aspersions on people in the second, reflect "conceptual combinations" of uncombinable attributes into false categories, and such "category mistakes'' (Ryle, 1949) are then asserted (by some) to reflect the real world. But what if we want to talk about a world without Vietnamization, cultural deprivation, meloncats, and grue things? Cassirer (1953) suggests that there is always "tacit reference to another intellectual criterion" (p. 7) in justifying why useful and sensible concepts should arise. It is this criterion that, while clearly critical to why knowing takes the specific shape it does, is never discussed by concept theorists.

We take these troubles as clear danger signs for the received theory of concepts. If any are insoluble—and some have suggested just this for Goodman's "grue" paradox—it implies that we have construed the whole matter incorrectly. Cassirer makes some suggestions to deal with these difficulties, and we consider these explicitly together with our own in a later section. But first we must examine what may be an even larger problem for concept theories: the problem of learning.

Is Concept Learning Possible?

This is a trick question, to be sure, but it may be a trickier question than most cognitive psychologists are aware. Surely nobody would wish to dispute that there is, in a layman's sense, concept learning. And if there is no "concept learning" for psychologists who would study (or who thought they were studying) it, then it would appear that a rather large branch of what passes for cognition would have to declare bankruptcy. That the question is indeed a tricky one is amply attested to by the problems of the *Meno* (cf. Sesonske & Fleming, 1965). And recently J. A. Fodor (1975) has modernized and recast these arguments, proposing that current psychological theorizing admits of no coherent process describable as "concept learning." More recently, Fodor (1980) has said it even more strongly: "the very *idea* of concept learning is, I think, confused" (p. 143).

Fodor's argument is bracingly simple. Concept formation, as we reviewed earlier, is generally conceived in current-day cognitive psychology as a kind of hypothesis-testing and -confirmation. The internally posed hypotheses amount to internal representations of one form or another that are tested or "matched" against the input. Hypotheses that do not match are discarded, and when the correct hypothesis (predicting the correct input) has been selected, the concept is acquired. But where do the hypotheses come from? Whatever the "language" of internal representations is, it must, according to Fodor, be rich enough to express all the correct hypotheses (concepts) in the first place in order to "project" them onto the data. In a similarly styled argument where the topic is *language acquisition* rather than concept learning, Fodor (1975) says, "one can learn [a language] *L* only if one already knows some language rich enough to express the extension of any predicate of *L*" (p. 80). When someone "learns" a concept one must already "have" that concept; what one really learns is only that that concept is "true" of the world (or not). This amounts to what Fodor (1984) himself terms a "mad-dog" nativism.

The responses to Fodor's arguments in the cognitive science community have been interesting in their general lack of vigorous reaction and in their paucity of credible alternatives. Dennett (1977) and Pylyshyn (1981), for example, recount Fodor's arguments but make no attempt to rebut them. Dennett's main complaint is that the position is "hard to swallow," but asks, "what are the alternatives?" (1977, p. 268), the latter in paraphrase of Fodor's claim is that the aforementioned theory of concept learning is the only one we've got. Marks (1978) says of a quote from Fodor (1975) similar to our earlier quote (Fodor, 1975, p. 80) only that it is "one of the seemingly scandalous conclusions we must tolerate if we take cognitive psychology seriously" (p. 111). Wasow (1978) also feels there is no problem, but he misunderstands Fodor and takes him to be making a Turing-machine argument, viz. that only two symbols and three operations are required to perform any algorithm. This is, Wasow assures us, hardly an excessive native endowment. And Stich (1982) is unabashedly positive in his response to a still more recent version of what he calls "Fodor's controversial conceptual nativism" (Fodor, 1981), calling it a "masterful presentation" of an "elegant argument" and protesting only that the view is not fully established because "definitions are only one way of constructing complex concepts" (Stich, 1982, pp. 420–421). By the latter, Stich has little more in mind for alternatives other than "prototypes" and "frames" (p. 421), which, Fodor would surely argue, are still couched in the representational medium or what he calls "mentalese." Only P. S. Churchland (1978) criticizes Fodor's views as "thoroughly misconceived" (p. 149) but her arguments mainly protest that mentalese has been made too rich and too fixed (p. 154). This criticism is only as explicit as Fodor's proposals about the structure of mentalese, and those proposals are none too explicit. In the end, Churchland seems to give up the ghost to Fodor's "best theory in town" argument, again only protesting that "theoretical vacuums" like these ought to be "just . . . the thing to stimulate the faculties" of researchers. Finally, Marshall (1981)—perhaps he read Churchland (1978)—says that Fodor's argument is "generally regarded as misconceived," but quickly adds that "no counterargument is known nor any convincing alternative account of learning whereby the conclusion can be avoided" (p. 614).

No mere quibbling nor poking at the edges of Fodor's argument will make it go away; it follows simply enough from its premises. And because he wishes to endorse a psychology based on those premises, this causes Fodor himself a certain unease. But he stoically resolves, "I shall endure what I don't know how to cure (p. 82)," all the while admitting an inclination to view his conclusions as a *reductio ad absurdum* of his representational-computational premises. That, however, is exactly what we take Fodor to have done, and consider ourselves to be among several cognitive psychologists who are indeed responding to Churchland's "vacuum." In fact, we take the matter to be a good deal more serious, as we see Fodor's arguments—and there are hints of this in the 1975 book that he does not fully pursue—to have near-epidemical consequences for styles of currently fashionable explanation in psychology, spreading readily to such time-honored topics as "perception," "judgment," "language acquisition" (all of which Fodor discusses), and beyond. In short, not only are "concept-learning" theories vulnerable to Fodor's argument, it seems that much of current cognition is equally vulnerable, and it is not clear if anything under the cognition rubric is immune.

Like Cassirer's critique, Fodor's arguments are a clear danger sign about certain seemingly obvious ways of studying and talking about cognition in general and concepts in particular. Rather than shrugging them off as interesting paradoxes, however, we prefer to take a route that avoids them altogether. An outline and some high points of that route are the topic of the next section.

CONCEPTS AND COGNITION IN OPEN SYSTEMS

To review: According to the generally received view, concepts are fundamentally *internal representations* that symbolize and classify (categorize) in a medium that is somehow language-like (predicates, features lists, propertied images). As far as can be determined, virtually every aspect of our existence, save possibly feeding, fighting, fleeing, and reproducing, but including most situations describable as remembering, expecting, perceiving, thinking—even learning, if it existed—are ultimately answerable to and constrained by this representational conceptual system. This surely makes the latter one of the most ubiquitous entities in all of psychology. Yet this view seems to have painted itself into an empirical corner and is in addition subject to various theoretical perplexities and paradoxes.

Assessing the many infirmities of the received view, it seems to us that what is most multiply responsible is the tacit but systematic omission of the *environment* as an important part of the theory. If the nature of concepts is significantly constrained (even if not exclusively determined) by the way the world is, then this would appear a serious omission. Indeed, the notice that it is to the environment that most concepts refer remains underdeveloped (Putnam, 1975). This seems peculiar to us, because without the environment the very idea of concepts is superfluous. The programmatic concern with psychology "as a science of mental life" or "a science of behavior" may have locked us in at square one with half-theories about everything. We are *not* suggesting a regression to a focus on the stimulus but rather the correction of a further omission of the necessary reciprocity between an organism and its environment. It is the purpose of this section to pursue some implications both logical and psychological, formal and informal, of taking environments seriously as places within which, among other things, "mental life," "behavior," and "symbol use" occur. In so doing, we attempt to unravel the tangled web of problems discussed in earlier sections. Our design is the retrograde of what has gone before, beginning with Fodor, then moving to Cassirer, and finally ending up with some general implications for empirical research on categories and concepts.

Fodor's Fallacy

The most immediate and in some ways the most profound consequence of having a formal place in one's theory for an environment as something in which organisms are embedded is that only in so doing can one consider the organism as an *open* instead of a *closed* system (von Foerster, 1960). Applications of information theory to problems in psychology failed precisely because of the debilitating need for the theorist to specify all the possible outcomes and their respective probabilities in advance. Applications of formal language-like systems with their predicate calculi, it would seem, are doomed to fail for the same kind of reason: All the potential predicates must be there in advance. In considering something that changes and develops in time, like a melody, a poem, or a person, both applications must take the entire (developmental) sequence as *given* in order to exhaustively enumerate possibilities (or predicates). Neither of these approaches, by their very design, are adequate to model open systems, and both obviously beg all questions of origin for systems that change or have a history (e.g., "how did the system come to acquire (just) those predicates?"). The good news is that people like Fodor (and, e.g., Chomsky) are simply mistaken with regard to the lack of an alternative, for organisms as open systems that do not "represent" states of the world in an explicit representational medium, we argue strongly, are not subject to Fodor's fallacy.

Let us consider the following argument, a variation of Fodor's: Because Darwinian mechanisms, like mechanisms of concept acquisition, are essentially *selection* mechanisms, no new species can come into existence. Cellerier (1980) advances this proposition as an analogue to what he calls Fodor's *cogito ergo non sum* principle, from which it would then follow that "*Homo sapiens* does not exist." There is no construal of the term "species" that makes the argument intelligible, of course; it is simply false, because there is no construal of the term "closed system" that adequately describes the context in which evolution takes place. On another level, consider chemical reactions. Would anyone ever suggest that no new substances can be created in a chemical reaction, because everything that is created is a "product" of what was there to begin with? And again the answer is no: If the system in which the reaction takes place is open to its surroundings, it is clear that substances may be "selected" from the environment that are not necessarily contained in the original reaction. Only a closed system is doomed to form substances or structures that are permutations of the original elements. On a larger scale, let us look at human society and ask, is it the case that there are no new tools, or new inventions in the history of humanity? We would invite those taking Fodor's position to write that history.

These informal arguments are in fact grounded in a formal basis. Workers in the theory of dynamical—as opposed to symbol—systems, have shown that apparently simple systems described by differential (or difference) equations can literally transcend their initial conditions. The behavior of so-called chaotic attractors (Hofstadter, 1981; R. Shaw, 1981) gives clear examples of inherently unpredictable behavior, even behavior that appears strongly stochastic, in a completely deterministic system. The behavior itself may be very orderly, but "information is created" (Abraham & C. Shaw, 1983; R. Shaw, 1981) in the system to make the behavior unpredictable and make the variation it exhibits appear partially random even though it is not. And on a related front, Prigogine (1976) has shown that an open system that is strongly coupled to its environment may be subject to undampable fluctuations that drive the system to a new state of greater complexity and organization not in any sense "contained" in the initial description of the system (see also Prigogine, Allen, & Herman, 1977). In the early state of the system, the fluctuations are mere "noise" relative to the system's character. "Order out of chaos" is the system selectively exploiting the richness of this noise ("white noise" literally contains energy at all frequencies), *taking what it needs* from its environment (von Foerster, 1960). And the converse, "chaos out of order," reflects the unpredictability of a system in an unpredictable environment that is continuously—at least in part—of its own making. R. Shaw (1981) says of turbulent motion that it is "continuously generated by the flow itself" (p. 106).

Systems such as these exhibit a large number of qualitatively different behaviors that correspond in complex ways to states of their environment. They do *not* "represent" the states of the environment however specific their behavior may be to those states, nor is the set of possible states limited by the (initial) system description *except* insofar as as a set of "observables" of the system are explicitly chosen by a scientist who would study its behavior as a set of "axes" on which to "plot" system trajectories. But there is no great profundity in the fact that if a scientist measures x, y, and z in a system, he will characterize all of its states in terms of x, y, and z.

Formal systems *qua* formal systems of course do not change as they are being studied. Yet we should not forget that even (indeed, especially) the most powerful formal system or "language" is never really closed in the sense of "complete." The irony of Gödel's incompleteness theorem, as Hofstadter (1979) points out, is that it is the very expressive power of the system that makes it able to represent true statements that are not "theorems" of the system. Any attempted augmentation of the system will by its own explicitness lead directly to a method for constructing a new true nontheorem (Hofstadter, 1979), thus perpetuating the incompleteness.

The real culprit, we think, is in the construal of perception—and all other processes described in the same style, but particularly perception—as a symbolic *matching* process. Descriptions of the world, if they are to be matched to some internal symbol or representation, must be translatable into the same form as that to which they are to be matched. How could anything new ever get in? If the input was not in a matchable form—describable in the internal language—the system would be unable to make any sense of it. To make matters worse, it is customary for theorists not of an ecological persuasion to describe the world in a language that is incommensurable with experience (Runeson, 1977; cf. Turvey & Shaw, 1979). The alternate strategy, foreshadowed in the beginning of this chapter, is to describe environmental states and organismic states in the same language and talk about internal states as *coordinating with* and not *corresponding to* (or representing) environmental states. Incommensurable properties can never get "into" a system, but under the proffered view, we would have instead commensurable properties that can come to be *shared* by two interacting subsystems (organism and environment) of a larger system in which they are both embedded. In this kind of formulation, Fodor's fallacy never arises. (See Chapters 8, 10, and 11, this volume, for specific examples of attempts to redescribe special environments.)

On Vanishing Intensions and Useless Concepts

By the schema for the "common feature" idea about concepts, the instances we experience might be represented as *abc, ade, afg,* and the resulting "abstracted" concept would be *a*. As we noted earlier, Cassirer criticizes this kind of concept as merely "annihilating the peculiarity" of the instances. In a world where objects are bundles of features and perception is a matching process, a concept is a partial match (at best). By this account, as Smith and Medin (1981) readily admit, even a "feature" is a "concept." But the feature idea may itself be an illusion, if the *a* of *abc,* because of its interactions with *b* and *c* and *bc,* functions differently than the *a* of *ade* (McCabe, 1984). A concept should embrace, not ignore, the variability in its instances. Nor will it do to pay a kind of theoretical lip service to this variability (v) by rewriting the concept $a \pm v$. Instead, following through on the ideas from the previous subsection, we must consider an "instance" as presenting information to us that is not bounded by internally given predicates that external features must match. Even to symbolize such information is problematic (cf. Gödel again), but, understanding that the following symbols symbolize for the *scientist* and not inside the mind of the organism, we might have instances of the concept *a* as ax_1y_1, ax_2y_2, ax_3y_3. The resulting concept would be not *a* but *aXY;* better, $af(x)g(y)$; and better still, $af_1(x)f_2(y)$, emphasizing that the functions f_1, f_2 are linked. The principal difference is that the concept is no longer merely a *part* (*a*) of something of which each instance ax_1y_1 or *abc* is a whole. We have, not just a common feature or features, but a general object of the same form as its instances, one that moreover exhibits the form of variation(s) characteristic of the concept. The concept in its full spelndor is something that both encompasses all of its instances and specifies instances not yet encountered (see Chapters 2, 3, and 6, this volume).

Cassirer says that a genuine concept should not "disregard the peculiarities and particularities which it holds under it," but should instead "show the *necessity* of the occurrence and connection of just these particularities" (1923/1953, p. 19, original emphasis). The hallmark of the concept is not the uniformity of its instances, as the prototype theory chided the "classical" definitional theory. But, we hasten to chide the prototype theory, nor is it the unprincipled variability of instances about some (arbitrary) conjunction of feature values. Neither uniformity nor variability, but *necessary connection* among the instances is what marks a genuine and complete concept.

The form of the concept that we have offered here is richer and more complex than the standard view. This in part reflects a richer notion of an environment as a source of information about concepts, an environment that must be coordinated with and not merely represented (although the latter may be sufficient for a computer). A possessor of this kind of concept may do more than merely summarize, he may discover and even invent new examples that satisfy the concept. But if a rich environment is an inexhaustible supply of concepts, it becomes important to stipulate constraints that will limit or at least distinguish concepts in a reasonable way. In the traditional view, a set of internally given predicates was to have performed this constraining function, but it constrained too much in some ways and not enough in others: Too much in that it made concept learning an impossibility, and not enough in that useless and nonsensical concepts were as easy to "construct" as ones that actually marked a significant (as opposed to merely true) property of one's environment (cf. Barrett, 1978; Chapter 9, this volume).

In the spirit both of providing an example of such a constraint and of treating the formation of concepts as a species of coordination with one's environment, we strongly recommend Gibson's (1977, 1979) notion of *affordance* (environmental support of an organism's intentional activities) and the reciprocal notion of *effectivity* (Shaw, Turvey, & Mace, 1982), the latter of which can be thought of as an affordance of the organism from the environment's point of view. We would suggest that the earliest proto-concepts are, not the things that words are eventually used to designate, but affordances. For an infant, what is the world divided into but things that afford eating, grasping, and nurturance? (And reciprocally, to what should the perceptual systems of attentive caregivers be especially attuned to if not the needs of their young? See Chapter 12, this volume.) To be human, of course, is to be able to go beyond such basic needs and appreciate things by virtue of their form as well as their function. But here, the classic aesthetic judgment that "form follows function" may serve as a model for the rest of cognition. And in our cognitive life, we still insist that a concept have a certain utility or we will not employ it in our thinking about and interacting with the world. Our students' cries for "relevance" in what we select to teach them can be thought of as a request for concepts that afford a certain conceptual leverage on the world as it is (directly) perceived and acted upon. A concept like "meloncat," though it is unambiguous and can even be true of the world (i.e., "There goes a meloncat." "Right."), does not pass a kind of cognitive affordance test; it has no useful meaning except in the conceptual environment of Osherson (1978) and, to some extent, the present chapter. Of course, if one is a philosopher, one had better understand the concept "grue," even though one encounters it only in environments like philosophy journals and seminars; after all, these are the very environments in which philosophers must learn to survive.

Symbolic environments populated by words and ideas constitute a logical place to look for cognitive analogues to affordances and effectivities. Freed from the straitjacketing idea that all intelligent transactions with our environments should be considered as internal "symbol processing," we are left with a more restricted, constrained use for "symbols," and may perhaps be able to give them proper consideration in a psychological context for the first time (see Chapter 4, this volume). A sketch of how some of this might look is as follows: Consider that living things like ourselves have coevolved with their environments to have effectivities useful in those environments. If we consider effectivities as possibilities for action, we can even say that inanimate objects "have effectivities," though they are usually dependent on some kind of interaction with animate parts of their environments for these effectivities to be realized. Just as an animal's teeth can pierce objects (have a piercing effectivity), so can an inanimate human artifact like a knife, the difference being that the knife must be thrown by some agent (although it may realize its effectivity if it is, say, knocked off a workbench during an earthquake). When employed by someone as a tool, the knife becomes an extension of the person, literally creates a coupling that shifts the organism/environment boundary in a temporary way. Now, before the person picks up the knife, its properties are presented to the person as *affordances*. When a person picks up a knife and wields it, an affordance is transformed into an effectivity. In the symbol, as in the tool, we find the same collapsing of affordance and effectivity. The *word* knife can also create a piercing-event, but, appropriately enough, only in symbolic environments. Symbolic environments, however, are neither in our head nor are they closed systems. "The pen is mightier than the sword" is an eloquent testimony to the power of symbolic environments to have palpable effects on nonsymbolic ones, the very metaphor of piercing being an especially salient reminder of such effects. And if it be protested that all of this talk of the powers of words is itself metaphorical, we would reply that metaphors are terribly important vehicles for comprehending our diverse environments, through perception and language alike (see Verbrugge, 1977, 1980). One of the most important criteria for useful concepts that go beyond directly detectable affordances of our nonsymbolic environments may turn out to be that they are metaphors, either for environmental events or for other concepts, that induce a novel means of comprehending those events and concepts. Successful scientific theories, for example, are certainly this sort of thing. (See Chapters 1 and 2, this volume, for further applications of affordances to ideas in cognition.)

Empirical Postscript: Wherefore Concepts?

Doing a psychological experiment is difficult enough, but doing a *good* psychological experiment, from the ecological perspective, is a most exacting enterprise, and fraught with pitfalls. The main reason is that the laboratory is *only one kind of environment* and a rather curious one at that, despite its advantages. If we want to know about how concepts are *used* rather than just know how certain simplified and mechanized tasks on concepts are performed (Neisser, 1983), the limitations of the laboratory as a sole, or even a primary, source of data and evidence become immediately and painfully clear. Some primary data should come, *inter alia,* from things people actually say and write. In a variation of a method due to Dewey and Bentley (1949; cf. also Bentley, 1954), scientists would do well to examine, not laboratory protocols, but real-world examples of concept use, such as letters, memoranda, newspaper articles, speeches, conversations, radio and television broadcasts, and the like, to see in each case how words are used to convey ideas and constrain the thinking of the receiver. In the spirit of bringing concepts out of the heads of persons and into the public arena, we are moved to look at concepts not merely as a means for thinking but as a means for communicating our thinking to others. When this is successfully done, one has induced the hearer or reader's own thinking to follow a certain route among a certain relational layout of concepts.

But this, of course, is only about concepts only as they are reflected (sometimes, filtered) through language, and, as we have seen, quite a few perfectly good concepts, e.g., affordances, are translatable to words only in a makeshift, jerry-built way (''sit-on-ability,'' to consider one of the simpler examples). Concepts are equally revealed by things people do as by things they say (see Chapter 7, this volume); words and actions can sometimes contradict one another, and actions can even contradict other actions (see Chapter 13, this volume). An ecological approach would thus hold that the way people interact with objects in their environments reveals something about their concepts. This observation leads to the revealing of an eccentric bit of classification in present-day psychology; research in what is commonly called ''problem solving,'' being about the discovery of new uses for old objects (e.g., Weisberg & Suls, 1973), would seem from the present perspective to be a valuable part of the study of *concepts.* Of course, *words* too are objects that can be tried in new uses, and these, as we alluded to before, are what we usually call metaphors. It goes without saying that metaphoric comprehension, as a kind of linguistic analogue to problem solving—"new uses for familiar tools/objects"—would occupy an equally important status in an ecologically styled research program on concepts. We would expect a corresponding decrease of research into "literal meanings" or "lexical features" of words (e.g., Honeck & Hoffman, 1980; Katz, 1972).

REFERENCES

Abraham, R. H., & Shaw, C. (1983). *Dynamics: The geometry of behavior: Vol. 2. Chaotic behavior.* Santa Cruz, CA: Aerial Press.

Adams, J. A. (1967). *Human memory.* New York: McGraw–Hill.

Anderson, J. R. (1978). Arguments concerning representations for mental imagery. *Psychological Review, 85,* 249–277.

Armstrong, S, L., Gleitman, L. R., & Gleitman, H. (1983). What some concepts might not be. *Cognition, 13,* 263–308.

Barrett, W. (1978). *The illusion of technique.* New York: Anchor Books.

Bentley, A. F. (1954). *Inquiry into inquiries.* Boston: Beacon Press.

Bourne, L. E., Jr. (1968). Concept attainment. In T. R. Dixon & D. L. Horton (Eds.), *Verbal behavior and general behavior theory.* Englewood Cliffs, NJ: Prentice–Hall.

Bower, G. H., & Trabasso, T. (1963). Concept identification. In R. C. Atkinson (Ed.), *Studies in mathematical psychology.* Stanford: Stanford University Press.

Bruner, J. S., Goodnow, J., & Austin, G. (1956). *A study of thinking.* New York: Wiley.

Brunswik, E. (1949). *Systematic and representative design of psychological experiments.* Berkeley: University of California Press.

Cassirer, E. (1953). *Substance and function.* New York: Dover. (Originally published, 1923)

Cellérier, G. (1980). Some clarifications on innatism and constructivism. In M. Piattelli-Palmarini (Ed.), *Language and learning: The debate between Jean Piaget and Noam Chomsky* (pp. 83–87). Cambridge: Harvard University Press.

Churchland, P. S. (1978). Fodor on language learning. *Synthese, 38,* 149–159.

Collins, A., & Quillian, M. R. (1969). Retrieval time from semantic memory. *Journal of Verbal Learning and Verbal Behavior, 8,* 240–247.

Dennett, D. C. (1977). Critical notice [Review of *The language of thought*]. *Mind, 86,* 265–280.

Dewey, J., & Bentley, A. F. (1949). *Knowing and the known.* Boston: Beacon Press.

Fodor, J. A. (1975). *The language of thought.* New York: Crowell.

Fodor, J. A. (1980). Fixation of belief and concept acquisition. In M. Piattelli-Palmarini (Ed.), *Language and learning: The debate between Jean Piaget and Noam Chomsky* (pp. 143–149). Cambridge: Harvard University Press.

Fodor, J. A. (1981). *Representations*. Cambridge: M.I.T. Press.

Fodor, J. A. (1984, February). *Observation reconsidered*. Talk delivered at U. C. San Diego.

Gibson, J. J. (1977). The theory of affordances. In R. E. Shaw & J. Bransford (Eds.), *Perceiving, acting, and knowing* (pp. 67–82). Hillsdale, NJ: Lawrence Erlbaum Associates.

Gibson, J. J. (1979). *The ecological approach to visual perception*. Boston: Houghton–Mifflin.

Goodman, N. (1973). *Fact, fiction, and forecast* (3rd ed.). Indianapolis: Bobbs–Merrill.

Hofstadter, D. R. (1979). *Godel, Escher, Bach: An eternal golden braid*. New York: Basic Books.

Hofstadter, D. R. (1981). Strange attractors: Mathematical patterns delicately poised between order and chaos. *Scientific American, 245*(5), 22–43.

Honeck, R. P., & Hoffman, R. R. (1980). *Cognition and figurative language*. Hillsdale, NJ: Lawrence Erlbaum Associates.

Katz, J. J. (1972). *Semantic theory*. New York: Harper & Row.

Levine, M. (1969). Neo-noncontinuity theory. In G. H. Bower & J. Spence (Eds.), *The psychology of learning and motivation* (Vol. 3). New York: Academic Press.

Luria, A. R. (1969). *The mind of a mnemonist* (L. Solotaroff, Trans.). New York: Avon Books. (Original work published 1965)

Marks, C. E. (1978). [Review of *The language of thought*]. *Philosophical Review, 87*, 108–116.

Marshall, J. C. (1981). Cognition at the crossroads [Review of *Language and learning*]. *Nature, 289*, 613–614.

McCabe, V. (1984). A comparison of three kinds of knowing: categorical, structural, and affirmative. *Journal of Mind and Behavior, 5*, 433–448.

Meyer, D. E. (1970). On the representation and retrieval of stored semantic information. *Cognitive Psychology, 1*, 242–299.

Neisser, U. (1983). Components of intelligence or steps in routine procedures? *Cognition, 15*, 189–197.

Osherson, D. N. (1978). Three conditions on conceptual naturalness. *Cognition, 6*, 263–289.

Osherson, D. N., & Smith, E. E. (1982). Gradedness and conceptual combination. *Cognition, 12*, 299–318.

Prigogine, I. (1976). Order through fluctuation: Self-organization and social system. In E. Jantsch & C. H. Waddington (Eds.), *Evolution and consciousness: Human systems in transition* (pp. 93–133). Reading, MA: Addison–Wesley.

Prigogine, I., Allen, P. M., & Herman, R. (1977). The evolution of complexity and the laws of nature. In E. Laszlo & J. Bierman (Eds.), *Goals in a global community (Vol. I*, pp. 5–63). New York: Pergamon.

Putnam, H. (1975). The meaning of "meaning." In K. Gunderson (Ed.), *Minnesota sutdies in the philosophy of science: Vol. 7. Language, mind, and knowledge* (pp. 131–193). Minneapolis: University of Minnesota Press.

Pylyshyn, Z. W. (1981). The nativists are restless! [Review of *Language and learning*]. *Contemporary Psychology, 26*, 501–504.

Rey, G. (1983). Concepts and stereotypes. *Cognition, 15*, 237–262.

Rips, L. J., Shoben, E. J., & Smith, E. E. (1973). Semantic distance and the verification of semantic relations. *Journal of Verbal Learning and Verbal Behavior, 12*, 1–20.

Rosch, E. (1978). Principles of categorization. In E. Rosch & B. B. Lloyd (Eds.), *Cognition and categorization* (pp. 27–48). Hillsdale, NJ: Lawrence Erlbaum Associates.

Rosch, E., & Mervis, C. B. (1975). Family resemblances: Studies in the internal structure of categories. *Cognitive Psychology, 7*, 573–605.

Rosch, E., Mervis, C. B., Gray, W. D., Johnson, D. M., & Boyes-Braem, P. (1976). Basic objects in natural categories. *Cognitive Psychology, 8*, 382–439.

Runeson, S. (1977). On the possibility of "smart" perceptual mechanisms. *Scandinavian Journal of Psychology, 18,* 172–179.

Ryle, G. (1949). *The concept of mind.* New York: Barnes & Noble.

Sesonske, A., & Fleming, N. (Eds.). (1965). *Plato's Meno: Text and criticism.* Belmont, CA: Wadsworth.

Shaw, R. E., Turvey, M. T., & Mace, W. (1982). Ecological psychology: The consequence of a commitment to realism. In W. Weimer & D. S. Palermo (Eds.), *Cognition and the symbolic processes* (Vol. 2, pp. 159–226). Hillsdale, NJ: Lawrence Erlbaum Associates.

Shaw, R. (1981). Strange attractors, chaotic behavior, and information flow. *Zeitschrift Naturforschung, 36a,* 80–112.

Smith, E. E., Balzano, G. J., & Walker, J. (1978). Nominal, perceptual, and semantic codes in picture categorization. In J. W. Cotton & R. L. Klatzky (Eds.), *Semantic factors in cognition* (pp. 137–168). Hillsdale, NJ: Lawrence Erlbaum Associates.

Smith, E. E., & Medin, D. L. (1981). *Categories and concepts.* Cambridge: Harvard University Press.

Stich, S. P. (1982). The compleat cognitivist [Review of *Representations*]. *Contemporary Psychology, 27,* 419–421.

Turvey, M. T., & Shaw, R. E. (1979). The primacy of perceiving: An ecological reformulation of perception for understanding memory. In L.-G. Nilsson (Ed.), *Perspectives on memory research: Essays in honor of Uppsala University's 500th Anniversary* (pp. 167–222). Hillsdale, NJ: Lawrence Erlbaum Associates.

Verbrugge, R. R. (1977). Resemblances in language and perception. In R. E. Shaw & J. Bransford (Eds.), *Perceiving, acting, and knowing* (pp. 365–389). Hillsdale, NJ: Lawrence Erlbaum Associates.

Verbrugge, R. R. (1980). Transformations in knowing: A realist view of metaphor. In R. P. Honeck & R. R. Hoffman (Eds.), *Cognition and figurative language* (pp. 87–125). Hillsdale, NJ: Lawrence Erlbaum Associates.

von Foerster, H. (1960). On self-organizing systems and their environments. In M. C. Yovitz & S. Cameron (Eds.), *Self-organizing systems* (pp. 31–50). New York: Pergamon.

Wasow, T. (1978). [Review of *The language of thought*]. *Synthese, 38,* 161–167.

Weisberg, R., & Suls, J. M. (1973). An information-processing model of Duncker's candle problem. *Cognitive Psychology, 4,* 255–298.

VISUAL EVENTS

What is learned when we remember things we have seen? The obvious answer of "the things themselves" is wrong, or at best incomplete, for it neglects the possibility that relations among the things might contribute to learning. If learning about visually apprehended objects and events is more a matter of finding relations than storing copies, then we must find a different answer to the "what is learned" question.

A long tradition of experiments on various kinds of "picture memory" exists that attempts to address these issues. A popular way to amend the answer to "what is learned" that emerges from this tradition runs something like the following: Visually experienced objects and categories are said to possess features, and a primary means of "finding relations" among objects and events is accomplished by codifying them in terms of *shared features* (see Chapter 5, this volume). But without specifying what these features might be, what properties of optical stimulation a perceiver might be sensitive to, this formulation appears sufficiently general and sufficiently vague to be nearly immune to decisive confirmation, and it places correspondingly little constraint on the real form of the theory.

There is another way to construe the whole matter of finding relations that is much more congenial to an ecological view of event cognition. In this alternative view, a perceiver's search for relationships is geared specifically to ways in which something seen may be *transformed* into something else seen. A good example of this transformationally-based view of visual perception applied to a picture memory context comes from a set of studies done in 1971 by Franks and Bransford. They constructed a set of pictures, each picture a different arrangement of simple geometrical forms, designed so that individual pictures could be mutually transformed into one another by well-defined transformations, such as permutations of objects over locations. A variety of different transformations were used, and several transformations could be combined with one another to give rise to a variable of "transformational distance." Any pair of pictures in the experiment could be evaluated with respect to this variable by counting up the number of transformations needed to map one into the other. A hypothesis about what is learned can be formulated in these terms: To remember what they have seen, subjects learn both the transformations and the essential invariant (however complex) properties that are preserved by them. To be sure, it *may* be possible to speak of the latter as "features," but this misses the point that invariants are specifically interdefined with a set of transformations that preserve them; a different set of transformations would specify a new set of invariants.

Franks and Bransford (1971) found strong support for their hypothesis. What subjects remembered having seen was strongly predicted by transformational distance between a given picture and the "base" picture from which all transformed versions were originally derived (and from which the set of transformed instances therefore had a minimum average transformational distance). This "base" picture, even if had never before been seen, acted as a "prototype" for the invariant structure preserved by the transformations generating the ensemble of pictures. Subjects easily rejected pictures generated by applying new transformations to the base as not being part of what they had seen before. A simple "feature frequency" model which counted up how often particular shapes appeared in particular locations instead of counting up transformations could not predict the results of these experiments.

Though Franks and Bransford's experiments used artificial materials and contrived transformations, their results have clear implications for more naturally occurring visual events. What their perspective does is to make us focus on the naturally occurring transformations that connect and relate different forms of the "same" object or event. These transformations include rotation and translation for rigid objects, projective transformations for two-dimensional representations of objects (i.e., pictures), and growth transformations for living creatures.

Chapter 6, by **Jenkins, Wald, and Pittenger,** presents a further articulation of the ecological perspective on memory for pictures. The authors propose that what is remembered is a whole event rather than parts of an event that are somehow stored and later connected. The experiments described in Chapter 6 illustrate the idea of generativity particularly well, presenting stimuli that specify a system of relationships in which individual stimuli cohere as well as additional stimuli that have not yet been presented. Jenkins et al. suggest that the perceiver does not confront every event with a fixed set of "feature detectors," rather events create their own features through the invariants they exhibit over time; events in this sense are self-defining.

In Chapter 7, **Braddon** views cognition as isomorphic to the reciprocal relationship between perception and action. The experiments in this chapter show that memory operates differently under active participation (perception/action) than under passive observation (perception/mentation), and that remembering routes and remembering landmarks along routes are differentially affected by participatory perceiving. Braddon's work may also be seen as related to the redefinition of "schema" presented in Chapter 2.

REFERENCES

Franks, J. J., & Bransford, J. D. (1971). Abstraction of visual patterns. *Journal of Experimental Psychology, 90,* 65–74.

6 Apprehending Pictorial Events*

James J. Jenkins
University of South Florida

Jerry Wald
Honeywell Corporation
Minneapolis, Minnesota

John B. Pittenger
University of Arkansas at Little Rock

CONTENTS

Many psychologists believe that all higher mental processes must be built up ''from the bottom.'' They believe that higher mental events are to be explained in terms of general processes operating in some context-free manner on elementary units defined at discrete segments of time. For such approaches, fundamen-

---

*Portions of this chapter were originally published in W. Savage (Ed.) *Perception and Cognition: Issues in the Foundations of Psychology*. Minnesota Studies in Philosophy of Science, 1978. University of Minnesota Press, Minneapolis. Copyright © 1978 by The University of Minnesota.

tal questions inevitably involve putting the world together again. Thus, special memories and comparators must be postulated to relate experiences over time. An event as simple as a tonal glide or a mere awareness of movement must be constructed somehow from frozen, instantaneous "snapshots" of elemental information. Then, when such experiences are "glued together," this approach must struggle to assemble each composite event with others of the "same sort" in order to arrive at general concepts. The problem of knowing that two disparate events are instances of the same concept before the observer recognizes the concept then becomes an impressive and baffling paradox (cf. Shaw & Pittinger, 1978).

Our position is that we can avoid these paralyzing paradoxes by making a different fundamental assumption, namely, that *events,* rather than static patterns, are the primary focus of perception and cognition. For present purposes we may regard events as pertaining both to objects and to changes or transformations defined over objects. We must note, however, that although objects and transformations are conceptually distinct, they are not independent of one another. Objects, for example, may be in part defined as those "things" left invariant under certain transformations such as translation. It is best, perhaps, to regard objects and transformations as two aspects of an event.

To help clarify this view we may recall some properties of objects that are said to be conserved under certain transformations, properties that contribute to the meaning of *object.* Consider, for example, Piagetian experiments on "conservation." The point of the experiments for our purposes is not that properties are invariant (or conserved) under all possible changes that may occur; indeed, it is just the opposite. *Some* properties are conserved under *some* types of changes or alterations, and those properties left invariant contribute to the meaning of the object within that situation. For example, *number* of marbles is conserved over various spatial arrangements of the marbles but it is not conserved over the operation of running the marbles through a grinder or smashing them with a sledgehammer. *Volume* of a liquid is conserved over various transformations of shapes of containers, but it is not conserved over evaporation, loss through spilling, addition of more liquid, drinking some of the liquid, and so forth. *Amount* of matter is conserved over translation, reshaping, amalgamation and subdivision but not over burning, addition, subtraction, eating, or dissolving. It is precisely the relation between the type of change and the property of concern that is being investigated in such experiments. For the sophisticated organism the crucial perception is that the operations performed on the material in question do or do not constitute a type of change that affects the property, and hence the object, whose invariance is at test. It makes no sense to talk about the conservation of number, volume, or matter without talking about the nature of the changes involved.

In the aforementioned examples it is easy to lose sight of the importance of the transformational aspect of an event: The object and its properties seem to predominate. But the importance of change cannot be overlooked. In many domains we know that the rate of change itself is a critical determinant of perception. Michotte's classic experiments demonstrate that the relative rates of movement of two objects striking one another determine whether the event is seen as "entrainment," "launching," or "triggering" (Michotte, 1963). And in other domains it is the style of change that alone specifies the object under change. Johansson (1975) has made elegant motion pictures of "point-light people" that show the power of change in the configuration of lights over time. These films were made in the dark and show only the patterns of movement and the disappearance and appearance of point-light sources mounted at the joints of the human subjects being pictured (shoulders, elbows, wrists, hips, knees, and ankles and a single light at the crown of the head). In a static frame of the film, an observer sees nothing but an unorganized jangle of lights. In the running film the moving patterns of lights are sufficient to specify not only the actions of walking, running, dancing, approaching, receding, and transversing, but they enable the observer to specify that the moving "object" is a human of a particular sex.

For the moment consider how the "bottom–up" theorist has dealt with the kinds of experiments we have just outlined. A common approach is to postulate the existence of "time-tagged" static images from which the information can be obtained to specify the relevant movement or derive the rate of change that is the critical variable in determining the perception. This by no means solves the problems, however. If one takes the information from the dynamic display and stores it in a series of static displays, then one must somehow scan the static displays over time to retrieve the necessary information from them. This reintroduces exactly the same problem that the static storage was designed to solve; for how do we extract the relevant information without presupposing some change detector in the scanning mechanism itself?

In addition it should be observed that a new problem is created by postulating static displays, namely the problem of sampling rate. As is well known, a sequence of static displays in the visual domain creates a stroboscopic effect that creates false perceptions of motion when the sampling rate interacts with the rate of movement being sampled. (Recall the backward turning wheels and airplane propellers that we so often see in motion pictures.) It is a serious deficiency in sampling theories that such phenomena are never observed in natural visual perception. One possible solution to *that* problem is to suppose that the sampling rate is variable depending on what kind of phenomenon one is observing, but this involves one in the paradox of knowing what one is perceiving before one perceives it so that one can adjust his sampling rate accordingly.

It seems to us that it is both more realistic and more reasonable to try to come to grips directly with events over time than to create problems for ourselves by reinventing Zeno's paradox of the arrow in flight being at rest in a frozen moment in time. If one avoids the assumptions that create the paradox, one may well escape having to try to find its resolution.

SOME EXPERIMENTS ON PICTORIAL EVENTS

Many years ago, Esper (1925) published an experiment demonstrating that people may learn more than they have experienced. He presented subjects with pictures of four forms, each of which appeared in four different colors, and required the subjects to learn the names that he had systematically paired with each colored form. The labeling system was such that the shape of the form determined the first syllable of the name and the color of the form determined the second syllable. Instead of presenting all 16 instances of the colored forms, however, Esper withheld two particular instances. Following training on the 14 items, he tested all 16 items in a naming test. He found that the subjects correctly named the two new items when they were presented. Surprisingly, the subjects could not even say which items were old and which items were new. Thus, Esper demonstrated that when there is a systematic relation between stimulus variation and response variation, subjects may learn the complete system of relations even though they do not see all the members, and that once they learn the *system,* they may not even know which instances they have seen and which they have not.

Esper's study is not just a selected curiosity; many studies of this sort have been conducted (see Esper, 1973, for an account). In attempting to explain the Esper results, one is forced to conclude that subjects go beyond learning of the finite set of stimuli with which they have been presented. The stimuli presented to the subjects specify a system of relations within which the individual stimuli cohere, and it is this system as well as the individual stimuli that subjects are learning. Thus, when presented with any set of related stimuli (i.e., coherent stimuli) subjects may acquire two forms of knowledge, knowledge of the particular stimuli experienced (Foss, 1968) and knowledge of the underlying coherent system of relations (Segal, 1962–1963). Any experimental outcome will be some product of both of these two bases of knowledge, the relative contribution in any particular situation being determined by a host of factors.

We should also note that such findings are not limited to particular experimental paradigms; analogous findings obtain with purely perceptual materials (Franks & Bransford, 1971; Posner & Keele, 1968; 1970; Strange, Keeney, Kessel, & Jenkins, 1970; see also Chapter 3, this volume; Chapter 7, this volume).

The general conclusion supported by all these experiments is that what one remembers depends on the generative power of the set of instances to which the subject has been exposed. In short, as Garner (1974) has noted, experimental subjects do not deal in some simple fashion with only the stimuli the experimenter presents. Rather, they respond on the basis of a set of possibilities that the occurring stimuli may be said to define or *generate.*

These findings stand in sharp contrast to work implying that visual memory is precise and virtually unlimited. Shepard (1967) and Standing and his colleagues (Standing, 1973; Standing, Conezio, & Haber, 1970) have demonstrated that if subjects are shown large numbers of unrelated pictures (up to 2,000), they can identify them with high accuracy on a forced-choice recognition test. The key word here is *unrelated:* Each slide is a slice of a separate event, unassimilated and unassimilable except as a discrete event in itself. It constitutes, then, an event with a frequency of one exposure that is later to be compared with some other unique event, which has a frequency of zero in the subject's experience. Put in this way, the recognition of large numbers of slides may not seem to be such a dramatic feat as we had first supposed. As long as the events stay separate and unique and have frequencies of zero or one, there is little remarkable about knowing which is which.

Striking evidence that effects are different when the picture to be remembered bear some relation to each other is found in a study by Goldstein and Chance (1970). These investigators discovered that memory for pictures was seriously impaired when the pictures were all of the same genre: all ink blots, all faces, or all snowflakes. When the "experimental event" becomes one of viewing related, though highly discriminable, members of a class of objects, a decrement in absolute recognition is observed.

Perhaps a *gedanken* experiment is appropriate at this point. Suppose that we took a motion picture of some easily recognized type of event. Now suppose that we take all the odd-numbered frames of the film and splice them together, and all the even-numbered frames and splice them together. If we show the odd-numbered sequence to an observer and then show him the even-numbered sequence, he will almost certainly report that he is seeing the same event. We would be surprised if he reported that he had never seen the second film before, although in the technical, physical sense, he has not.

The *gedanken* experiment suggests a continuum of relatedness running from the intact movie on one end, through a series of frames with an increasing number of intervening frames removed, to the presentation of a series of scenes of isolated events of the Shepard, Haber, and Standing variety on the other end. Reflecting on this potential continuum enticed us to approach the event perception problem through a series of still pictures that were in themselves separate and distinct enough that the question of discriminability of stimuli would not arise but which, taken together, presented a dynamic event: something like a picture story or a slide show that tells a story.

The questions we posed were the following: If subjects saw an appropriately ordered sequence of pictures that was sufficient to give them the necessary information for an event, would they give us evidence that they had experienced that event in its entirety? Would they, for example, falsely recognize pictures of the event that they had not seen before? Would they be able to reject pictures that were highly similar to the pictures seen but which violated some invariant of the event or some detail of the observation?

We decided to begin with some natural but simple, everyday types of events: a woman making a cup of tea, a teenage girl answering the telephone, and, as a kind of control event, some pictures of people at a party. The first two cases clearly told a story. In the first, a woman standing beside a table in a dining room unwrapped a tea bag and put it in a cup on the table. She left the room and returned with a sugar bowl that she put on the table. She left again and returned with a tea kettle from which she poured water into the cup. She returned the kettle to the kitchen, came back into the room, sat down at the table, removed the tea bag from the cup, added sugar, and took a cautious sip of tea. Pictures were taken from a fixed station point, with the camera oriented so that the woman was always near the center of the picture.

In the second event, pictures were again taken from a fixed station point, A girl appeared in the doorway, crbssed the room, and picked up the phone. She talked for a few moments while standing, then sat at the desk on which the phone rested, put her feet up on the desk, smiled and laughed, put her feet down, and hung up the phone.

The third event *could* have been construed to make a loose story but the pictures were taken from two different station points and no particular story was apparent. A graduate student was shown arriving at a party, walking across a room, sitting on a couch with other students, and talking to a visitor (who was also shown alone). Several new people came and went from subsequent pictures, which were mainly of a particular corner of the room.

For each event, "control" pictures were taken. For the Tea Sequence, additional pictures were taken with a new brightly colored object on the table with the tea things, with the woman wearing glasses, with the woman pouring water with her left hand instead of her right, with the camera very close to the table, and with the camera at a new station point across the table. Control pictures for the Telephone Sequence involved changes in distance of the camera from the girl and different postures at the desk with the phone. Controls for the Party Sequence were other pictures of the party from the same station points. The pictures involved the same people but they were in different postures and different combinations.

Two-thirds of the pictures taken of the Tea Sequence and the Telephone Sequence were presented to subjects for learning; every third picture in the sequence was removed. For recognition testing, subjects were shown equal numbers of (1) a (randomly ordered) subset of the original pictures (Originals), (2) the removed pictures that belonged in the series but had not been previously seen (Belonging slides), and (3) the pictures that did not fit the sequence (Controls). Slides were shown to subjects twice during original learning.

The results of the experiments were very gratifying. For the Tea Sequence, 80% of the Originals were recognized as originals, 50% of the Belonging slides were falsely called originals, and only 10% of the Controls were falsely called originals. For the Telephone Sequence, 94% of the Originals were recognized as originals and 42% of the Belonging slides were falsely called originals, whereas only 3% of the Controls were called originals. As we had expected, the Party scenes behaved differently from the Tea Sequence and Telephone Sequence events. The results are more in agreement with the traditional picture memory studies discussed earlier; Originals were correctly recognized 83% of the time, but both Belonging and Control slides were falsely called originals less than 10% of the time.

A fair interpretation of these data seems to be that if a series of pictures show an event taking place over time, the subjects will apprehend the event. Having done this, subjects were largely unable to reject pictures that fit the specifications of the event experienced. Specific memory for individual pictures was outweighed by the abstract or general memory for the event experienced. At the same time, the Control slides showed us that subjects were quite sensitive to both the general constraints and invariant details of events; thus some aspects of memory were enhanced. Pictures that violated the constraints or invariants of the experienced event were detected as new, even if their elements strongly resembled those in the original pictures.

The elements of our experiments strongly resemble traditional studies of isolated pictures, but the phenomena are very different. Traditional studies use hundreds or thousands of isolated, unrelated pictures and obtain high levels of picture recognition with only one presentation. In our studies of coherent events, less than two dozen slides were shown twice, yet we obtained high levels of *false* recognition for Belonging slides.

Some additional evidence that we are looking at a very different set of phenomena came from a further experiment, where members of a class were presented with the Tea Sequence on three successive class days. Each time, the Tea Sequence was shown twice at the beginning of class and the same recognition test was given at the end of class. Now, isolated picture recognition is very sensitive to frequency effects, in particular, once subjects have seen pictures used as "lures" in the recognition test, their ability to distinguish original pictures from such lures is greatly reduced. That did not happen in this experiment. The results on all 3 days were virtually identical, subjects getting neither better nor worse.

Furthermore, it was found that over successive trials certain slides tended to polarize, that is, the accepted slides became even more widely accepted and the unaccepted slides became even less well accepted. This we see again as evidence that the event rather than the individual slide is the important construct. It is also suggestive evidence that even though the event is well defined on the first occasion, it may become even better specified with repeated exposures.

FURTHER EXPLORATIONS

Temporal Order, "Similarity," and Event Cohesion

The major conclusion we draw from the studies we have just described is that events are primary. We can specify events with a sequence of slides and influence subjects' recognition responses when they perceive the coherence of the events. In this way our results resemble those of Esper and others.

When the experimenter specifies the structure of a system with a set of systematically related stimuli, subjects may learn (or "pick up") that system. However, in the case of pictorial events, what is the nature of the relations that specify the event? An obvious, but overly simple suggestion is that it is the raw, physical similarity of the slides in the original set that makes them cohere. This cannot be the whole story, given the results from our Control slides. The next studies shed additional light on this question.

The first thing we tried was randomizing the original presentation order for each of the three picture sequences. We predicted that the randomization would do nothing whatsoever to recognition of the Party Sequence. If no event was picked up when the pictures were shown in their original sequence, there was no reason to suppose that an event would be created by their randomization. We predicted specific picture recognition as before, and that is exactly what we observed. The results for the Party pictures duplicated those of the first experiment.

We did not know what to predict for the organized events. One might suppose that some events are so intrinsically ordered that any presentation of details can be correctly ordered by an observer. If this is the case, the event will be apprehended in spite of random ordering. On the other hand, if the event is intrinsically only weakly ordered, perhaps specific memory for individual pictures will be evident.

In fact, we observed both of these outcomes. The Tea Sequence pictures, even though randomly presented, yielded the same results observed earlier. The Telephone pictures, however, did not. When the Telephone Sequence was presented randomly, the test series yielded excellent recognition of the Original slides, but almost no false positives to the Belonging slides (or the Control slides). Although we cannot at present specify the source of the coherence of the Tea Sequence as opposed to the Telephone Sequence, we see such specification as an attractive research possibility.

The fact that the Telephone Sequence breaks down when it is presented in random order is useful in that it furnishes valuable information about the role of picture similarity. Obviously, picture similarity could not be the source of the false positives originally observed for Belonging slides in this sequence. If the false positives had been due to simple picture similarity, there is no reason for the order of presentation to make any difference at all. It is tempting to think that the Telephone Sequence is close to some critical point on the dimension between the split movie and the array of isolated events just discussed. The set of pictures is apprehended as a coherent event when the appropriate order of presentation is followed but the individual pictures are insufficiently interdependent to be perceived as much more than a set of unrelated pictures when the order is scrambled. Thus, in some cases, order in time can be an important source of information in specifying possible alternative events. This may happen especially when there is insufficient information to specify or demand a particular temporal order within the event itself.

The Orbiting Event

Some of our strongest results, and an instructive lesson, come from a series we have called "Orbiting." This series shows an octagonal tray sitting on a black background. In the center of the tray is a large jar. The various pictures show the tray and jar immobile while a small saltcellar moves from one location to another around the rim of the tray through each vertex and each midpoint between vertices. Sixteen pictures make up the series and complete the orbit. The learning series was prepared by drawing randomly two slides from every set of three slides in order (so that the missing slides would not be periodic). As before, the sequence was shown twice. The subjects were then tested on five slides from the Original series, five Belonging slides and five Control slides that violated some aspect of the event (distance, perspective, relation of the salt cellar to the rim, reversal of jar and saltcellar, missing objects). The results were striking. Our subjects correctly recognized Original slides as originals 89% of the time. They incorrectly identified Belonging slides as originals 73% of the time and *never* identified Control slides as originals (0%).

The instructive lesson happened serendipitously as we were examining the control slides for the Orbiting event. Our photographer made one slide that fit the series perfectly well but used a different position for the light sources. This slide is interesting because an observer knows immediately that it is not one of the series but the source of the difference is not apparent for some time. Then one becomes suddenly aware that the shadows are wrong, something that almost no one would specify if asked to describe the picture. This points out to us that any invariant in the situation can become important. The invariants are accepted as the defining properties of the event or constraints on "what counts" in the pictures. One becomes aware of these invariants when they are violated, although they may not be given in the description of the event or even be available in consciousness (see Garner, 1974, for more on this point). It seems to us that the converse of this also holds. If something varies freely in the learning series (e.g., the quality of lighting in the original Tea Sequence), it is ruled out as a defining property of the event and unless this variable reaches extreme values in the test series, it will be ignored. What is important here is that what is taken to be invariant or deviant for any event will be defined over the course of the event itself. In this sense events are self-defining and they may be studied as such.

Left–Right Orientation in Events

Studies bearing on the power of events to specify their own important characteristics have been carried out by Robert Kraft, who was interested in a special aspect of picture memory. Kraft pointed out to us that picture memory could hardly be like images because left–right orientation was often not preserved in picture memory. When Standing, Conezio and Haber (1970) tested subjects for their knowledge of whether a slide was reversed or not, they found a marked drop in the accuracy of orientation information over 24 hours although subjects were still highly accurate in distinguishing pictures that they had seen from new pictures. In Kraft's own work on memory for orientation of human profiles, he found virtually chance identification of the original left–right orientation, even when subjects were warned that they were going to be tested on orientation.

From the point of view espoused in this chapter, we would expect that if an event had a natural movement direction through space that was intrinsic to it, subjects should be able to remember orientation far above chance, because orientation would be defined over (and hence be a defining property of) the event. Kraft and Jenkins (1977) developed three picture sequences that portrayed events flowing to the left and to the right. Each event had both left-going and right-going actions but they were part of the overall event in a natural way that made the orientation of objects and movements an integral part of the story.

One group of subjects saw these pictures in random order and in random left–right orientation as a control for memory for orientation of individual slides. These subjects, when tested on left–right orientation, performed poorly (67% correct). A second group of subjects saw the pictures in correct left–right orientation but in randomized order. These subjects apprehended the events and performed very well in left–right orientation tests (91% correct). In fact, subjects who saw the pictures in the correct orientation and the correct order did not do much better than this (94% correct). Kraft found that subjects who were given the event in the correct orientations and order could assign even Belonging slides that had never been seen to the appropriate orientation 90% of the time. Thus, when orientation is an integral property of an event, subjects pick up and retain this information readily in the course of apprehending the event. But when orientation is simply an arbitrary property of an individual slide, subjects are not very successful in remembering it.

We think this work is important because it begins to clarify the nature of picture memory. Through research like this we may better distinguish the abstract representation of a perceived event from the common-sense notion of a "good image" that seems to dominate thinking in this area.

Events with Changing Station Point

All the materials so far have been developed from the perspective of the static observer, yet this is only one kind of visual experience that accompanies events. Information is also available over time to an observer who is moving through an environment (Gibson, 1966). Accordingly, we undertook an experiment where the observer moves and the landscape is still. The event was a walk across campus. The pictures were taken early one Sunday morning and show the campus empty of people. Every 20 paces or so the walker (J.P.) took a photograph looking straight ahead on his walk. Control pictures included other scenes of the same campus, other pictures of some of the same buildings taken from positions off the walk, and scenes taken along other walks at the University.

Subjects performed very much like those previously studied with events from stationary points of observation: 82% of the Originals were correctly identified as having been presented before and 83% of the Belonging slides that were simply interspersed along the walk were falsely recognized. Thus, the Belonging slides were indistinguishable from the slides that were actually presented. Randomly ordering the slides during learning led to similar results: Originals 76%, Belonging 68%. (Controls were falsely recognized 11 and 8% of the time for ordered and random conditions, respectively.)

These experiments with the moving observer allowed us to determine how much of the false recognition effect was attributable to the general knowledge subjects had of the physical campus and how much was attributable to the visual information present in the slide series alone. To exploit this circumstance, we performed the same random and ordered experiments on a similar population of students at another university. These students, of course, could not be expected to identify any of the buildings or have any knowledge of the general campus layout. If the false positives in the original experiments were attributable to extensive knowledge of the constraints of the campus and the nature of the walk, then the naive subjects should show little or no false recognition of Belonging slides. If, on the other hand, the walk is specified as a coherent visual event in itself, then subjects from another campus may be expected to show the same phenomena of false recognition.

The repetitions of the experiments with the second population of subjects yielded several interesting comparisons. The subjects who saw the ordered series responded in the usual fashion of subjects viewing some coherent event. They recognized Original slides 85% of the time, Belonging slides 54% of the time, and Control slides 4% of the time. The subjects who saw the randomized series responded somewhat more profusely to all cases: Originals 89%, Belonging 66%, and Controls 9%.

When the data for these groups are compared with those of the students who knew the campus, the parallel is remarkable. The data for the randomized presentations are almost exactly the same (except that students who did not know the campus were somewhat more likely to recognize correctly the Original slides than students who did know the campus). The data for the ordered presentation, however, show a striking difference in the recognition rate for the Belonging slides. The subjects who knew the campus believed that they had seen the Belonging slides 83% of the time whereas those who did not know the campus believed that they had seen the same slides only 54% of the time.

It appears that this series of pictures reveals both the nature of coherence of a new visual event and the contribution of personal knowledge to that event. The series is sufficient to specify the event in enough detail to make the interpolated slides "familiar" even to an outsider or even when presented in random order; but at the same time personal knowledge and correct temporal-spatial order specify the total event even more fully. .

Frankly, we had not expected so strong an outcome. Even with two viewings, the slides leave the naive observer with the impression that he knows very little about the walk. Yet, one of the things that he does know is that a walk is specified. Almost always one sees the path itself in a relatively constant position on the screen. This invariant alone is sufficient to reject some of the Control slides, but it will not, of course, reject any Belonging slide. Yet it cannot be the whole story, because some Belonging (and Control) slides with this detail are rejected anyway. The outcome has sensitized us to the fact that real events may have many more sources of coherence than we typically notice. It challenges all of us as scientists to specify such sources.

Findings of Our Studies

The studies to date provide a set of demonstrations that are quite convincing at the phenomenal level. We have clearly shown that subjects can and do apprehend natural events portrayed over a series of slides. Subjects describe what they have perceived *as an event,* rather than as a collection of slides, and their behavior on subsequent recognition tasks is influenced in powerful ways by that perception. Subjects often believe they have seen Belonging slides that, in fact, they have not seen. Subjects do not believe they have seen highly similar Control slides that differ from the original experience with respect to either static or dynamic invariants defined over the original set; that is, they detect discrepancies in station point, lighting, direction of action, event-specific transformations and relations, presence or absence of objects, and so on.

We have also shown that analogous phenomena can be obtained under highly varied conditions. Most important, perhaps, is the demonstration that the moving observer over the still environment is just as much a natural event as the dynamic event presented to the stationary observer. Equally interesting are the demonstrations that artificial events (such as Orbiting) can be constructed and that such events may show greatly enhanced experimental effects. The promise here is that of greater control and careful evaluation of the contribution of specific aspects of the visual presentation to the coherence of the event.

Wider Implications

At the general level these studies can be seen as adding to the evidence already available showing that any set of slides implies some set of possible alternatives. In particular, we see these experiments as *strong support for the position that coherent sets of slides, that is, slides that relate to each other in some systematic fashion, specify other stimuli that may or may not be presented.* Stimuli that are thoroughly specified are likely to be falsely recognized just because they fit all of the constraints or invariants of the system that has been apprehended. They may not be falsely recognized if they are only weakly specified or if there is some aspect of the particular stimulus that makes its very absence a salient feature of the presentation.

We see events as natural wholes that are, so to speak, perceived through the slides, rather than built up from the slides. The slides are windows through which the event is glimpsed, rather than Tinker Toys that are used to construct some kind of event-like edifice. We believe that events define their own invariants over time and we now believe that there are many more sources of coherence in real events than we had previously imagined. Perhaps any characteristic that can be specified in the visual array could become an invariant for some kind of event. Conversely, random variation in any aspect of an event may signify allowable variation and result in that aspect's being "ruled out" as a property that is relevant to that event.

We see a wealth of evidence suggesting that these experiments give rise to two kinds of knowledge, specific knowledge of what was seen in the experiment and extensive, general knowledge of the event itself. In the extreme case of unrelated materials the two levels are the same; the independent slides presented are single representatives of the individual events experienced. As the event level comes to differ from the particular slide level, the two kinds of knowledge may coexist independently. At the extreme of relatedness, knowledge of the event itself may totally dominate knowledge of the specific inputs.

Several of our findings reflect the presence of these two levels of knowledge. Our subjects describe the event, rather than the slides, when we ask them what they have seen. When the events are apprehended, subjects show the false recognition of Belonging slides; when events are not apprehended they do not. Frequency effects play little or no role in the recognition data when coherent events are perceived, although they are important when one deals with unrelated events.

We believe that we have shown that information is specified over time and that we have developed a technique for assessing the importance of the time course of the display in studying the event. The difference in natural versus random order displays offers us an opportunity to evaluate the contribution of time and rate information to the quality of an event. Some of the events we have studied so far (e.g., the Tea Sequence) seem to be so well specified or so constrained that random presentation does not prevent their veridical perception. Others are much less constrained (the Telephone Sequence) and lose their single-event quality under randomization.

The "Bottom-up" Approach

It is doubtless apparent to the reader at this point that the research reported here does not make contact with the "bottom-up" approach that we mentioned at the beginning of the chapter. The present research could be regarded as specifying some things for the "bottom-uppers" to explain. But more than this, our research reflects a difference in basic goals.

Our attempt is to study the perception of events and the characteristics of stimulus presentations that give rise to the apprehension of events. We are not trying to explain *how* the subjects apprehend these events, we are simply trying to say *what supports* the apprehension. We see the perception of the event as primary and the enumeration of elements and specifics as secondary, for only after the event is apprehended can it be analyzed appropriately.

We see the selection of materials to be studied as crucial and feel that the dramatic differences between the phenomena associated with unrelated pictures and the phenomena associated with related pictures are an important warning to investigators about permissible generalizations from impoverished materials and artificial laboratory settings. We feel that attempts to work with "frozen" stimuli are doomed to irrelevance or failure because they are forced to address problems that arise from asking the wrong questions.

With respect to our experiments we see several thorny problems for the "bottom–up" analysis. First, what is it that is taken from each individual slide and remembered? We think the evidence is fairly strong that whatever an image might be, it is not some sort of picture in the head; it is not another photographic representation. Second, what kind of device scans the stored representations? It seems to us that it must be some kind of dynamic "change detector," which does not solve the problem but changes it from one of scanning the real world to one of scanning a set of static representations. If there are such change detectors, why not let them work directly on the world, rather than on some less rich representation of the world? Third, given that our subjects seem to respond to event-specific invariances, how could the device get along with anything less than universal storage of all possible aspects of every visual representation? How would such a device discard the random changes from slide to slide but detect and represent as crucial the dynamic invariances? In brief, even in our simple experiments we see a set of unyielding questions that threaten us with the paradoxes we mentioned at the beginning of the chapter.

We can sidestep these problems by focusing on the event as the primary percept. We believe that the human being is a marvelous device, shaped by millions of years of evolution, and capable of apprehending real events. We do not need to wait for a solution of the analytic processing dilemmas (that we have created for ourselves) before we start to work on understanding event perception. We can simply move in the opposite direction, away from an exclusive concern with the machinery of the organism and toward the structure of the world. We can try to understand what is perceived and what will provide sufficient ground for a coherent perception before we try to specify how it is done.

Directions of Research

Starting with the assumption that events are primary, we are led to study a novel set of questions.

We believe that the line of investigation that we are pursuing can be readily extended. We can ask what kinds of variables increase coherence in events of a given kind, without expecting to obtain transsituational answers. We can begin to separate a subject's knowledge of the stimuli presented from his knowledge of the event specified. We can ask under what circumstances we find subjects unable to reject instances that belong to an event even when they were not seen as part of the event. We can evaluate the role of past experience and knowledge of the observer in contributing to the coherence of an event. And we can explore the manner in which a dynamic event creates its own "features" through the invariants it manifests over time.

These are exciting questions that we think will furnish new stimulation for psychologists of all orientations. They are questions that can be investigated right now; they do not have to wait on new processing metaphors or new solutions to old paradoxes. They may not appeal to those who believe that the job of the psychologist is to postulate processing models that will deal with any and all kinds of possible information. If one believes that is the psychologist's task, our approach will, indeed, be seen as something outside of the mainstream or even outside of psychology itself. We, of course, would disagree. It will be interesting to see what each approach offers in the long run.

ACKNOWLEDGMENTS

The research reported in this paper was supported by grants to the Center for Research in Human Learning, University of Minnesota from the National Science Foundation (GB 17590), The National Institute for Child Health and Human Development (HD 01136), and the Graduate School, University of Minnesota. The second author was a predoctoral trainee of the National Institute for Child Health and Human Development under Training Grant, HD 00098. The third author expresses thanks to the University of Arkansas for a travel grant, which made collaboration possible. The authors are happy to express their appreciation to Martin Wurthman and Vincent Berg who helped with the photographic work involved in these studies. The debt that the authors owe to Robert Shaw for intellectual stimulation and inspiration is evident throughout the chapter. It is gratefully acknowledged.

REFERENCES

Bransford, J. D., Barclay, J. R., & Franks, J. J. (1972). Sentence memory: A constructive versus interpretive approach. *Cognitive Psychology, 3,* 193–209.

Bransford, J. D., & Franks, J. J. (1971). The abstraction of linguistic ideas. *Cognitive Psychology, 2,* 331–350.

Bransford, J. D., & McCarrell, N. S. (1974). A sketch of a cognitive approach to comprehension: Some thoughts about understanding what it means to comprehend. In W. B. Weimer & D. S.

Palermo (Eds.), *Cognition and the symbolic processes.* Hillsdale, NJ: Lawrence Erlbaum Associates.

Chase, W. G., & Simon, H. A. (1973). Perception in chess. *Cognitive Psychology, 4,* 55–81.

Esper, E. A. (1925). A technique for the experimental investigation of associative interference in artificial linguistic material. *Language Monographs of the Linguistic Society of America, 1,*

Esper, E. A. (1973). *Analogy and association in linguistics and psychology.* Athens, Ga.: University of Georgia Press.

Foss, D. J. (1968). An analysis of learning in a miniature linguistic system. *Journal of Experimental Psychology, 76,* 450–459.

Franks, J. J. J., & Bransford, J. D. (1971). Abstraction of visual patterns. *Journal of Experimental Psychology, 90,* 165–174.

Garner, W. R. (1974). *The processing of information and structure.* Potomac, MD: Lawrence Erlbaum Associates.

Gibson, J. J. (1966). *The senses considered as perceptual systems.* Boston: Houghton–Mifflin.

Goldstein, A. G., & Chance, J. E. (1970). Visual recognition memory for complex configurations. *Perception and Psychophysics, 9,* 237–240.

Gough, P. B. (1972). One second of reading. In J. F. Kavanagh & I. G. Mattingly (Eds.), *Language by ear and by eye.* Cambridge: MA: The M.I.T. Press.

Haber, N. R. (1970). How we remember what we see. *Scientific American, 222*(5), 104–112.

Jenkins, J. J. (1974a). Can we have a theory of meaningful memory? In R. E. Solso (Ed.), *Memory and cognition: The second Loyola symposium.* Potomac, MD: Lawrence Erlbaum Associates, 1–20.

Jenkins, J. J. (1974b). Remember that old theory of memory? Well, forget it! *American Psychologist, 29,* 785–795.

Johansson, G. (1975). Visual motion perception. *Scientific American, 232*(6), 76–88.

Kavanagh, J. F., & Mattingly, I. B. (1972). *Language by ear and by ear.* Cambridge, MA: The M.I.T. Press.

Kraft, R. N., & Jenkins, J. J. (1977). Memory for lateral orientation of slides in picture stories. *Memory and Cognition, 5,* 397–403.

LaBerge, D., & Samuels, S. J. (1974). Toward a theory of automatic information processing in reading. *Cognitive Psychology, 6,* 293–323.

Michotte, A. (1963). *The perception of causality.* London: Methuen & Co., Ltd.

Neissor, U. (1967). *Cognitive psychology.* New York: Appleton Century Crofts.

Posner, M. I., & Keele, S. W. (1968). On the genesis of abstract ideas. *Journal of Experimental Psychology, 77,* 353–363.

Posner, M. I., & Keele, S. W. (1970). Retention of abstract ideas. *Journal of Experimental Psychology, 83,* 304–308.

Postman, L. (1975). Verbal learning and memory. *The Annual Review of Psychology, 26,* 291–335.

Segal, E. M. (1962–1963). Stimulus perception as a function of response set (Doctoral dissertation, University of Minnesota, 1962). *Dissertation Abstracts, 23,* 3994. (University Microfilms No. 63–2331).

Shankweiler, D. P., Strange, W., & Verbrugge, R. R. (1977). Speech and the problem of perceptual constancy. In R. E. Shaw & J. D. Bransford, (Eds.), *Perceiving, acting and knowing: Toward an ecological psychology,* Hillsdale, NJ: Lawrence Erlbaum Associates.

Shaw, R. E., & Pittenger, J. B. (1978). Perceiving change. In H. L. Pick & E. Saltzman (Eds.), *Modes of perceiving and processing information.* Hillsdale, NJ: Lawrence Erlbaum Associates.

Shaw, R. E., & Wilson, B. E. (1976). Conceptual knowledge: How we know what we know. In D. Klahr (Ed.), *Cognition and instruction.* Hillsdale, NJ: Lawrence Erlbaum Associates.

Shepard, R. N. (1967). Recognition memory for words, sentences and pictures. *Journal of Verbal Learning and Verbal Behavior, 6,* 156–163.

Standing, L. (1973). Learning 10,000 pictures. *Quarterly Journal of Experimental Psychology, 25,* 207–222.

Standing, L., Conezio, J., & Haber, R. N. (1970). Perception and memory for pictures: Single-trial learning of 2500 visual stimuli. *Psychonomic Science, 19,* 73–74.

Strange, W., Keeney, T., Kessel, F. S., & Jenkins, J. J. (1970). Abstraction over time of prototypes from distortions of random dot patterns. *Journal of Experimental Psychology, 83,* 508–510.

Verbrugge, R. R. (1974). *The comprehension of analogy.* Unpublished doctoral dissertation, University of Minnesota.

7

Thinking on Your Feet: The Consequences of Action for the Relation of Perception and Cognition

Steven S. Braddon
Sacred Heart University
Bridgeport, Connecticut

Among cognitive psychologists, the idea that perception is an active process is uncontroversial. Yet, as Michaels and Carrello (1981) note, the meaning of the phrase "active perceiver" needs far greater attention. Usually, cognitive processes such as inferencing and hypothesis-testing are taken to constitute the activities of active perceivers. Rarely are physical actions such as traveling and exploring considered relevant to perceiving and knowing. The purpose of this chapter is to examine some of the consequences for cognitive theory and research when perceivers are allowed to move as well as to think.

For more than a decade, Roger Shepard and his colleagues have investigated the relationship between mental representation and perception. They suggest that people have evolved the capacity to mentally represent objects in a way that is second-order isomorphic with object perception (Shepard & Cooper, 1982, Ch. 1); that is, the transformation of an object (e.g., by rotation or folding) and the analogous internal cognitive transformation of the object's representation are held to exhibit many of the same properties (Shepard & Feng, 1972; Shepard & Metzler, 1971), although not necessarily sharing any first-order similarity—the representation does not literally resemble the object (Shepard, 1968).

Although Shepard connects representations to their perceptual origins, an important assumption has not received sufficient attention. The theory of second-order isomorphism tacitly assumes that *passive* observation is the paradigm process by which representations of real-world objects are obtained. The physical transformations in Shepard's experiments happen "out there" in front of the perceiver/spectator. Thus the character of object perception derives from what *objects* do, not what *people* do in the world. In short, the second-order isomorphism perspective fails to consider that perceivers are not only observers and representers of object transformations but also actors who generate or induce those transformations.[1]

Thus when Shepard (and a majority of cognitive psychologists) puts subjects through their paces, the paces are usually mental. The search for information takes place over a cognitive surface rather than the terrestrial surfaces of the physical environment. Whereas subjects have traveled many cognitive miles searching for, constructing, and retrieving answers to questions posed by experimental tasks, very little *real* distance has been traveled and very few actual objects located, constructed, or retrieved. It would appear that cognitive studies have not given serious consdieration to the role of action in cognitive processes.

Many researchers have demonstrated that when action accompanies perception, task performance is altered, sometimes dramatically (Bach-y-Rita, 1972; Bairstow & Laszlow, 1979; Gibson, 1962). How does the inclusion of action in perception bear on the matter of second-order isomorphisms? One effect may be that second-order isomorphisms no longer hold. Let us consider an experiment in mental paper folding by Shepard and Feng (1972). Subjects in the experiment were shown a line drawing of an unfolded cube consisting of six connected squares. An arrow pointing to an edge was drawn on each of two of the squares. The task was to carry out the process of mentally assembling the cube and to determine, as rapidly as possible, whether the two arrows met tip to tip. Latencies increased linearly with the total number of squares mentally carried.

Shepard and Feng assumed rather than examined the properties of the perceptual side of the isomorphism, but Braddon and Warner (1980) tested explicitly whether the paper-folding task provided evidence of a parallel between conception and perception; they directly compared mental paper folding with the perception of the physical activity of paper folding. Data showed that the "conceptual" folders replicated the linearity obtained by Shepard and Feng, but the "physical" folders produced a relatively flat function. A cube requiring a total of eight squares to be manually carried took no longer to fold than a cube requiring just two squares to be manually carried.[2]

---

[1]For present purposes, active and passive observation are portrayed as mutually exclusive. Many roles, however, involve both styles of perceiving. For example, a football referee is both a spectator and an active participant (Warren, 1978).

[2]Though the cube is composed of only six squares, eight total squares can be carried in the folding process if Shepard & Metzler's (1971, Experiment 2) definitions are adopted. When a particular square is folded, it may be connected to and therefore "carry along" one or more other squares.

The difference between conception and perception found by Braddon and Warner can be attributed to the qualities contributed by action to perception that are not mirrored in conceptual processes. For each fold, the mental paper folder must cognitively track the new positions and orientations of the squares and arrows. Each additional square increases the cognitive load and systematically increases decision time. In contrast, for physical paper folding the hands "remember" without difficulty the changing orientation of the squares throughout the process, and the location of the arrows is perceptually available. Thus it is not surprising that the carrying along of additional squares does not have an equivalent influence on performance in the two conditions.

Although active perceiving presents challenges for the second-order isomorphism concept, it is conceivable that Shepard and his colleagues never intended the isomorphism to embrace active perceiving. Perhaps cognitive processes do accurately model processes of passive observation. Does mental rotation, for example, mirror what a perceiver sees when watching someone or something carrying out that transformation? This notion gains some plausiblity when we consider that mental transformation tasks typically begin with the presentation (and therefore, observation) of one or two stimuli upon which the cognitive operation is then performed (e.g., Shepard & Metzler, 1971). As other intermediate positions of the transformation are added, the conceptual process becomes less and less distinguishable from an act of observation. There is, however, a problem with the equating of perception with passive observation. The evolutionary significance imputed to second-order resemblances would seem to require conceptual processes to model active, participatory perception, not passive observation (Shepard, 1981; Shepard & Cooper, 1982).

THE ADAPTIVE VALUE OF COGNITIVE PROCESSES THAT MODEL REALITY

Shepard (1981) argues that in the evolution of higher organisms a perceptual mechanism was favored that accurately represented basic transformations of physical objects. Internalized "rules" enable a family of cognitive operations to be executed the outcomes of which mirror reality. Most important among these outcomes are the planning of action and the anticipation of perceptual information (see also Corballis, 1982; Clark, 1943, Ch. 5). For example, engineers usually design bridges and conceptually evaluate their (the bridges') safety before attempting construction. This procedure avoids both unnecessary expense and risk to life.

Shepard makes the further claim that cognitive modeling exists because of its survival value. He suggests that:

> the success of a hungry cat waiting at a hole for the reemergence of a mouse depends on the speed and accuracy with which the cat is prepared to perceive and to

respond to that emergence when and if it occurs. But the readying of the appropriate perceptual representation and the control of the appropriate motor response, alike, take place in the internal, rather than the external, domain of the cat. (p. 292)

If Shepard's analysis of how mice are caught is correct then it appears that cognitive and perceptual activity are indeed functionally equivalent. The analysis, however, does not hold up. The cat's conceptual processes cannot accomplish the assigned tasks because the information required to act accurately is not internally available. The speed and direction of the mouse as it emerges from the hole and attempts to escape are external to the cat. How can the cat be prepared with the "appropriate perceptual representation" unless it has extraordinarily precise forcesight of the mouse's moves and the chase that follows? It is hard to see exactly how a cognitive process that models the prey's behavior would offer any evolutionary advantage. The predator would benefit only if the prey happened to appear at just the place with just the speed that was cognitively modeled at that time. Any other internal state of affairs would cause error and delay in the cat's predation that increases with the discrepancy between the cat's preparations and the mouse's actual behavior (cf. Cooper, 1976). Because these latter outcomes will be more numerous, it is not clear how, on Shepard's account, cats catch mice with such finesse.

This cat and mouse story indicates that mental modeling could not have evolved for the purposes suggested by the second-order isomorphism framework. Events in the real world are rarely so predictable that cognitive plans or preparations can be relied upon for the information that enables precise behavior. An engineer's success or failure in planning and predicting also depends often on environmental factors beyond control.

To take an extreme case, few could have predicted or cognitively modeled the circumstances that precipitated the 1949 collapse of the Tacoma Narrows bridge. In fact, it was a pattern of regular vortexes inherent in the total situation that caused the collapse; *unique* environmental conditions were required to produce such an effect. Stevens (1974) states: "With a steady wind of forty-two miles per hour blowing across a thirty nine foot wide roadway, vortexes peeled off from one edge and then the other and caused the bridge to twist on itself, first one way and then the other" (p. 65). On a far smaller scale, the cat's success or failure depends on the same sort of environmental interactions rather than on internal modeling. It is the actual perceptual and behavioral *interplay* of the cat and mouse that guides the cat rather than a simulacrum solely under the predator's cognitive control. The claim that conceptual processes model perceptual processes does not adequately clarify the nature of such interplay in that second-order isomorphisms focus on representation rather than physical activity. The experiments to be reported here examine the role of action in the acquisition of knowledge. How does passive observation compare with the active observation that accompanies purposeful and active behavior?

MEMORY AND ACTIVE PERCEPTION: THREE
EXPERIMENTS

The series of studies considered here examined active and passive perceivers (alternately, "actors" and "observers") in a novel spatial task. Four environmental routes were learned with and without accompanying behavioral activity. Both quantitative and qualitative differences were expected in the knowledge acquired about the routes through the two styles of perceiving. Such outcomes would highlight the need for cognitive psychologists to clarify *what sort* of perceptual processes are meant to be isomorphic with conceptual processes. The tasks selected for these experiments did not require that subjects engage in the image transformations characteristic of second-order isomorphism research. Nevertheless, the actor-observer manipulation bears on the functional parallel of perception and cognition because it promises to address the question of whether passive observation is representative of all perceptual processes.

Part of the idea for the present research derives from differerences in the roles of automobile driver and passenger. A common intuition is that drivers acquire knowledge of a region better than passengers. A person can be driven to a destination several times and yet be unable to find it when first placed in the driver's seat. What does the driver know that the passenger does not?

The developmental literature is informative on this question. There is considerable agreement that environmental knowledge progresses from attention to landmarks by 3-year-olds to an adult's comprehension of global spatial layout (Cohen & Schuepfer, 1980; Hazen, Lockman, & Pick, 1978; Siegal & White, 1975). Furthermore, evidence indicates that active, self-guided exploration fosters the growth of integrated environmental knowledge in children better than passive exploration, such as being led around by an adult (Feldman & Acredolo, 1979; Hazen, 1982).

The contrast between active and passive modes of exploration is clearly present in the driver–passenger case. One transports, the other is transported. Perhaps then, passengers do not easily make the transition to drivers because in their role as more passive observers, they, like young children, attend to different information, landmarks, or salient details, rather than the route connecting them. Conversely, drivers, the active participants, know the route as a whole but less well as a set of individual landmarks. On this analysis, if a new landmark were substituted for an old one on a familiar route, observers should detect this landmark change more often than actors. If, instead, the actual path of the route were altered, we would expect actors to be better than observers at detecting the change.[3]

---

[3]Braddon (1980, Ch. 2) develops the implication of these hypotheses for the analogue-propositional knowledge debate (see Block, 1981, Ch. 6–8).

Experiment 1

Two groups of active observers and two groups of passive observers saw four sequences of seven "route elements," each route element being either a picture or a word. A sample sequence is presented in Fig. 7.1a. The subjects' task was to remember the 28 items (four routes times seven route elements) for a subsequent recognition test. Each sequence of seven elements specified a route taken by a different geometric figure through a matrix of 16 squares. The composite route taken in the sample sequence is shown at the far right of Fig. 7.1a. (Subjects never saw this.) The pictorial route elements indicated the current matrix location of the figure; linguistic elements, the words "up," "down," "left," and "right," signified that the figure moved one square in the indicated direction.

The seated, passive observers saw slides showing three complete passes through the 28 route elements in the task. They were instructed to remember the separate items but were also encouraged to "follow" each route, i.e., to integrate the pictorial and linguistic elements into a coherent path. Identical instructions were given to the active observers except that they *walked* the four routes three times each. The 28 elements were presented to actors as a hand-held deck of cards. The environment in which the walks took place was a 4' × 4' matrix of 16 floor tiles marked off with tape.

A recognition test immediately followed. One of the active and one of the passive observer groups reversed roles for the test; the other two groups kept their original roles; that is, approximately half of the subjects who learned the route elements as active observers were tested as passive observers, and vice versa. For each of the four routes, four types of route segments, each three elements long, were devised (see Fig. 1b). OLD items consisted of three consecutive route elements excerpted "verbatim" from the longer routes. In contrast, NEW items introduced a novel element that detoured the segment off the course of the original route. The other two types of test segments, the BELONGING items, shared qualities with both the old and new cases. Each of these segments accurately traversed part of a route but included a specific route element not originally present. This was accomplished by substituting one pictorial element for its appropriate linguistic "translation," and vice versa. The BELONGING segments are interpreted as altering "landmark" information while preserving "path" information.

The 16 three-element route segments (four routes times four segment types) were presented on slides to passive observers or on cards to active observers who walked each test segment. An "old/new" recognition judgment followed each segment. Subjects answered "old" if they felt that the three elements were identical in all respects to three consecutive elements seen in one of the four initial routes, otherwise "new."

To summarize, four independent conditions were studied (passive or active observation at acquisition × passive or active observation at recognition.) If, as

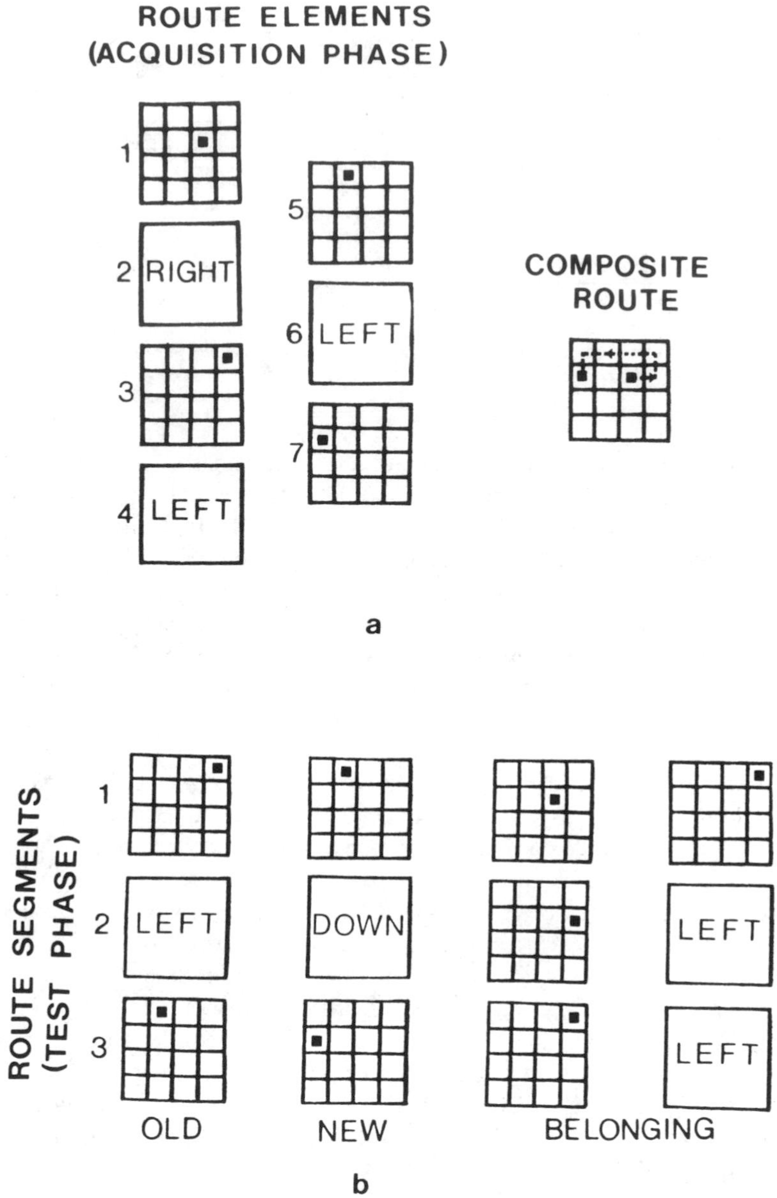

FIG. 7.1. (a) One of the four sets of acquisition route elements. The resultant route is at the far right; (b) the four types of route segments used in Experiments 1 and 2 to assess knowledge of the sequence shown in (a).

TABLE 7.1
Mean Proportion of Correct Recognition Judgments as
a Function of Route Segment Type (Experiment 1)

Group	Segment Types		
	Old	New	Belonging
PP	.77	.94	.50
PA	.56	.93	.43
AP	.57	.86	.47
AA	.58	.91	.58

Note: P = passive observation; A = active observation. The first letter in each pair denotes
the acquisition condition, the second, the test
condition.

hypothesized, observers are more attentive to "landmark" information than actors are, observers should recognize OLD segments and reject NEW and BELONGING segments more accurately than actors. BELONGING items provide the best opportunity to evaluate the hypothesis because for these, correct judgments could not be based simply on a decision whether a test segment route matched part of an acquisition route; that is, knowledge of the specific elements composing the routes was required for a correct response to BELONGING items.

Table 7.1 presents the mean proportion of correct recognition judgments in the four conditions collapsed over the four routes. The two types of BELONGING items did not differ, so these data were also combined. Little support was obtained in this first experiment for the hypothesis that seated observers remember route landmarks (i.e., route elements) better than do active participants. Although the relative accuracy of the PP group (passive observers throughout) on old items bore out predictions, the PA (passive then active) group, which was also seated throughout the presentation of the four routes, was less successful. For the complete set of 16 test items, recognition accuracy was not enhanced overall by passive observation during either the acquisition or test phases. However, an interesting, though unanticipated, interaction was obtained: A greater proportion of correct judgments were made to test segments when the subjects' activity in the two phases matched than when they did not (compare groups PP and AA with PA and AP in Table 7.1). This pattern was also found in an analysis including just the BELONGING items. Although the compatibility effect cannot account for the difference between the AA and PP groups, it appears that the match versus mismatch of activities across phases of the experiment exerted a stronger influence on performance than the identity of the activities per se.

Compatibility effects are common in memory research (Cohen, Weatherford, & Byrd, 1980; Smith, 1979; Tulving, 1979). Smith (1979), for example, found that recall of a word list was optimal when the classroom in which the list was learned was also the test environment. Reinstatement of context apparently provided reminders of the associations made between to-be-remembered items and the incidental objects in the room. Smith's "environmental reinstatement effect" suggests that part of the outcome of Experiment 1 may have been due to differences in the setting in which active and passive observers encountered the routes and test segments. In the second experiment, an attempt was made to equate better the contexts for active and passive observing. In addition, the PA and AP conditions were removed from the design. Finally, because performance on BELONGING items in Experiment 1 was virtually at chance, Experiment 2 altered instructions slightly in order to emphasize more strongly the importance of specific route elements.

Experiment 2

In this experiment, the active and passive observers were more nearly analogous to drivers and passengers. Paired subjects were seated side by side and had nearly identical views of the laboratory. A passive observer watched an actor move hand and arm through a tabletop version of the 16-square matrix. The four routes and 16 test segments were the same as in Experiment 1. All subjects saw the stimulus information on index cards held by the experimenter and were specifically instructed to attend carefully to the route elements. Immediately following acquisition, the deck of 16 test segments was presented to the pair of subjects. Again, the actor moved hand and arm through the test items while the observer watched. Subjects rendered an old/new recognition judgment in writing following each segment. There was no changing of roles, so in effect only PP and AA conditions were examined in this study.

Table 7.2 presents the mean recognition data from 10 pairs of subjects. Overall, passive observers were more accurate than active observers. The difference was most pronounced for the BELONGING items, which required noticing that a landmark, but not the route, had been altered. Despite instructions to attend to specific route elements, actors performed substantially worse than observers on BELONGING items.

The results of Experiment 2 support the view that an adequate characterization of perception must consider the behavior in which the perceiver is engaged. Action and passive observation were found to make unequal contributions to

TABLE 7.2
Mean Proportion of Correct Recognition Judgment as
a Function of Route Segment Type (Experiment 2)

Group	Old	New	Belonging
Passive	.68	.95	.60
Active	.68	.85	.39

knowledge of environmental events. If the second-order isomorphism claim is that conceptual processes correspond to perception-as-observation, then the disadvantage actors faced here is not addressed.

Experiment 3

The purpose of the third study was to replicate the actor–observer differences obtained in the previous experiment using a prompted recall test in place of recognition. In addition, the study provided a fairer assessment of the hypothesis that active observers would remember the routes better than passive observers. In both of the first two experiments, the instructions (and the test) had focused attention primarily on knowledge of route details—the sort of information that passive observers were expected to notice more readily. In Experiment 3 the path and the details of the route were emphasized equally and examined separately.

Subjects were tested individually. Active participants walked the four routes as in Experiment 1; seated observers were shown the route elements on cards by the experimenter as in Experiment 2 (the tabletop matrix was not present). Subjects learned both the four routes and the elements that comprised them. Two recall tests immediately followed the third pass through the sequence of route elements. For the route recall test, the task was to draw the four paths taken through the matrix, given the first route element as a prompt. For the route detail recall test, subjects recalled in writing the second through seventh elements of each route (because the first had already been provided). The two recall tests could be completed in either order or in alternation.

A recalled route was judged correct only if the path drawn exactly matched the actual one. The results of the route recall test are summarized on the left side of Table 6.3. As expected, active observers were more accurate at recalling the paths. For each of the correctly recalled routes, the number of correctly recalled route elements was determined. An element was judged correct only if it precisely matched the information that appeared in that serial position in the route. A score of zero corresponds to the (unlikely) case in which, although the route was correctly recalled, all the recalled details were incorrect. Simply put, such a case would signify that the route, as an abstract path, was learned, but not the specific components that gave rise to it. A score of six would indicate that

TABLE 7.3
Mean Percent Recall (Experiment 3)

Group	Routes[a]	Route Details[b]
Passive	52.3	69.6
Active	70.5	52.2

[a] based on four routes.
[b] based on six details per route.

accurate route recall was complemented by a precise recollection of all the uncued route details. The results of the route detail recall test are given as percentages on the right side of Table 7.3.[4] Here, in contrast to the route recall test, it was the passive observers who performed better, thus completing the predicted interaction between type of observation (active vs. passive) and type of recall (path vs. details).

The results of Experiment 3 clearly indicate that the skills of perceivers who passively observe and those who act are qualitatively distinct. Each mode of perceiving was seen to be better suited than the other for learning about a particular aspect of environmental routes. Passive observers excelled at retention of the components of the route; active observers excelled at retention of route "Gestalts."

Taken together, the results of Experiments 2 and 3 indicate that activity plays a significant role in the pursuit of knowledge. The strong implication is that observing an object and manipulating an object are not equivalent for perceivers. Cognitive theories that focus on one aspect of perception and not the other are incomplete.

TWO VIEWS OF COMPLEMENTARITY

Whereas second-order isomorphism research pursues the similarity between cognition and perception, the other side of this coin clearly deserves further attention: How are cognition and perception distinguished? How do they collaborate with, rather than substitute for, each other? In Shepard's (1981) more recent views, physical objects and their internal representations are treated more as complementary to, rather than merely isomorphic with, one another; transformations on objects and on representations are also complements of one another. In a complementarity, the members of the relation functionally mesh; in a second-order isomorphism, they are mutually substitutable. In some cases, there is no difference between the two relations. For example, two spoons can be put together to create a percussion instrument (a functional mesh) and can also be mutually substitutable in function (isomorphic). As Shepard's primary example demonstrates, however, a complementarity and a second-order isomorphism may be quite different. Shepard employs the relation of lock and key to illustrate the mesh between internal and external realms. The lock and key do not look alike. A lock clearly does not substitute for a key when each is used conventionally. One object does not do the work of the other. Nor are the transformations in which they participate isomorphic. Instead, the unique relation between

---

[4]For routes recalled incorrectly, the mean number of correctly recalled details for active and passive observers was 1.4 and 1.0, respectively.

the two objects is functionally defined; the key opens only the one lock. A similar functional relation bonds transformations on objects and on representations. What makes a lock and key complementary is that they are *interdefined,* not interchangeable. The meaning and value of one emerges only when the other is considered. Furthermore, a lock and key become functionally related only when they are used together in a *unified* action.

The concept of complementarity may be useful for understanding the relation between perception-in-action and conceptual processes (see also Chapter 2, this volume). Like a lock and key, physical transformation of an object (i.e., manipulation) provides information to a perceiver that its cognitive counterpart does not and vice versa. Because the two modes of knowing are not redundant, a person will benefit by joining them in accomplsihing a task, just as the lock and key are joined to effect an outcome. In this view, cognitive processes *extend,* rather than duplicate, perceptual skills. Because passive observation may in fact accurately model cognitive processes, the focus of second-order isomorphisms on duplication may appear to be adequate. Active perceivers, however, are different, as research presented here indicates. Does a complementarity relation link ongoing conceptual activity to perception-in-action?

Shepard's discussion of complementarity relations is less helpful on this question. Perceivers are consistently described as informed about the world not by ongoing actions but by information derived from internal modelings of events. Some of the practical problems with this view were addressed earlier in discussions of Shepard's (1981) treatment of cat predation. But logical problems also exist that lie at the putative origins of representations. Shepard appeals to evolution for the process that gives rise to these mental models. Internal models are claimed to allow an accurate construction of the external world given impoverished sensory information. Yet how could these models have evolved in the first place if the information essential to survival—that which is to be modeled—cannot be perceptually detected with reliability? Models of impoverished sensory input can only be impoverished themselves unless veridical knowledge of the world can be acquired through other than perceptual means (for similar arguments, see also Dennett, 1978, Ch. 1; Turvey & Carello, 1981; Turvey, Shaw, Reed, & Mace, 1981; Wilcox & Katz, 1981).

On the other hand, if the perceptual information required for survival (or any other purpose) is sufficient, available, and detectable, then the necessity of mental representations is open to question. Perceivers would not need to mirror internally the rules that govern the objects and transformations of the external world because the environmental events could be perceived directly, without mediation or internal copying.

Perception without mediating cognitive processes is a hallmark of the ecological perspective pioneered by J. J. Gibson (1979) and extended by researchers in ecological psychology. This view supports an analysis of complementarity congenial to a melding of perception-in-action with conceptual processes. Working within the ecological tradition, Shaw and Turvey (1981) argue that perceiving is complementary with acting, not with internal processes: "Perception is the mechanism that functions to inform the actor of the means the environment affords for realizing the actor's goals. Correspondingly, . . . action is the mechanism that functions to select the means by which goals of the actor may be effected" (Shaw & Turvey, 1981, p. 378). Underlying this complementarity is the logical dependence or coreferentiality of animal and environment; that is, the environment is defined in terms that are tailored to how a perceiver/actor lives (as opposed to a definition in species-neutral vocabulary). Similarly, an animal is defined as a set of perceptual and behavioral capacities to explore what its environment offers. An environment described with reference to an animal is the affordance structure of that environment (Gibson, 1977); conversely, an animal described with reference to an environment defines the animal's effectivity structure (Shaw, Turvey, & Mace, 1982). Each of these structures is a kind of isomorphism of its own. Affordances focus on the functional fit of environment to animal. Effectivities view this relation from the animal's perspective.

Like a lock and key, the complementary relation between affordance and effectivity—between perceiving and acting—forms a unity. Perceiving does not functionally resemble acting in the sense that their respective processes are substitutable. Rather, perceiving and acting are mutually constrained. The literal fit of key into lock depends equally on the ability to handle the objects appropriately, to perceive that possible relation between the objects, and to guide the action perceptually to completion. The plausibility of the ecological view is reinforced by findings that complex actions can be visually regulated (Lee, Lishman, & Thomson, 1982) by information, contained in the "perceptual present," about what is yet to happen (e.g., impending collision, cf. Schiff, 1965; Schiff & Detwiler, 1979). If anticipation can be described in noncognitivistic terms, attempts to extend the ecological approach to planning and preparing should be vigorously pursued.

Certainly, there are conceptual processes not amenable to perceptual explication. Thinking, reasoning, and imagining extend the skills of active perceiving. Constraints such as gravity and speed of motion that limit real actions are not imposed on cognitive action. Perhaps the usefulness of thought is not so much that it models perception but rather that it can abstract away from and reflect on perception. On this view, creativity and insight would result from the *merger* of conceptual and active perceptual processes and not lie solely in the processes of the conceptual domain.

SUMMARY AND CONCLUSIONS

The emphasis on this chapter has been on a critical analysis of the claim that conceptual processes resemble perceptual processes by a second order isomorphism. Several weaknesses in this claim were identified. Most importantly, the isomorphism failed to capture the interdependence of perception and action.

Evidence from three experiments indicated that passive and active observers come to know different qualities of simple environmental routes. Passive observers remembered the routes as an array of individual elements or landmarks whereas actors remembered routes as connected paths.

Both the putative evolutionary basis and apparent everyday applications of a "second-order" resemblance between conceptual and perceptual processes were faulted on logical and practical grounds. The assumption of the unreliability of perceptual input makes the development of an accurate cognitive model difficult to explain. However, if this assumption is abandoned, the need for such a model is open to question. It was also argued that, contrary to the second-order isomorphism framework, mental representation alone cannot effectively guide perception and action. Arguments for the complementarity of perception and cognition did not appear to overcome these problems, but the concept of complementarity does promise to illuminate the relation between perception and action. In the ecological view the processes of perceiving and acting are considered complementary activities, interdefined but not interchangeable. Control for these activities is distributed in a relation between animal and environment and not contained in a conceptual mechanism. As for conception itself, the possibility was offered that the attendant cognitive processes enter into a higher order complementarity with perceiving/acting.

The English critic G. K. Chesterton once remarked that "There are no rules of architecture for a castle in the clouds." Clearly though, there are rules for a castle built on the ground. Thinking ordinarily differs from active perceiving but the two must mesh to yield creative accomplishments. By keeping subjects stationary, experimenters treat passive observation as the paradigmatic case of information acquisition and treat action as an influence on performance better minimized than explored. The data and theory presented in this chapter suggest that if subjects spent more time thinking on their feet, cognitive psychology would be more firmly grounded in reality.

ACKNOWLEDGMENTS

The research presented in this chapter is based on the author's dissertation submitted in partial fulfillment of the requirements for the Ph.D. at the University of Connecticut. I thank the editors of this volume and Catherine T. Best for their helpful comments. The secretarial assistance of Marian Ruzicka and Mary Tsalapatanis is gratefully acknowledged. Correspondence should be addressed to the author at Lever Research, Inc., 45 River Rd., Rm. 805, Edgewater, N.J. 07020.

REFERENCES

Bach-y-Rita, P. (1972). *Brain mechanisms in sensory substitution*. New York: Academic Press.
Bairstow, P. J., & Laslow, J. I. (1979). Perception of movement patterns: Tracking of movement. *Journal of Motor Behavior, 30*, 311–317.

Block, N. (Ed.). (1981). *Imagery*. Cambridge, MA: MIT Press.

Braddon, S. S. (1980). *The roles of participation and observation in the perceiving and remembering of figural-symbolic events*. Unpublished doctoral dissertation, University of Connecticut.

Braddon, S. S., & Warner, K. (1980, September). *A comparison of mental and physical paper folding*. Paper presented at the 88th meeting of the American Psychological Association, Montreal.

Cohen, R., & Schuepfer, T. (1980). The representation of landmarks and routes. *Child Development, 51*, 1065–1071.

Cohen, R., Weatherford, D. L., & Byrd, D. (1980). Distance estimates of children as a function of acquisition and response activities. *Journal of Experimental Child Psychology, 30*, 464–472.

Cooper, L. A. (1976). Demonstration of a mental analog of an external rotation. *Perception & Psychophysics, 19*, 296–302.

Corballis, M. C. (1982). Mental rotation: Anatomy of a paradigm. In M. Potegal (Ed.), *Spatial abilities: Development and physiological foundations*. New York: Academic Press.

Craik, K. J. W. (1943). *The nature of explanation*. Cambridge, England: Cambridge University Press.

Dennett, D. C. (1978). *Brainstorms*. Bradford, VT: Bradford Books.

Feldman, A., & Acredolo, L. (1979). The effect of active versus passive exploration on memory for spatial location in children. *Child Development, 50*, 698–704.

Gibson, J. J. (1962). Observations on active touch. *Psychological Review, 69*, 477–491.

Gibson, J. J. (1977). The theory of affordances. In R. E. Shaw & J. Bransford (Eds.), *Perceiving, acting, and knowing*. Hilldale, NJ: Lawrence Erlbaum Associates.

Gibson, J. J. (1979). *The ecological approach to visual perception*. Boston: Houghton–Miffin.

Hazen, N. L. (1982). Spatial exploration and spatial knowledge: Individual and developmental differences in very young children. *Child Development, 53*, 826–833.

Hazen, N. L., Lockman, J. J., & Pick, H. L. Jr. (1978). The development of children's representations of large-scale environments. *Child Development, 49*, 623–636.

Lee, D. N., Lishman, J. R., & Thomson, J. A. (1982). Regulation of gait in long jumping. *Journal of Experimental Psychology: Human Perception and Performance, 8*, 448–459.

Michaels, C. F., & Carello, C. (1981). *Direct perception*. Englewood Cliffs, NJ: Prentice–Hall.

Schiff, W. (1965). Perception of impending collison. *Psychological Monographs, 79*, (Whole No. 604).

Schiff, W., & Detwiler, M. L. (1979). Information used in judging impending collision. *Perception, 8*, 647–658.

Shaw, R. E., & Turvey, M. T. (1981). Coalitions as models for ecosystems: A realist perspective on perceptual organization. In M. Kubovy & J. R. Pomerantz (Eds.), *Perceptual organization*, Hillsdale, NJ: Lawrence Erlbaum Associates.

Shaw, R., Turvey, M. T., & Mace, W. (1982). Ecological psychology: The consequences of a commitment to realism. In W. Weimer & D. Palermo (Eds.), *Cognition and the symbolic processes II*. Hillsdale, NJ: Lawrence Erlbaum Associates.

Shepard, R. N. (1968). Cognitive psychology: A review of the book by U. Neisser. *American Journal of Psychology, 81*, 285–289.

Shepard, R. N. (1981). Psychophysical complementarity. In M. Kubovy & J. R. Pomerantz (Eds.), *Perceptual organization*. Hillsdale, NJ: Lawrence Erlbaum Associates.

Shepard, R. N., & Cooper, L. A. (1982). *Mental images and their transformations*. Cambridge, MA: MIT Press.

Shepard, R. N., & Feng, C. (1972). A chronometric study of mental paper folding. *Cognitive Psychology, 3*, 228–243.

Shepard, R. N., & Metzler, J. (1971). Mental rotation of three-dimensional objects. *Science, 171*, 701–703.

Siegal, A. W., & White, S. H. (1975). The development of spatial representations of large scale environments. In H. W. Reese (Ed.), *Advances in child development and behavior* (Vol. 10). New York: Academic Press.

Smith, S. M. (1979). Remembering in and out of context. *Journal of Experimental Psychology: Human Learning and Memory, 5,* 460–471.

Stevens, P. S. (1974). *Patterns in nature.* Boston: Little, Brown.

Tulving, E. (1979). Relations between encoding specificity and levels of processing. In L. S. Cermak & F. I. M. Craik (Eds.), *Levels of processing and human memory.* Hillsdale, NJ: Lawrence Erlbaum Associates.

Turvey, M. T., & Carello, C. (1981). Cognition: The view from ecological realism. *Cognition, 10,* 313–321.

Turvey, M. T., Shaw, R. E., Reed, E. S., Mace, W. M. (1981). Ecological laws of perceiving and acting: In reply to Fodor and Pylyshyn (1981), *Cognition, 9,* 139–195.

Warren, R. (1978). The ecological nature of perceptual systems. In E. C. Carterette, & M. P. Friedman (Eds.), *Handbook of Perception* (Vol. 10). New York: Academic Press.

Wilcox, S., & Katz, S. (1981). The ecological approach to development: An alternative to cognitivism. *Journal of Experimental Child Psychology, 32,* 247–263.

IV

LINGUISTIC EVENTS

A popular strategy in the recent study of cognition has been to treat language as the fundamental area of inquiry and attempt to cast other phenomena in linguistic terms. Perception then becomes the process of constructing language-like descriptions about the world—often from a set of pre-packaged mental predicates. A view more coherent with the real world was launched with the classic study of Bransford and Franks (1971) on the "The Abstraction of Linguistic Ideas." This study revealed that language is mainly a carrier of meaningful real-world events and it is the meaning of events, not the linguistic vehicle, that is remembered.

The ascent to using meaningful materials in the study of remembering has been a slow and arduous one. For Ebbinghaus, meaning was something to be explicitly avoided, and nonsense syllables were the proper stimuli for studying learning and remembering. When it was recognized that nonsense syllables could have meanings that were idiosyncratic, rather than nonexistent, psychologists moved to words. But subjects were quick to discover relationships among the words, even if experimenters did not plan any, so psychologists moved to explicitly categorized lists. From here, it was but a short step to yet another natural form of organized relationship among words, the sentence. In recent years, the sentence, and its internal-representational equivalent, the proposition, have been widely accepted as the "proper" unit of memory.

Bransford and Franks took the whole matter one critical step further by presenting subjects with sentences that were themselves interrelated to form "intersententially defined ideas"—we would call them events—that could be summarized in long sentences like *The warm breeze blowing from the sea stirred the heavy evening air.* Four of these "event sentences" were used to generate smaller sentences each of which expressed part of the entire event. Bransford and Franks divided up the content of the event sentence into four such "atomic" sentences, each of which was called a ONE, and recombined these in varying numbers and combinations to form TWOS and THREES (the event sentence, by definition, was a FOUR). In a "sentence memory" experiment, they presented subjects with several ONE, TWO, and THREE sentences—but no FOURS— derived from the four event sentences. Though the sentences were presented in a random order, subjects unfailingly picked up the connections among them; what was learned was not some number of sentences but *four events.* This was strikingly demonstrated by the results of a recognition test. Subjects' confidence about which sentences they'd seen and which they hadn't was solely a function of the proportion of the total event content expressed by the sentence, so that recognition ratings were lowest for ONES, higher for TWOS, and higher still for THREES. In particular, the FOURS, which had never been presented, received the highest ratings of all. Sentences expressing similar ideas to presented sentences, but specifying some alteration in the event (NONCASES), were readily rejected by subjects.

Subjects were evidently not storing a representation of the presented sentences, because performance on sentences derived from the learned events was not at all a function of whether or not the sentences had been experienced before. What was learned was in fact *generative* with respect to sentential structures, in that one could always devise a novel sentence to describe some aspect of the experienced event. As a picture is worth a thousand words, perhaps an event is worth a thousand sentences.

So natural and compelling is this process by which meaningful events are "extracted" from sentences that we might wonder why it wasn't officially noticed sooner. To be sure, we were mired for a time in nonsense syllables and have still not completely shaken our bias against meaning. In a way Bransford and Franks's "linguistic ideas" is a misnomer, for the research shows us that, although the sentence is perhaps a "unit" of communication, it is by no means a unit of memory—but neither is a paragraph, a word, or any *linguistic* unit at all. The meaning of an event remembered can, and frequently does, transcend the syntax of the form in which it is originally expressed or experienced.

That the forms through which meanings are expressed can be very different is driven home to us forcibly in Chapter 8. There, **Poizner, Klima, Bellugi, and Livingston** present an analysis of the essential movement qualities through which linguistic processes take meaningful form in American Sign Language (ASL). Learning this language involves a change in one's perceptual attunement to general movement qualities in a way that is conducive to apprehending meanings through the ASL medium. The authors, through use of the point–light technique of Johansson, show that not only the general linguistic character of the signing events, but quite specific grammatical information, can be detected by attuned perceivers from the abstract motion patterns.

Chapter 9 examines semantic events in the English language. **McCabe** shows how recognition memory functions better for sentences that reflect significant real-world events than for sentences about events that are either salient, but unlikely to have real-world referents, or merely typical. The primacy of significance over salience and typicality reflects the importance of reciprocally defined properties of organism/environment relations, in contrast to properties that are purely mental or purely environmental.

REFERENCES

Bransford, J. D., & Franks, J. J. (1971). The abstraction of linguistic ideas. *Cognitive Psychology, 2*, 331–350.

8 Motion Analysis of Grammatical Processes in a Visual-Gestural Language*

Howard Poizner

Edward S. Klima
The Salk Institute for Biological Studies

Ursula Bellugi
The Salk Institute for Biological Studies
University of California, San Diego

Robert B. Livingston
University of California, San Diego

CONTENTS
Introduction: Modality and Language
Linguistic Movements Rendered as Dynamic Point-Light Displays
   Extracting Movement from Sign Form
   The Information in Point-Light Displays
   The Interplay Between Perceptual and Linguistic Processes
Three-Dimensional Computer Graphics and Linguistic Analysis
   Case Study of a Linguistic Dimension
   Biological Boundary Conditions on Language
Summary

INTRODUCTION: MODALITY AND LANGUAGE

Current research shows that American Sign Language (ASL) has developed as a fully autonomous language with its own complex organizational properties (Bellugi & Studdert-Kennedy, 1980; Klima & Bellugi, 1979; Lane & Grosjean,

*Portions of this chapter were originally published in *Motion: Representation and Perception* (Proceedings of the SIGGRAPH/SIGART Interdisciplinary Workshop). New York: Association for Computing Machinery, 1983. Reprinted with permission of the publisher. Association for Computing Machinery. New York, Copyright © 1983.

1980; Siple, 1978; Wilbur, 1979). Like spoken language, ASL exhibits formal structuring both at the level of internal structure of lexical units and at the level of grammatical scaffolding of sentences. ASL also reveals similarities to spoken language in its use of organizational principles such as constrained systems of features, rules based on underlying (as opposed to surface) forms, and recursive grammatical processes. Although ASL shares principles of organization with spoken languages, the formal devices instantiating those principles arise out of the very different possibilities of a visual-gestural mode.

Despite common principles of organization in signed and spoken languages, there are aspects of linguistic form in signed languages that stand out as most strongly resulting from the difference in modality. A fundamental difference between ASL and spoken language is in surface organization: Whereas spoken languages are notoriously linear and sequential, signed languages display a marked preference for simultaneous organization. The inflectional and derivational devices of ASL, for example, make structured use of space and movement, nesting the basic sign stem in spatial patterns and complex dynamic contours of movement. The multilayering of linguistic elements in ASL is a pervasive structural characteristic at all levels: the lexical items, the morphological processes, the syntax, even the discourse structure (Bellugi, 1980).

Signs of American Sign Language are related by a wide variety of inflectional and derivational processes. Different lexical items have families of associated forms, all interrelated by formal patterning based on modifications of the movement of signs in space. Thus a single root form, for example that glossed as ASK or QUESTION, has a wide variety of manifestations, shown in Fig. 8.1. These different forms mark grammatical categories such as Person, Number, Reciprocity, Temporal Aspect, and Distributional Aspect, as illustrated in the figure. They also constitute the basis for derivationally related noun–verb pairs and a host of other derivational processes (see Fig. 8.1). The variety of inflectional and derivational devices indicate that ASL is an inflective language, more like Hebrew, Latin, and certain African languages than like English or Chinese (Bellugi & Klima, 1980; Klima & Bellugi, 1979).

In the *kinds* of distinctions that are morphologically marked and the *degree* to which morphological marking is a favored form of patterning in the language, ASL is similar to some spoken languages. However, in the *form* by which its lexical items are systematically modified, ASL has aspects that are unique. Grammatical processes such as those illustrated in Fig. 8.1 are conveyed by changes in movement and spatial contouring and occur as superimposed but separable layers of structure. One of the most distinguishing and pervasive characteristics of ASL is the multilayered nature of its structural organization. In individual forms the lexical and grammatical components occur in distinct co-occurring layers, and most significantly, this layering is largely maintained in the surface structure of these forms. There is a separation in the dimensions of contrast used to build morphemes at each layer. Consider, for example, the

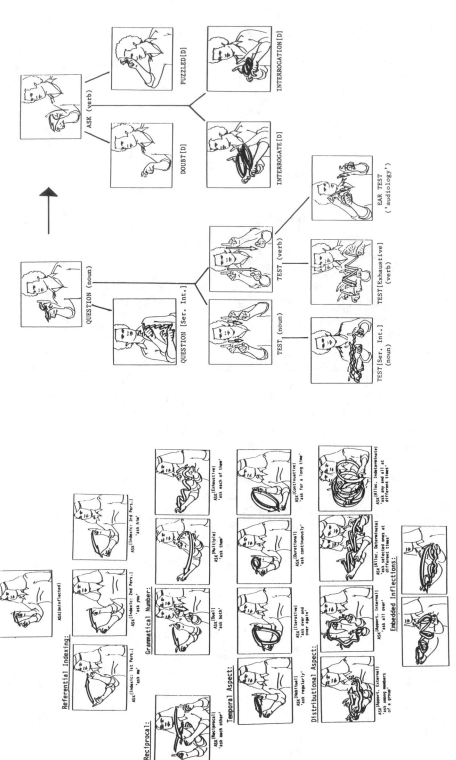

FIG. 8.1. A variety of morphological processes in ASL layered on a single root.

inflected form GIVE[‘to her’][Imperative]] representing the lexical morpheme meaning "to give," and two inflectional morphemes, one a pronoun-index morpheme for third person and, the other, the imperative morpheme. Let us build up this ASL utterance morpheme by morpheme. The lexical morpheme, like other lexical morphemes in the language, is represented by (1) a specific hand configuration (in this case, "O"), (2) a specific location (in this case, the space in front of the body), and (3) a specific movement-path shape (in this case, linear). These lexical components are themselves present in layered from (i.e., separate and co-occurring) in the surface. The third person pronoun-index morpheme has as its form a particular diagonal direction of movement, which is superimposed in layered fashion over all the other components of the form. The imperative morpheme is realized by a *tense* quality of movement, again, simultaneously spread over the entire form. From this example we can see that sign language is predominantly multilayered with respect to form, with additional levels of grammatical function mirrored by additional layers of form. In some morphologically complex forms, *sequencing* of contrasting values does occur within one or more layers, but this does not substantially change the picture of a predominantly layered organization. The layering in addition to the sequencing within layers is the basis for a very rich morphological system.[2]

We have identified some 50 different derivational and inflectional processes in ASL. Linguistic analysis has revealed that the derivational and inflectional forms do not merely differ in a holistic manner; rather, they differ along a limited number of spatial and temporal dimensions. *Spatial dimensions* such as geometric array (circle, line, arc), planar locus (vertical, horizontal), and direction of movement (upwards, downwards, sideways) figure significantly in the structure of inflections for such categories as Person, Reciprocity, Grammatical Number, and Distributional Aspect (see Fig. 8.1). *Temporal dimensions* or movement qualities such as tension (tense, lax), end-manner (continuous, held), and rate (fast, slow) figure significantly in the structure of inflections for Temporal Aspect, Focus, Manner, and Degree. Two additional dimensions— cyclicity (singular, reduplicated) and hand use (one hand, two hands)—interact with the others in the formation of inflections in several grammatical categories.

---

[1]Lexical bases of signs are denoted by English glosses in full capitals (e.g., GIVE). Bracketed labels, as in GIVE[‘to her’] refer to specific inflectional processes signs have undergone. Multiple bracketing, as in GIVE[‘to her’][Imperative] refer to hierarchically nested inflectional processes.

[2]Some spoken languages also have a multilayered organization. In Hebrew for example, a word is composed of a tri-consonantal lexical root at one layer and vowel patterning conveying inflectional and derivational morphemes as a second layer. The surface form of words in Hebrew is nonetheless linear, with consonants and vowels following one another. Thus, unlike spoken languages that show a pronounced layered structure, ASL forms retain their layered structure in the surface structure— components of the lexical root and derivational and inflectional morphemes all co-occur in a multi-layered structure.

Thus the large number of morphological processes in ASL are combinations of a limited number of formal dimensions of space and movement.

LINGUISTIC MOVEMENTS RENDERED AS DYNAMIC POINT–LIGHT DISPLAYS

Extracting Movement from Sign Form

In our research, linguistic analyses and experimental studies are linked together. We have the following objectives in carrying out our experimental investigations of movement in ASL. First, we believe our research may help to answer general questions about the importance of dynamic events in visual perception. Second, we are interested in whether the perception of movement is itself modified by the special linguistic experience of acquiring a visual-gestural language. Third, we want to subject the multilayered model of ASL to the strong test of isomorphism between posited elements of the linguistic structure and properties of the embodied utterance. In order to investigate linguistically significant movement in ASL experimentally, we needed a way to isolate movement of the hands and arms, that is, to extract movement from sign forms. We used small light-emitting diodes placed at selected spots on the body, adapting the "point–light" technique introduced by Johansson for studying the perception of biological motion (Johansson, 1975; see also Chapter 13, this volume).

With regard to our first objective, evidence from perception of dynamic events has already offered clues to such longstanding questions as the nature of so-called perceptual constancies and the organizing principles for the visual system. Johansson (1973, 1975), Cutting and Kozlowski (1977), Ullman (1979), and others have demonstrated the usefulness of studying perception of dynamic point–light displays, in which information about form is drastically reduced. In our research, we have extended this technique of studying biological motion to the complicated movement patterns within the linguistic system of ASL. We reduced the sign "image" to nine moving points of light, with the lights located at the major joints of the arms and hands (shoulders, elbows, wrists, index fingertips). We recorded signing in a darkened room, so that on the videotape only the pattern of moving points of light appears against a black background.

The Information in Point–Light Displays

Using our standard placement of nine lights, we found that signers could accurately *match* lexical and inflectional movements presented in dynamic point–light displays with movements presented in normal form on videotape. Signers, furthermore, could accurately *identify* ASL inflections presented in point–light displays and signs of a constant hand configuration. Indeed, the signs were identified almost as well when presented as point–light displays in two dimensions as when presented normally in three, reflecting in part the information that the moving points carry about depth. Having found that dynamic point–light displays can convey sign forms, we then sought to identify more precisely the information-carrying aspects of these point–light displays. We found, for example, that movement of the fingertips, but not of any other pair of points alone, was necessary for sign identification. In general, we found that the more distal the joint, the more information its movement carried for sign identification (Poizner, Bellugi, & Lutes-Driscoll, 1981).

Thus, even given such apparently reduced information, deaf signers are highly accurate at recognizing and identifying morphological processes of ASL presented in these point–light displays, demonstrating that patterns of dynamic movement contours form a distinct, isolable (but co-occurring) layer of structure in ASL. These results broaden the data base on the perception of dynamic point–light displays to include perception of dynamic shapes and trajectories of a formal linguistic system. In this domain, as in others, moving points of light exhibit a strong coherence, allowing perception of complex events to take place. These displays, furthermore, provide a foundation for the development of techniques that will allow the rigorous analysis and control over important stimulus parameters of ASL for psycholinguistic investigations. We have shown that point–light displays accurately convey lexical signs and morphological processes in ASL. In order to quantify such movement trajectories, we have developed procedures for the computer graphic analysis of these displays, and we present some first results of these analyses later. Before turning to these, we would first like to address the question of how experience with ASL affects the perception of dynamic movement displays (cf. our aforementioned second objective).

The Interplay Between Perceptual and Linguistic Processes

To pursue the interplay between perceptual and linguistic processes, we have contrasted the perception of movement by native deaf signers with hearing non-signers. We presented point–light displays of inflected and uninflected ASL signs to both groups for simple judgments of movement similarity. Multidimensional scaling and hierarchical clustering of judgments for the two groups of subjects revealed, in the first place, that lexical and inflectional movements were perceived in terms of a limited number of underlying dimensions. Secondly, the perceptual dimensions for the lexical level were in general different from those of the inflectional level (Poizner, 1983). This result supports, with perceptual data, our previous linguistic analysis; namely, that the linguistic fabric of the two levels of structure in ASL is woven from different formational materials. Furthermore, the perception of movement types within each level differs for deaf and hearing subjects, with perception of movement form tied to linguistically relevant dimensions for deaf subjects, but not for hearing subjects. Thus, the data suggest that acquisition of a visual-gestural language can modify the natural perceptual categories into which these movement forms fall (Poizner, 1981, 1983). Previous studies of the perception of formational categories of ASL have looked at static properties of signs such as configuration of the hands (Lane, Boyes-Braem, & Bellugi, 1976; Stungis, 1981) and location of the hands (Poizner & Lane, 1978). In these studies, the patterns of results for deaf signers and hearing nonsigners were the same; no modification of perception due to linguistic experience was found for static sign attributes. This suggests that perception of ASL *movement*—and perhaps movement in general—differs crucially from perception of static parameters such as handshape and location.

THREE-DIMENSIONAL COMPUTER GRAPHICS AND LINGUISTIC ANALYSIS

Figure 8.2 illustrates aspects of the computer graphic analysis of ASL's elaborate system of movement contrasts. Up to now there has been little precise quantification of the movement signal itself. We have developed methods for both accurate three-dimensional movement measurements and three-dimensional reconstruction of movement permitting interactive control over the movement signal (Loomis, Poizner, Bellugi, Blakemore, & Hollerbach, 1982). In our early studies, we digitized trajectory information frame by frame from the output of a single camera (Bellman, Poizner, & Bellugi, 1983). We now use a three-dimensional movement monitoring apparatus (the Selspot System-see Fig. 8.2a) designed to permit rapid high-resolution digitization of hand and arm movement. Two opto-electronic cameras track the positions of light-emitting diodes attached to the hands and arms and provide a digital output directly to a computer, which calculates three-dimensional trajectories. From the position measurements, the movements are reconstructed in three-dimensions (using an Evans & Sutherland Picture System—see Fig. 8.2b). Our system allows display and interactive control over the three-dimensional movement trajectory, so that various trajectory and dynamic characteristics can be calculated for any portion of the movement (see Fig. 8.3). Figure 8.3 presents illustrations of four ASL inflections together with the reconstructed movement of the fingertips. Velocity and acceleration of the hand along the movement path are shown for each inflection. A rectangular solid is drawn by the computer around the movement path to delimit the maximum deviation of the movement along each of the three Cartesian dimensions. The figure also shows a three-dimensional calibration index, 50mm on a side, which has been rotated with the data to calibrate absolute displacement along each of the three axes.

These procedures provide potent methods for extracting the movement from sign forms and for applying three-dimensional analyses to these movements.

With these procedures coupled to our linguistic analyses, we can address some basic issues in the organization and structuring of language. We link these two modes of analysis below in two domains. In one, the analysis of physical characteristics from three-dimensional reconstructions of movement helps reveal the physical correlates of linguistic dimensions and in the process, helps refine our

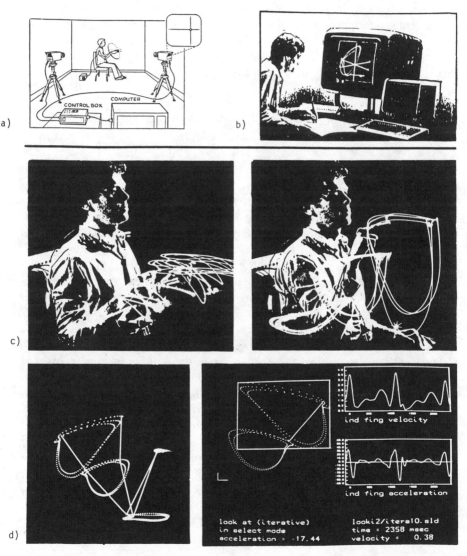

FIG. 8.2. Computer graphic analysis of ASL movement: (a) movement digitization by Selspot cameras; (b) Evans and Sutherland Picture System used to reconstruct digitized movements; (c) dynamic point–light displays; (d) three-dimensional computer graphic reconstructions.

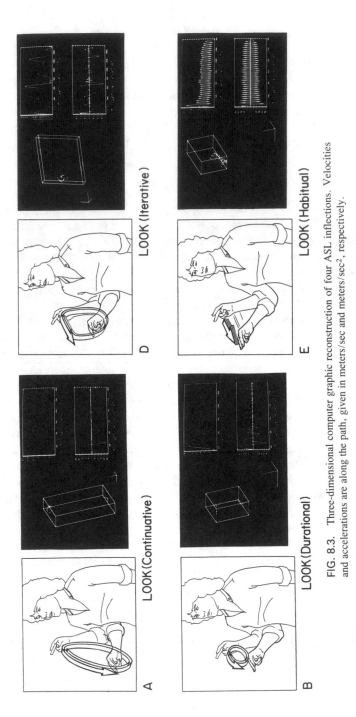

A LOOK(Continuative)

B LOOK(Durational)

D LOOK (Iterative)

E LOOK (Habitual)

FIG. 8.3. Three-dimensional computer graphic reconstruction of four ASL inflections. Velocities and accelerations are along the path, given in meters/sec and meters/sec², respectively.

understanding of the linguistic dimensions. In the second, we present a study designed to investigate the biological boundary conditions that may help determine the structure that sign languages take in general. From three-dimensional movement analyses we derive a visual-articulatory space in which some ASL movements are embedded. From the metric defined by a series of these spaces, we make predictions about contrasts that might be likely to appear in other sign languages, about the order of acquisition of movement forms by deaf children, and about the structure underlying perception of ASL movement forms.

Motion Analysis of a Linguistic Dimension

A discrete, if not binary, system of oppositions characterizes the "phonological" structure of ASL movement (Bellugi, 1980). The physical structure of ASL movement, however, is on the whole continuous in nature. It is therefore of interest to investigate the nature of the physical correlates of the "phonological" distinctions.

Investigations of the physical correlates of phonological segments in speech appear to reveal a lack of correspondence between segments in the signal and phonological segments (Liberman, Cooper, Shankweiler, & Studdert-Kennedy, 1967). It is possible that the situation may differ in sign for the following reasons. In the first place, the phonological structure of ASL retains its layered nature at the surface (e.g., the handshape retains its form throughout the movement). Furthermore, the elements of the separate layers differ dramatically in their composition (e.g., handshape vs. location vs. movement shape vs. movement quality), and the layers are independently controllable, so to a large extent they do not interact with one another. Finally, in sign, unlike speech, movements of the articulators themselves, rather than their effects, are directly observable. We should expect that this would result in less of a discrepancy between an articulatory and a visual description of the movement event. For one "phonological" opposition in ASL, *evenness*, we have already found a relatively direct mapping between the structure of the signal and the phonological distinction.

We have posited 11 spatial and temporal linguistic dimensions along which inflectional-derivational processes differ from one another. (For a fuller discussion see Klima & Bellugi, 1979.) In our first linguistic analysis, we characterized some inflectional forms as *even* (e.g., Durational, Habitual) and some as *uneven* (e.g., Continuative, Iterative); that is, under some inflections, movement appears nearly constant in velocity (*even*), whereas under others there is a clear acceleration (*uneven*). Our assignment to these categories was in general accordance with the judgments of native informants and other researchers.

In order to investigate the physical manifestation of this linguistic dimension, we segmented movement cycles into two portions roughly corresponding to movement of the verb stem and return movement to the beginning position for the next cycle. In the case of LOOK[Habitual] (see Fig. 8.3), the division can be made at the end of the movement outward from the signer's body; for LOOK[Continuative] and LOOK[Durational], segmentation is performed along the major axis of a movement trajectory along an ellipse. In general, we have found that many repetition cycles and some single-cycle movements can be thought of as consisting of two parts, although in some cases a finer segmentation is necessary.

In order to capture that aspect of the signal conveying *evenness* or *unevenness* of movement, a variety of forms were first segmented into the two major parts of each repetition cycle, and peak velocities were measured for each segment. Figure 8.4a presents peak velocities across half cycles for LOOK[Continuative], LOOK[Habitual], and LOOK[Durational]. The solid line represents peak velocity of the first half cycle, and the dashed line, peak velocity of the second half. Figure 8.4a shows that for LOOK[Habitual] the hand reached about the same maximum velocity moving away from the body as when returning toward the body for all except the first of 16 cycles. Similarly, maximum velocity of the first half cycle of each cycle of LOOK[Durational] was about the same as the second half. However, for LOOK[Continuative], the maximum velocity in the first half cycle was nearly three times that of the second half. The Continuative inflection, as it turns out, has been considered to have an *uneven* quality of movement, whereas Habitual and Duration inflections have been considered to have an *even* movement quality.

To evaluate the possibility that differential peak velocities across half cycles may indeed index this aspect of ASL movement, ratios of maximum velocity of the first half of the movement cycle to the second half were calculated for 15 multipart ASL movements. The median ratio across repetition cycles was used as a measure of the evenness of the movement. Figure 8.4b presents these median ratios. When the hand moves faster in the first half cycle than in the second, the ratio is greater than 1.0; when the movement is faster in the second half, the ratio is less than 1.0. The figure shows that the ratios vary from about .2 to 2.8, with a cluster of points at 1.0. The two dashed lines in the figure form a boundary around movements that have been described linguistically as being *even*. The three movements above this group and the one movement below it have all been classified as *uneven*. Thus, as Fig. 8.4b indicates, the distribution of velocity ratios corresponds without exception to the linguistic classification of the opposition *even/uneven* and therefore provides a quantitative index of this movement attribute. Thus, in the case of *evenness,* we have found a correspondence between signal properties and "phonological" components. We have made substantial progress in uncovering the physical correlates of other posited distinctions, including those of *tense* and *restrained* manner. We are particularly pleased about the possibility of capturing the physical correlates of these latter two movement attributes, because their descriptions have been couched in purely articulatory terms.

The preceding analysis is by no means comprehensive but is intended to illustrate a general approach to developing a visual "phonetics" of sign language movement.

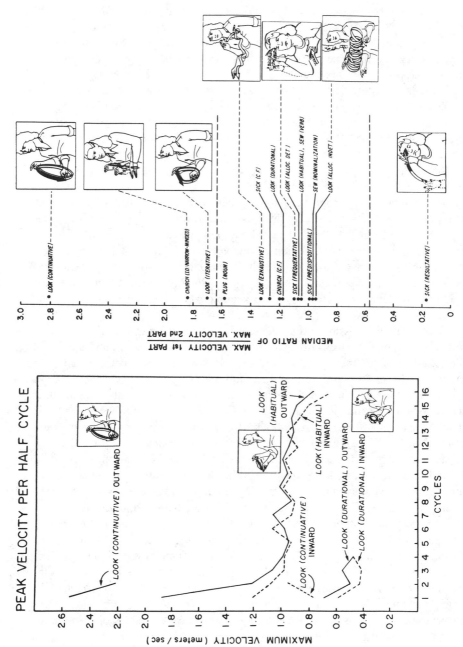

FIG. 8.4. Physical correlate of a phonological opposition (evenness).

166

Biological Boundary Conditions on Language

The second domain in which we link computer graphic analysis and linguistic analysis is the search for biological boundary conditions on linguistic form. If specific requirements of perception and motor control inherent in characteristics of the transmission system help determine "phonological" structure, then the "phonological" structures of signed and spoken languages should differ correspondingly. This issues is all the more interesting in light of the fact that in humans, specialized structures and functions have evolved for spoken communication: vocal tract morphology, lip, jaw and tongue innervation, and mechanisms of breath control have all undergone evolutionary change from nonhuman primates to man that have shaped the vocal apparatus into a more efficient transmission system for the production of a variety of sounds (Lenneberg, 1967; Liberman, 1970, 1974; Liberman, 1975).

In many ways the transmission system of sign language (visual-gestural) is radically different from that of speech and offers remarkably different possibilities and constraints. The auditory system, for example, is particularly adept at temporal discrimination (Julesz & Hirsch, 1972) and, indeed, speech exhibits strong temporal patterning. The visual system is extremely well suited for spatial discrimination and for simultaneous processing of visual parameters. Common to both modes, however, is the pressure for rapid and efficient communication. Our previous studies have suggested that the rate of transmitting propositional information in ASL is about the same as that in English, despite radical differences in the size of the articulators and the time required to produce basic lexical items in the two modes (Klima & Bellugi, 1979). The pressure towards maximizing output rate and the differing capacities of the transmission modalities could very well help shape the form taken by languages. Liberman (1982), in fact, has suggested that phonetic segments of speech are complexly encoded in the acoustic signal in order to bypass certain sensory limits of the auditory system such as the resolving power of the ear. If, as Julesz and Hirsch (1972) suggest, the resolving power of the eye for temporal differentiations is far less than that of the ear, then this boundary condition may well have an effect on shaping the surface form of visible language.

Deriving Visual-Articulatory Spaces.   In this chapter we present one visual-articulatory space into which a subset of ASL movements fall. The sign forms used for this mapping all involve repetition of movement. These forms were mostly ones inflected for temporal aspect and degree, inflections that convey duration or recurrence over time and, in the case of "degree," the relative intensity of the state of action. The nature of the dimensions of the spaces we derive and the positioning of movement forms in the spaces should reveal the ways in which ASL has used the possibilities of the visual-gestural modality to create its movement contrasts.

Each sign form from which the movement was to be extracted was made in canonical form. The movement was then digitized and reconstructed in three dimensions. We tried quantifying the movements in a number of ways, including the kinematic parameters of duration, amplitude, velocity, and acceleration. From these measurements, we constructed low-dimensional spaces in which the movements were located. We motivated our selection of particular spaces by the degree to which they revealed relevant linguistic relationships.

The rhythmic properties of many ASL morphological processes are part of their essential defining characteristics. For example, the inflections for Continuative and Durational aspect are distinguished essentially by their rhythmic properties throughout cycles of movement. We present one method of quantification, Fourier analysis, particularly relevant to cyclic movements. Fourier analysis allows the description of rhythmic (and spatial) structure of events by summing suitable sinusoidal components.

Figure 8.5 presents the Fourier spectra of movement components in the sagittal and vertical directions for the LOOK[Continuative] and the LOOK[Durational] inflections. The sign forms used in this study have their primary movement components in these directions. Line drawings of the two inflected signs and three-dimensional reconstructions of the movements are also presented. The spectra for the Continuative inflection exhibit a first major peak at .80HZ., reflecting a basic repetition rate of .8 cycles per second. Higher harmonics occur at integral multiples of this fundamental frequency, with their amplitude (in dB) decreasing in a roughly linear fashion. The Durational inflection, however, shows a very different pattern of Fourier components. First of all, its fundamental repetition rate is 1.68 hz., approximately twice as fast as that of the Continuative. Unlike the relatively high energy of the harmonics of the Continuative, the Durational shows essentially one major energy component (the fundamental) with very reduced harmonics. Spectra of movements with sinusoidal components in the sagittal and vertical directions are precisely what we would expect for the smooth, circular, repeated movement of the Durational inflection. Because the Continuative inflection has an uneven rhythm, however, its spectra show substantial energy components at the higher harmonics corresponding to this difference in dynamics. The amplitudes of the harmonics relative to the fundamental, and the frequencies at which they occur, together provide a concise index that captures relevant relationships among ASL movement forms.

Figure 8.6 illustrates one visual-articulatory space for 11 cyclic ASL movements. This figure presents energy of the 3rd harmonic relative to the fundamental versus energy of the 2nd harmonic relative to the fundamental for the movement component in the sagittal axis (toward and away from the signer's body). The figure shows several clusters of movement forms. *Even* movements without any endmarking—points A,B,C—form a tight cluster in the upper right corner of the figure (all have energy concentrated at the fundamental). Diametrically opposite to these movements lie movements that are uneven in quality: points G

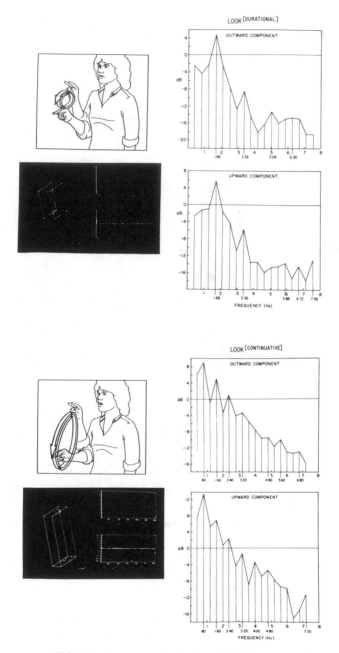

FIG. 8.5.   Fourier spectra for two ASL inflections.

169

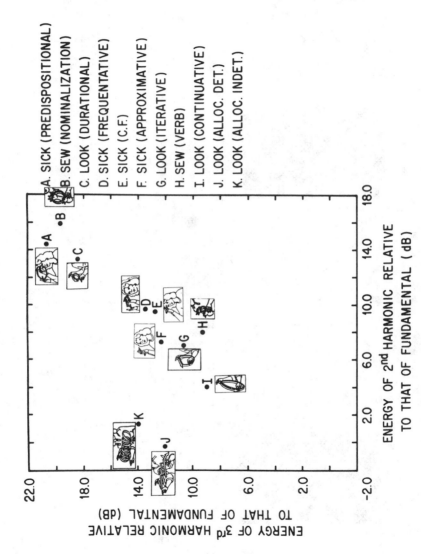

A. SICK (PREDISPOSITIONAL)
B. SEW (NOMINALIZATION)
C. LOOK (DURATIONAL)
D. SICK (FREQUENTATIVE)
E. SICK (C.F.)
F. SICK (APPROXIMATIVE)
G. LOOK (ITERATIVE)
H. SEW (VERB)
I. LOOK (CONTINUATIVE)
J. LOOK (ALLOC. DET.)
K. LOOK (ALLOC. INDET.)

ENERGY OF 2nd HARMONIC RELATIVE
TO THAT OF FUNDAMENTAL (dB)

ENERGY OF 3rd HARMONIC RELATIVE
TO THAT OF FUNDAMENTAL (dB)

FIG. 8.6.   Visual-articulatory space for some cyclic ASL movements.

and I are forms having high energy at the 2nd and 3rd harmonics as well as at the fundamental. Points D, E, and F lie intermediate along this major axis of the figure, and are *even,* but *endmarked.* The final two points in the figure, J and K, are grouped together, away from the other movements, and exhibit amplitudes of the 2nd harmonic equal to or greater than that of the fundamental. The Allocative Determinate (J) and Allocative Indeterminate (K) are the only two movement forms of the figure that are displaced from the sagittal axis, a movement characteristic important both to the linguistic structure of the morphological processes and to the perception of these processes (Klima & Bellugi, 1979; Poizner, 1983). Fourier components reflect this pattern of displacement. Thus this preliminary construction of a physical space of movements already captures, in terms of signal properties, relevant relationships among movement forms that were independently posited as linguistically relevant. This approach should illuminate the physical basis for these linguistic relationships.

From the metrics that such spaces define, as we can make predictions about the following three areas: (a) the general form that sign languages take; (b) the order of emergence of featural contrasts as the child acquires the languages; and (c) structure underlying perception of movement. We predict, specifically, that those contrasts that are minimally separated in the space (a) are less likely to appear universally in other sign languages, (b) will emerge late in the child, and (c) are more easily confused in perception. For example, from the space presented in Fig. 8.6, the contrasts *even/uneven* and *displaced/nondisplaced* are salient properties of the movements. We predict that the linguistic oppositions underlying these contrasts will be likely to appear in other sign languages and will be easily recognized by perceivers.

Modality Issues.   Derivation of the physical spaces underlying the sounds of speech has also been attempted by some investigators. There is a growing realization that the science of phonetics can produce insights for the understanding of phonological structure (Ladefoged, 1980; Lindblom, 1978; Ohala, 1974; Mac-Neilage & Ladefoged, 1976). Lindblom and his colleagues have tried to map out how the phonological structure of vowels is shaped by physical requirements of speech perception and production (Liljencrantz & Lindblom, 1972; Lindblom, 1978, 1979). Lindblom derives a possible acoustic-auditory space based on a model of vocal-tract articulation. Within this acoustic-auditory space, he calculates, by algorithm, the maximal separation for a vowel system with a given number of vowels. Lindblom then compares these calculated vowel spaces with those observed in the world and finds a strikingly good match. Maximizing perceptual contrast seems a strong determinant of the phonological structure of vowel system.

Although the work of Lindblom and his colleagues is very intriguing, they have as yet attempted to derive spaces only for steady-state vowels, sounds that are somewhat artificial in speech (Strange, Jenkins, & Edman, 1977; Strange,

Verbrugge, Shankweiler, & Edman, 1976). The severe acoustic-phonetic problem that dynamic speech sounds show (i.e., the apparent lack of correspondence between acoustic and phonetic segments) may be a limiting factor in this domain. The study of sign language has advantages in the exploration of determinants of phonological structure and may prove an especially fruitful domain. We are encouraged by our initial studies that we will not face the same kind of acoustic-phonetic problem that has plagued researchers in speech.

SUMMARY

Movement of the hands and arms through space is an essential element of both the lexical structure and the grammatical structure of ASL. It is in patterned changes of the movement of signs that many grammatical attributes, in particular, are represented. These grammatical attributes occur as isolable superimposed layers of structure, as demonstrated by the accurate identification by deaf signers of these attributes presented only as dynamic point–light displays. Three-dimensional computer graphic analyses were applied in two domains to quantify the nature of the ''phonological'' (formational) distinctions underlying the structure of grammatical processes in ASL. In the first, we showed that for one opposition, *evenness/unevenness* of movement, a ratio of maximum velocities throughout the movement perfectly captures the *linguistic* classification of forms along this dimension. In the second, we mapped out a two-dimensional visual-articulatory space that captures relevant relationships among movement forms that were independently posited as linguistically relevant. The fact that we are finding direct correspondences between properties of the signal and properties of the ''phonological'' system in sign language may arise in part because in sign languages, unlike spoken languages, the movements of the articulators are directly observable, and, also in part, because of the predominantly layered organization of sign language.

ACKNOWLEDGMENTS

This work was supported in part by National Science Foundation Grant #BNS81–811479 and by National Institutes of Health Grants #HD13249 and #NS19096, to the Salk Institute for Biological Studies. We are extremely grateful to Dr. John Hollerbach and Dr. Emilo Bizzi, Psychology Department, Massachusetts Institute of Technology, and to Dr. Erik Antonsson and Dr. Robert Mann of the Massachusetts Institute of Technology, Laboratory for Human Mechanics and Rehabilitation, for making available and providing assistance in acquiring data with their Selspot Movement Monitoring Systems, which made possible the research into three-dimensional reconstruction and analysis of sign movement. We thank Dr. Harlan Lane for the suggestion to apply Fourier analysis to quantify sign movement, and Dr. Sandra Hutchins for very helpful discussions of the Fourier analyses.

REFERENCES

Bellman, K., Poizner, H., & Bellugi, U. (1983). Invariant characteristics of some morphological processes in American sign language. *Discourse Processes, 6,* 199–223.

Bellugi, U. (1980). The structuring of language: Clues from the similarities between signed and spoken language. In U. Bellugi & M. Studdert-Kennedy (Eds.), *Signed and spoken language: Biological constraints on linguistic form* (pp. 115–140). Dahlem Konferenzen. Weinheim/Deerfield Beach, FL: Verlag Chemie.

Bellugi, U., & Klima, E. (1980). Morphological processes in a language in a different mode. In W. F. Hans, C. Hofbauer, & P. R. Clyne (Eds.), *The elements: Linguistic units and levels.* (pp. 21–42). Chicago: Chicago Linguistic Society.

Bellugi, U., & Studdert-Kennedy, M. (Eds.). (1980). *Signed and spoken language: Biological constraints on linguistic form.* Dahlem Konferenzen. Weinheim/Deerfield Beach, FL: Verlag Chemie.

Cutting, J. E., & Kozlowski, L. T. (1977). Recognizing friends by their walk: Gait perception without familiarity clues. *Bulletin of the Psychonomic Society, 9,* 353–356.

Johansson, G. (1973). Visual perception of biological motion and a model for its analysis. *Perception and Psychophysics, 14,* 201–211.

Johansson, G. (1975). Visual motion perception. *Scientific American, 232,* 76–89.

Julesz, B., & Hirsch, I. J. (1972). Visual and auditory perception: An essay of comparison. In E. E. Davis & P. B. Denes (Eds.), *Human communication: A unified view.* New York: McGraw–Hill, 283–340.

Klima, E. S., & Bellugi, U. (1979). *The signs of language.* Cambridge, MA: Harvard University Press.

Ladefoged, P. (1980). What are linguistic sounds made of? *Language, 56,* 485–502.

Lane, H., Boyes-Braem, P., & Bellugi, U. (1976). Preliminaries to a distinctive feature analysis of handshape in American sign language. *Cognitive Psychology, 8,* 263–289.

Lane, H., & Grosjean, F. (Eds.). (1980). *Recent perspectives on American sign language.* Hillsdale, NJ: Lawrence Erlbaum Associates.

Lenneberg, E. (1967). *Biological foundations of language.* New York: Wiley.

Liberman, A. M. (1970). The grammars of speech and language. *Cognitive Psychology, 1,* 301–323.

Liberman, A. M. (1974). The specialization of the language hemisphere. In F. O. Schmitt & F. G. Worden (Eds.), *The neurosciences: Third study program* (pp. 43–56). Cambridge, MA: MIT Press.

Liberman, A. M. (1982). On finding that speech is special. *American Psychologist, 37,* 148–167.

Liberman, A. M., Cooper, F. S., Shankweiler, D. P., & Studdert-Kennedy, M. (1967). Perception of the speech code. *Psychological Review, 74,* 431–461.

Lieberman, P. (1975). *On the origins of language.* New York: Macmillan.

Liljencrantz, J., & Lindblom, B. (1972). Numerical simulation of vowel quality systems: The role of perceptual contrast. *Language, 48,* 839–862.

Lindblom, B. (1978). Phonetic aspects of linguistic explanation. *Studio Linguistics, 23,* 137–153.

Lindblom, B. (1979). Experiments in sound structure. *Revue de Phonetique Appliquee.* Belgique: Universite de l'Etat Mons, *51,* 155–189.

Loomis, J., Poizner, H., Bellugi, U., Blakemore, A., & Hollerbach, J. (1982). Computer graphic modeling of American sign language. *Computer Graphics, 17,* 105–114.

MacNeilage, P., & Ladefoged, P. (1976). The production of speech and language. In E. Carthette & M. P. Friedman (Eds.), *Handbook of perception VII.* New York: Academic Press, 75–120.

Ohala, J. J. (1974). Experimental historical phonology. In J. M. Anderson & C. Jones (Eds.), *Historical linguistics II: Theory and description in phonology.* (Proceedings of the First International Conference on Historical Linguistics. Edinburgh, 2–7 September 1973.) Amsterdam: North Holland, 353–389.

Poizner, H. (1981). Visual and "Phonetic" Coding of Movement: Evidence from American sign language. *Science, 212,* 691–693.

Poizner, H. (1983). Perception of movement in american sign language: Effects of linguistic structure and linguistic experience. *Perception and Psychophysics, 33,* 215–231.

Poizner, H., Bellugi, U., & Lutes-Driscoll, V. (1981). Perception of American sign language in dynamic point–light displays. *Journal of Experimental Psychology: Human Perception and Performance, 7,* 430–440.

Poizner, H., & Lane, H. (1978). Discrimination of location in American sign language. In P. Siple (Ed.), *Understanding language through sign language research.* New York: Academic Press, 271–287.

Siple, P. (Ed.). (1978). *Understanding language through sign language research.* New York: Academic Press.

Strange, W., Jenkins, J. J., & Edman, T. R. (1977). Identification of vowels in "vowel-less" syllables. *Journal of the Acoustical Society of America, 61,* S39(A).

Strange, W., Verbrugge, R. R., Shankweiler, D. P., & Edman, T. R. (1976). Consonant environment specifies vowel identity. *Journal of the Acoustical Society of America, 60,* 213–224.

Stungis, J. (1981). Identification and discrimination of handshape in American sign language. *Perception and Psychophysics, 29,* 261–276.

Ullman, S. (1979). *The interpretation of visual motion.* Cambridge: MA: MIT Press.

Wilbur, R. (1979). *American sign language and sign systems: Research and applications.* Baltimore: University Park Press.

9 Memory for Meaning: The Ecological Use of Language

Viki McCabe
University of California, Los Angeles

CONTENTS
Introduction
Theories of Meaning
An Experimental Comparison of Salience, Typicality, and Significance
General Discussion and Implications
  Intrinsic vs. Extrinsic Factors
  A Note on Bias
  Summary and Implications

Cognitive research often focuses on either stimulus properties or mental processes. Both approaches implicitly assume that mind and matter, animal and environment, are quite separate. For example, research focused on stimuli attributes memorability to stimulus salience or noticeability (due to contrast effects or "solo status") without examining observer contributions (McArthur & Post, 1977; Taylor & Fiske, 1978; Von Restorff, 1933). On the other hand, research focused on mental processes attributes memorability to "mental construction" of generically typical schemas (through abstraction and generalization), assuming that properties of stimuli do not specify their own generic class.[1] (Bartlett, 1932; Bransford & Franks, 1971). Each research area neglects one side of the cognitive equation. This neglect obscures an important point; the human mind and the stimulus environment in which it participates have coevolved. In the interests of survival, it seems reasonable that a creature's mental processes be yoked in some way to the specifications of its environment, and that the meaning

---

[1]An alternate explanation of how we know generic typicality eschews constructive processes and suggests that we detect invariants that directly specify class (cf. McCabe, Chapter 1, this volume).

of those specifications be in some way a function of the needs and intentions of the participants of that environment (Gibson, 1966, 1979).

An alternative view combines stimulus and observer into a single "cognitive" unit or event. The mental and environmental participants in this event have a privileged relationship based on reciprocal fit and significance. Reciprocal fit occurs when the physical properties of the environment provide functional support for a creature's intentions, needs, or goals. Significance reflects the value of this support to such a creature. From this view, perceptual systems are tuned to resonate to and select reciprocally calibrated environmental specifications. Such specifications would capture selective attention and have privileged processing channels for cognitive processes such as memory, which are then piggy-backed on the perception of environmental significance. This is not to say that the typical "meanings of things," their essential generic summaries, do not influence memory. Nor does it imply that salience, which reveals that something "means something different" from its surround, is of no import. It does suggest that "meaningfulness" or significance along with salience and typicality may, with respect to memory, all be part of a single cognitive event.

In short, meaning can be partitioned into three levels of relevance for cognitive processes such as memory. A fundamental level of meaning, "salience," reflects the separation of an item from its surround, its discriminability from "nothing" to "something" (That is a thing). This level probably has its strongest effect on attention. A second level of meaning involves an item's status as a member of a generic class (That thing is an X). This level of meaning probably modulates recognition and identification. A third level of meaning involves an item's importance to someone or some group (its functional value) and reflects its significance (That X is valuable). This level of meaning would probably have its primary effect on judgment and action. All three levels would influence memory.

Taken separately, however, each level of meaning seems to place it in a different location. Salience implies that meaning is a property of the stimulus. Generic typicality implies that meaning is constructed in the mind. Functional significance implies that meaning is in the unique relationship between a particular stimulus and a particular mind. Although the view in this chapter is that salience, typicality, and significance are levels of meaning of the same cognitive event, there have been a number of theories that place meaning in only one of these locations (possibly to discount it altogether).

THEORIES OF MEANING

During the hegemony of behaviorism, Watson (1920) remarked that "the question of meaning is an abstraction, a rationalization, and a speculation serving no useful purpose" (p. 103). This radical behaviorist position discounted mental processes and considered that meaning was located in the mind. In effect, Watson considered the concept of meaning to be useless.

The Gestalt psychologist Koffka (1935), on the other hand, believed that meaning was important and that it was available in the invitational qualities of an object: "a fruit says 'Eat me'; water says 'Drink me'; thunder says 'Fear me' " (p. 7). This invitational quality accounted for both what the object had to offer and what the perceivers found meaningful to their needs. Although Koffka's idea of meaning was implicitly rooted in the relationship between an observer and an object, and Gestalt theory believed that mental isomorphs paralleled empirical events, meaning was described as a stimulus property.

When behaviorists had answered most of the questions they could reasonably ask using lever-pressing paradigms, the concept of mental mediation was added to their theoretical assumptions (Bandura, 1972; Osgood, 1964; Osgood, Suci, & Tannenbaum, 1957). The meaning of a stimulus was considered to be equivalent to the behavior it elicited, but this position allowed for unobservable aspects whereby behavior was conditioned to representational mediation processes. For example, an infant bottle that was perceptually salient at feeding time came to "mean" milk because it elicited the same sucking response. Because of mental mediation, one stimulus could stand for another. From the mediation perspective, meaning was located in the stimulus and was construed as equivalence.

Eventually Chomsky's work in linguistics and the problems involved in understanding language acquisition forced a confrontation between the empiricists' belief in the primacy of stimulus variables and the rationalist's insistence on the possibility of innate mental structures (Chomsky, 1959, 1968; Skinner, 1957; Weimer, 1973). Chomsky challenged traditional theory by proposing (1) that it would be impossible for a young child to "learn" language within the short time in which children appear to accomplish this task, and further (2) that children were capable of recognizing and producing novel sentences that they had never "learned." Chomsky, therefore, proposed that language competence was innate and that meaning was conferred by deep syntactical structure on semantic content. For Chomsky, meaning was in the mind.

A synthesis of the empiricist and rationalist positions was effected by cognitive psychologists such as Gibson (1966), Neisser (1976), Shaw and Bransford (1977), Jenkins (1977), and Turvey and Shaw (1979). They began to look at behavior in more interactionist ways and concluded that both reactive emitted behavior such as lever pressing and active spontaneous behavior such as language learning occurred within and were organized around their contexts (both implicit and explicit). Behavior was seen as rational, purposive, and organized by the meaning inherent in the total event in which it occurred. Instead of being located in the stimulus of the empiricist or the mind of the rationalist, meaning was seen as a function of the interaction of both (Shaw & Bransford, 1977). Meaning was not seen as invested in things or in the words that represent things but in the relations between things that constitute an event. Bransford and Mc-

Carrell (1974) explain, "The semantic content of a particular linguistic message is created only as the comprehender, guided by the linguistic cues, specifies conditions under which the abstract relations can be realized given his knowledge of the world" (p. 215). In this view, meaning is considered to be that set of real-world relationships (between the cognizer and cognized, modulated by context) that constitute the information interface of an event.

This information interface is summarized in J. J. Gibson's concept of affordance (Gibson, 1966, 1979). An affordance is a perceptually available compatibility relationship between a particular animal and the environment in which it participates. According to Gibson, for example, a crevice affords shelter to a lizard but not to an elephant, and a chair affords sit-upon-ability to a human but not to a fish. Lizards and humans thus perceive the specifications that inform them about the support offered by crevices and chairs, respectively. Elephants and fish would have no such perceptions. In Gibson's terms, meaning is the reciprocal calibration of the properties of the environment with respect to the needs and intentions of a species or individual. Meaning is not merely in the mind or in the stimulus. It is the affordance structure of a particular species/environment or person/environment relationship. For Gibson, humans perceive the meaning of a chair as its sit-upon-ability rather than either its salience or its typicality with respect to a generic category. A fish probably perceives a chair quite differently or possibly does not perceive the chair at all. Each species perceives that part of the environment that is species-significant, a reasonable account for why perceptions are often different both between and within species. Perception is a function of selection and selection varies with significance and circumstance.

One way to picture the notion of an information interface is as an event where reciprocal frames of reference intersect. For example, any object can be considered a "brute entity" until it is interpreted, that is, until its relationships to other things are grasped (Dewey, 1933). As a brute entity, an object can have as many interpretations as it has possible functions. Envision this set of alternative functions as intersected by a contextual frame of reference that limits the possible meanings of that object to those which are appropriate for that physical and social context. The contextual contribution is simultaneously intersected by a cognizer's frame of reference; this frame operates to understand the object in light of a person's intentions and goals with respect to that object. The meaning of something emerges as an event that includes the possible functions of that something relative to its context for a particular person or group of people.

For example, to a health conscious mother, beef liver provides a vitamin-rich source of inexpensive protein, which is appropriate to serve for dinner. She believes that liver is healthy and values it accordingly. Liver is a significant or meaningful item for her. It affords her nutrition. To her 9-year-old son, beef liver is a blight on the universe, which may be appropriate to feed the cat if you hold your nose. Although its effects are negative, liver is still significant to the boy. It affords him distress. In certain African tribal ceremonies the beef liver becomes a divining device for a shaman, who acts as though he believes liver has secret answers that endow it with significance. And for a creature like a cow, a liver is just an organ that stores glycogen. The mother will probably remember beef liver when she is searching for ways to balance her budget; her son will remember beef liver when he has a bout of "what a horrible childhood I've had"; the shaman will remember beef liver when he has to perform certain rituals; and the cow, like many of us to whom liver is unimportant, will never think about or remember beef liver at all.

To review: Meaning is considered here as composed of three levels—salience, typicality, and significance. These correspond to three levels of perceiving and reflect varying degrees of articulation of the relationships between perceived entities and the events in which they are embedded. Salience reflects "figure-ground" differentiation of entities from their event contexts, typicality reflects more specific properties of the entities-in-themselves that are common to similar entities, and significance articulates still further properties as relativized by possible contexts of interaction.

In the present view, perceiving is an inherently meaningful activity. More than this, perceiving is considered the root source of meanings (cf. Verbrugge, 1980). Like perceiving, remembering is also regarded as fundamentally driven by meaning, which means that it is fundamentally driven by constraints in the real world of perceiving. From this perspective, it becomes important to ask about the relative influence of these various levels of meaning upon the cognitive process of remembering.

Salience and typicality, taken separately, seem to indicate incompatible properties. Typicality suggests familiarity and frequency whereas salience suggests novelty and uniqueness. Salience emphasizes stimulus properties (unique status) and typicality emphasizes observer properties (mental construction). If salience and typicality could be manipulated separately, would one be more influential on memory processes? Or might significance, which emphasizes compatibility relationships between stimulus and observer, be a more comprehensive factor and thus have more influence on memory than salience or typicality?

Existing research that systematically manipulates salience and typicality—but not significance—shows that in laboratory experiments both of these variables give rise to general effects that are similar for most observers; such effects thus reflect extrinsic determination by class norm in relation to the probability of a stimulus' occurrence. In contrast, significance, in both the laboratory and the larger world, is an intrinsic factor that binds a stimulus and observer into one unit reflecting the particular importance of a stimulus for a particular observer or group of observers. The relationship defining the stimulus/observer event is necessarily one of compatibility, and compatibility relationships by nature are intrinsically determined.

From a significance perspective, extrinsic factors that are less relevant to the observer's concerns may be less influential than intrinsic factors upon cognition.

This perspective does not debate that solo items (that stand out from surrounding items) might capture attention but adds that those items could also be dismissed as irrelevant and thus not be as readily remembered. Although factors such as solo status may be perceptually salient to everyone, they may not be important to anyone. Concomitantly, a significance perspective suggests that even though typical circumstances may constitute the bulk of a person's real-world knowledge, typical circumstances might be ignored if they are not compatible with that person's current interests. However, variables do exist that produce effects that are both general and intrinsic; variables that have continual or recurrent significance for most people; variables that are both typical and significant in that they affect everyone and are important to everyone. These variables usually fall into two categories: those determined by biological constraints (e.g., food), and those determined by social import (e.g., status). One variable that is significant for both biological and social reasons is gender. This is so because biologically based sexual and reproductive drives have become yoked to elaborate social rituals and prescriptions that are learned and implemented continually by members of any social group. In most cultures gender is used to help structure the social system and thus is ubiquitous in that system. Traditional gender-related circumstances are thus both typical and significant.[2] In contrast, nontraditional gender-related circumstances would be salient because they would be atypical and thus unique. They would, however, have few real-world referents and thus might be irrelevant to people's needs and intentions.

It is suggested that when everything else is held constant, circumstances that are gender-traditional are more significant to most people than similar circumstances where gender is either atypical or irrelevant. If gender-traditional circumstances are more significant, it is asserted that they will also be more memorable. An empirical test of these ideas follows.

AN EXPERIMENTAL COMPARISON OF SALIENCE, TYPICALITY, AND SIGNIFICANCE

The study at hand examined the relative effects of salience, typicality, and significance on memory. This was accomplished by comparing recognition for three types of sentences that varied on a gender dimension but were matched for syntactic form, rhythm, and the frequency with which their constituent words are used in the English language (Kucera & Francis, 1967).

The three types of sentences depict people who are either gender-nontraditional, gender-traditional, or gender-neutral with respect to common social roles. The first type of sentence depicts nontraditional people who are unique on a

---

[2]This does not constitute an endorsement of the gender-related ordering of the present social structure but rather a description of what might be considered typical within that structure today.

gender dimension and thus perceptually salient. For example, "The *brawny typist* made coffee for the boss." These sentences are labeled nontraditional (NT). The second type of sentence depicts people who are gender-traditional in the same sorts of roles. For example, "The *sweet typist* made coffee for the boss." These sentences are labeled traditional (T). The third type of sentence also involves typical people in common traditional roles but these people are neutral on the gender dimension. For example, "The *ideal patient* gave the records to the nurse." These sentences are labeled neutral (N). Traditional and neutral sentences were designed—and rated by a separate group of subjects—to be equally typical of the culture, but the suggestion is that the gender dimension makes traditional sentences more significant.

The foregoing permits an assessment of the relative effects of salience, typicality, and significance, as follows. If salience is the most important determinant of recognition memory, then nontraditional sentences should be remembered best. We might suppose that, all other things being equal, gender-related events are more salient than gender-neutral events, so altogether one would predict the ordering NT > T > N from best to worst recognition. On the basis of typicality, T and N sentences are equal and higher than NT sentences, so T = N > NT would be predicted. The predictions according to significance are similar to typicality, but with the critical differentiation of T and N, therefore T > N > NT. From a significance perspective the important property of the nontraditional sentences leading to the prediction of lowered recognition is that they reflect content with few real-world referents and therefore are largely *irrelevant*. In this sense, the significance perspective embodies the suggestion that memory is a function of real-world referents of sentences rather than the sentences themselves; succinctly, the sentences are considered transparent to their (real-world) referents.

Eighty subjects—40 males and 40 females—were given a set of acquisition sentences to study and were tested on a set of recognition sentences. Some of the sentences were of the form <adjective> <subject> <verb> <object> (adjective condition), others of the form <adjective> <subject> <verb> <pronoun> <object> (pronoun condition), where the pronoun refers to the subject of the sentence. The traditionality of sentences was manipulated by the adjective-subject relation, e.g., "the sweet typist" versus "the brawny typist." Actions described by the verb phrases were always appropriate to the subject. Sentences with pronouns could vary not only in their traditionality as defined but also in the congruity of the subject-pronoun relation, e.g., typist-her (congruent) versus typist-his (incongruent). During recognition, some of the adjective-condition sentences were shown again (T, N, or NT Repeated), and some were shown with a new adjective (Tsw, Nsw, or NTsw—Switched Adjective). New pronoun-condition sentences were also shown during recognition, that were either Congruous (TC, NC, or NTC) or Incongruous (TI or NTI—there are no NI sentences because it is not possible to have an incongruent pronoun in neutral

TABLE 9.1
Examples of the Eleven Sentence Types Used in the Acquisition and
the Recognition Sets

	Traditional	Neutral	Nontraditional
Repeated	The sweet typist served coffee to the boss.	The ideal patient gave records to the nurse.	The delicate politician issued orders to the staff.
Switched Adjective	The distinguished politician issued orders to the staff.	The irritable patient gave records to the nurse.	The brawny typist served coffee to the boss.
Added Congrous Pronoun	The reckless economist traded his blue chip stocks.	The lonely child helped his science teacher.	The powerful fashion model served tea in her salon.
Added Incongruous Pronoun	The reckless economist traded her blue chip stocks.	None.	The powerful fashion model served tea in his salon.

sentences). Examples of these 11 types of recognition sentences are displayed in Table 9.1.

The task for subjects was to indicate for each sentence in the recognition set whether they had seen it before, and how confident on a scale from 1 to 3 they were of their judgment. After recognition testing, subjects completed sex-role attitude scales.

The results are shown in Table 9.2. Table entries are mean confidence ratings multiplied by +1 for "Old" responses and −1 for "New" responses. For the moment, we restrict our attention to the Adjective condition sentences: the Repeated sentences and their controls, the Switched Adjective sentences. We see that although subjects distinguished old from new sentences, they tended to respond "old" as a function of significance. For both types of sentences, the observed ordering is T > N > NT.

The proportion of "Old" responses independently of confidence ratings is shown in Table 9.3. Because of the extremely low-false alarm rates to neutral

TABLE 9.2
Means of Recognition Scores for Eleven Types of Sentences that Were Rated
on a Scale from −3 to +3

	Repeated	Switched Adjective	Congruous Pronoun	Incongruous Pronoun
Traditional	.88 (T)	−.34 (TSW)	.41 (TC)	−1.25 (TI)
Neutral	.24 (N)	−1.19 (NSW)	−.14 (NC)	−
Nontraditional	−.29 (NT)	−1.39 (NTSW)	−.15 (NTC)	−1.37 (NTI)

Note: The abbreviation for each sentence type is next to its mean score.

TABLE 9.3
Proportion of Mean Positive Responses for Each Sentence Type

	Repeated	Switched Adjective	Congruous Pronoun	Incongruous Pronoun
Traditional	.88	.37	.65	.26
Neutral	.61	.04	.48	–
Nontraditional	.34	.02	.56	.21

and nontraditional (Nsw and NTsw) sentences, a signal detection analysis was rendered inadvisable. However, if one examines the pattern of "old" responses given in Table 9.3 (both hits and false alarms), certain qualitative statements seem appropriate. First, the fact that the false alarm rates for the neutral and nontraditional sentences are about equal whereas the corresponding hit rates are rather different indicates that the hit rate for the neutral sentences represents actual memory sensitivity rather than response bias. If it were bias, then the mean of the false alarms for the neutral sentences (.04) should be substantially higher. This result is not surprising if one considers that sentences receive their meaning in reference to typical real-world circumstances and that the neutral sentences reflect more real referents in the real world than the nontraditional sentences. Because other research has shown that people tend to remember written material in light of their real-world knowledge base (Bransford, Barclay, & Franks, 1972), it seems reasonable that people would tend to remember typical real-world circumstances as depicted in neutral sentences better than salient atypical circumstances as depicted in the nontraditional sentences.

However, the high false alarm rate for the novel traditional sentences (Tsw) may indicate a response bias for traditional sentences. It cannot be due to a general response bias to say yes because, again, that would affect all conditions. Nor can it be a bias channeled by prototypical schemata, because traditional and neutral sentences were judged equally typical. So perhaps what is operating is a simple preference for traditional sentences.

It is more difficult to separate preference and significance because significant items can also be items that are preferred. But consider the following: Because significant content areas are of core concern, they may actually have a greater number of connections in real-world circumstances (gender may be widely relevant) than less significant content areas. This would give significant variables such as gender a wider distribution in most subject's real-world knowledge base when compared with less significant or less typical variables. In contrast to significance, preference should not necessarily work this way. A person may prefer pistachio to chocolate ice cream, but that does not necessarily indicate that pistachio ice cream carries significance for that person nor ensure pistachio ice cream a wide distribution in that person's real-world knowledge base. Additional comments on the plausibility of a "stereotypic bias" hypothesis and related matters are pursued in the general discussion.

Turning now to the Pronoun condition sentences, Table 9.2 clearly indicates that novel congruent pronouns were accepted as old more than novel incongruent pronouns. This effect is somewhat larger for traditional than nontraditional sentences, as we might expect from a significance perspective. Congruous pronouns tend to make both traditional and nontraditional sentences more traditional while leaving neutral sentences unchanged. Incongruous pronouns, on the other hand, make traditional sentences less traditional, but leave nontraditional sentences essentially the same. Incongruous pronouns do not apply to neutral sentences. The results here seem straightforward. Novel pronoun additions are accepted as "old" to the degree that they depict real-world circumstances and enhance the significance of the sentence in which they are embedded.

A separate analysis was done on the data in Table 9.2 with the neutral sentences removed, allowing a direct comparison of the relative effects of repeating a sentence, switching its adjective, and adding a congruent or incongruent pronoun. A highly significant interaction confirms what one can observe by eye in the table. Although T sentences were judged as old more than TC sentences, the opposite was true for NT sentences, which were not judged as old as often as NTC sentences. In addition, Tsw sentences were judged old more than TI sentences, but NTsw sentences were, if anything, judged old less than NTI sentences. This analysis further confirms that the choice of old or new for the sentences presented is influenced by the sentence's degree of congruence with significant real-world referents. Thus for traditional sentences the pattern reflecting degree of "old" responses is $T > TC > Tsw > TI$ but for nontraditional sentences the pattern is $NTC > NT > NTI > NTsw$.

Overall, the results show a tradeoff between whether or not a sentence has been seen before, its degree of cultural significance, and the pronoun inferences that are acceptable. This can be expressed in a linear model:

$$M_i = b_0 + b_1 R_i + b_2 S_i + b_3 I_i$$

where

M_i = recognition memory for sentence i
R_i = whether or not the sentence has been seen before
S_i = the degree of significance the sentence reflects
I_i = the type of inference (congruent or incongruent pronoun) that is acceptable.

Then let

R_i = -1 for sentences not seen before, or
     = 1 for sentences seen before
S_i = 1 if sentence is significant (T, TC, Tsw), or
     = .5 if sentence is partially significant (TI, NTC, NTI), or

$$= 0 \text{ if sentence is neutral (N, Nsw, NC), or}$$
$$= -1 \text{ if sentence is not significant (NT, NTsw)}$$
$$I_i = 1 \text{ if congruous pronoun is added (TC, NC, NTC), or}$$
$$= 0 \text{ if no pronoun is added (T, Tsw, N, Nsw, NT, NTsw), or}$$
$$= -1 \text{ if incongruous pronoun is added (TI, NTI).}$$

Using a simple regression analysis, parameters of this model were estimated from the mean values for each type of sentence obtaining $b_0 = .316$; $b_1 = .606$; $b_2 = .567$; $b_3 = .681$. Not only the b's but also the standardized beta weights were all about equal. The model accounts for nearly 98% of the variance in the 11 means in Table 9.2, with the multiple correlation equal to .989. In a sense, S and I both amount to the same thing—significance—in the former case modulated by the adjective-subject relation. It is therefore appropriate to look at the multiple correlation between performance and the combination of these two variables. The correlation so obtained is .688, which compares favorably with the .568 correlation between performance and whether a sentence has been seen before or not (R). This is all the more striking if one bears in mind that it is the *latter*—whether a sentence appeared in the acquisition set—that the subjects were supposed to be judging, but it is the former that is a better predictor of their behavior.

Turning finally to the results for the sex-role attitude scales, it was found that differences in recognition were related to individual differences in attitudes. This is what should occur from a significance perspective, because significance is a function of specific organism-environment relations, even with a variable such as sex-role traditionality, which is of generally high significance to most people. The relevant correlations were not high, but bear in mind that any variable that varied greatly in significance across individuals would have been unsuitable for demonstrating overall statistical effects averaged across subjects. This tradeoff seems unavoidable, being inherent in the relation between the concept of significance as defined in this chapter and the concept of statistical "significance" as determined by uniformity of effects over persons.

GENERAL DISCUSSION AND IMPLICATIONS

The results show that people can generally distinguish between *old* and *new* sentences but they are most likely to respond "old" to both *old* and *new* sentences that are congruent with the real world, reflecting gender-traditionality and thus significance. For people with the most traditional attitudes towards gender, this effect is enhanced. People also tend to say "old" to sentences that reflect typical rather than atypical content. In fact, the less significant and the more atypical the sentence content is, the more likely people are to say "new" to sentences that are actually *old*. The pattern that best reflects degree of influence on memory appears to be significance (intrinsic importance) > typicality (real-world representativeness) > salience (ability to stand out).

Intrinsic versus Extrinsic Factors

Salience, in the form of contrast, uniqueness, or solo status, may not be important enough in laboratory experiments to hold its own against significance. But in the real world, salience, typicality, and significance are not separate but often combine in the same perceptual display. For example, a male robin's salient red breast is typical for that species and significant as a sexually relevant display (Lack, 1943). The key is that in this real-world circumstance neither the salience nor the typicality inherent in the red breast are extrinsic factors that affect all birds or even all robins at all times. The male robin's red breast only affects interested parties: female robins during mating season and rival male robins engaged in boundary disputes. Red breasts are differentially significant. They are also tied to most robins' core concerns—retention of territory and reproductive success. Salience and typicality as described in the social and cognitive literature bypass these intrinsic factors (because stimulus and observer are treated separately) and look for extrinsic factors that yield general effects. It is not debated that certain perceptually salient factors may modulate initial attention better than others. What is at issue is whether extrinsic factors that obtain general effects are as useful to measure memory for the real world as intrinsic factors that obtain specific effects. Gender-typical information for both robins and humans is an *intra*species intrinsic factor tied to the species' core concerns. Salience as solo status of any type is an *inter*species extrinsic factor that is usually not of core concern to any organism. Because memory must be adaptive if organisms are to survive, it is reasonable to suppose that they are more likely to remember things with intrinsic importance.

Perhaps this point can be enhanced by two parallel examples from learning psychology. General laws of learning such as the Law of Contiguity and the Law of Effect were thought to hold over all species, for all stimuli, at all times. In short, they were thought to produce general effects. If things co-occurred they would be associated and if they did not co-occur, no associative bond would be formed. However, Garcia and Koelling (1966) showed that if one exposes rats to either a taste stimulus or an audio-visual stimulus paired either with radiation that causes delayed nausea or with footshock, only the taste stimulus tends to become associated with nausea and only the light and noise tend to become associated with footshock. It appears that "contiguity" can be stretched to hours when a significant activity such as learning to avoid "poisoned" food is at stake. But contiguity has little effect when the relationship between the conditioned and unconditioned stimulus is not significant for the species tested.

In the same spirit, Allison, Larson, and Jensen (1967) reversed the procedure of Miller's (1951) classic instrumental responding experiment, in which rats learned to turn a wheel in order to escape from the electrified white half of a box to the safe black half. Allison et al. showed that rats had trouble learning to flee from black to white whether they had been shocked in the black half or not, yet easily learned to run from white to black under either shock or no-shock conditions. In fact, rats are naturally nocturnal animals that live in dark areas. The suggestion is that light and dark are differentially significant to rats; dark is associated with familiarity and safety whereas light is associated with strangeness and danger regardless of the administration of shock or the Law of Effect. Thus both learning and memory appear to be a function of significance.

A Note on Bias

Other studies that have examined memory for gender-relevant material have obtained some results that are similar to those reported here (Deaux & Major, 1977; Kail & Levine, 1976; Lippa & Signorella, in press; see Bem, 1981, for a review of these studies). Rather than explaining the discrepancy between subjects' responses and presented material as a function of significant real-world circumstances, these studies suggest that the responses obtained are systematically in error due to stereotype schemas. The assumption is that people with such schemata process presented stimuli through a biased framework. It might be helpful to examine the bases for such a biased framework in order to discover whether the concept of bias is adequate to account for the results found in this study and in the studies just cited.

Bias versus Adaptation.   Trimming information by categorizing according to typicality and selecting information according to intrinsic interests are inherent to the cognitive processes of most species (McCabe, 1982). For example, ducks and geese flee the shadow of a hawk whether or not that shadow is cast by a real hawk or a cardboard outline simulating a hawk (Tinbergen, 1951). Ducks and geese are ''biased'' to detect this type of predator specification in order to survive. By these principles, eagles, in contrast, would be ''biased'' to ignore such information because it does not threaten their survival. Human beings have similar ''biases.'' Humans are able to detect a child's age level and tend to make care-giving decisions by attending to the child's cranial/facial proportion over other age-level indicators (McCabe, 1984; Chapter 12, this volume). Chimpanzee infants have faces with proportions similar to human faces, yet adult chimpanzees ignore this cranial/facial specification and attend to their infant's white tail tufts to make judgments of dependent status (Lawick-Godall, 1968). Adaptation and survival often depend on attention being selective along dimensions of significance. For example, while on a hike, one might best attend to escaping from an angry bear rather than to picking the flowers growing by the trail. Selectively attending to the bear surely compromises processing other available information and therefore creates in memory a potential bias towards bears. Indeed, one might never perceive nor remember that the flowers were there. In such cases, however, "bias" towards particular stimuli is to be expected. Consequently, to explain typical adaptive behavior as biased behavior seems scarcely helpful since the terms are closely allied under normal circumstances.[3]

Bias Versus Real-World Circumstances. If misperception, distortion, or bias is at work, these processes should work equally for traditional and nontraditional persons. If bias is at work when subjects who score high on sex-role traditionalism say "old" to (novel) traditional sentences, then bias should also be at work for nontraditional subjects, inducing them to say "old" to *nontraditional* material. However, this did not occur in the present study. On the other hand, if memory is for real-world circumstances (rather than a matter of biased schemas), responding "new" to both old and new nontraditional sentences is quite sensible. Presumably memory reflects the real world, and because nontraditional material has few real-world referents people tend to fail to recognize that type of sentence.

People tend to remember written material in light of their own real-world knowledge base (Bransford, Barclay, & Franks, 1972). Because gender-relevant orderings are ubiquitous in the social system, gender has widespread connections in real-world circumstances. This large network of connections makes gender-traditional material more easily available and thus produces different effects on traditional and nontraditional sentences (Tversky & Kahneman, 1973).

Summary and Implications

The results of this study are attributed to the priority (in recognition processes) of real-world circumstances that reflect the relationship between stimulus and observer and therefore are not merely extrinsically salient or typical but also intrinsically significant; this priority overrides recognition of depicted circumstances that are either atypical or typical but less significant. It is suggested that an attribution of distortion, bias, or error for these results may be due to several possible confusions. The first confusion is confounding memory for written material with memory for the referents of that material. Research has shown that people do not remember the sentences they read; they remember what those sentences mean in light of their own real-world knowledge base. As Whitehead (1948) noted, "There is not a sentence which adequately states its own meaning.

---

[3]This is not to say that there are no maladaptive biases. There are, and neuroses describe a number of them.

There is always a background of presupposition which defies analysis by reason of its infinitude'' (p. 73).

A second related confusion involves confounding what is inside people's heads (schemas) with what people's heads are "inside" (the world) (Mace, 1977). It does not seem appropriate to assign causal properties to internal stereotypic schemas for "biasing" memory toward sentences that depict external real circumstances (that it is adaptive to remember) and away from sentences that depict atypical circumstances with few real-world referents (that it is adaptive to forget).

The third confusion may be a previously unexamined source for the first two; it is the confounding of cognitive judgments with value judgments. In point of fact, people's heads are "inside" a real world where different prescriptive expectations are placed on people according to their gender. In addition, these prescriptions often order the availability of different roles to people with different genders. In effect, the *social system* is biased with respect to gender. The fact that people's memories reflect these social biases involves cognitive judgments. The fact that these social prescriptions may be neither realistic nor equitable for their recipients involves value judgments. What one remembers and how one might like to restructure the world one remembers are most likely two different phenomena. For example, one might infer that the people who are most interested in changing gender imbalances are probably also most aware of the actual frequency of occurrence of such imbalances. Would it be reasonable to attribute their accurate perception and memory of those gender imbalances to their attitudes and associated stereotypic schemas? This would imply that the gender imbalances could be in their heads rather than in the world. Although people's beliefs may certainly be influential in maintaining the social structure, this does not necessarily mean that their memories are in error.

In sum, this study has shown that recognition memory functions primarily to preserve real-world circumstances that are intrinsically significant. Laboratory manipulation of extrinsic factors such as salience or typicality contribute to cognitive events, but, in the absence of significance, they are less influential on recognition memory.

ACKNOWLEDGMENTS

The work described here is based on a doctoral dissertation completed at the University of California, Los Angeles in April, 1980. The author wishes to thank Letitia Anne Peplau, Thomas Wickens, and Patricia Greenfield for their excellent comments and consistent support throughout this project. Appreciation is also extended to Jerry Balzano, Robert Shaw, Robert Katz, and Gudrun Einarsdottir for reading this draft of the manuscript. Correspondence should be directed to Dr. Viki McCabe, Psychology Dept. UCLA, Los Angeles, CA 90024.

REFERENCES

Allison, J., Larson, D., & Jensen, D. (1967). Acquired fear, brightness preference, and one-way shuttlebox performance. *Psychonomic Science, 8,* 269–270.

Bandura, A. (1972). Social learning through imitation. In M. R. Jones (Ed.), *Nebraska Symposium on Motivation.* Lincoln: University of Nebraska Press.

Bartlett, F. A. (1932). *Remembering.* Cambridge, England: Cambridge University Press.

Bem, S. L. (1981). Gender schema theory: A cognitive account of sex-typing. *Psychological Review, 88,* 354–364.

Bransford, J. D., Barclay, J. R., & Franks, J. J. (1972). Sentence memory: A constructive versus interpretive approach. *Cognitive Psychology, 3,* 193–209.

Bransford, J. D., & Franks, J. J. (1971). The abstraction of linguistic ideas. *Cognitive Psychology, 2,* 331–350.

Bransford, J. D., & Franks, J. J. (1972). Sentence memory: A constructive versus an interpretive approach. *Cognitive Psychology, 3,* 193–209.

Bransford, J. D., & McCarrell, N. S. (1974). A sketch of a cognitive approach to comprehension. In W. B. Weimer & D. S. Palermo (Eds.), *Cognition and the symbolic processes.* Hillsdale, NJ: Lawrence Erlbaum Associates.

Chomsky, N. (1959). Review of B. F. Skinner, *Verbal behavior. Language, 35,* 26–58.

Chomsky, N. (1968). *Language and mind.* New York: Harcourt Brace Jovanovich.

Deaux, K., & Major, B. (1977). Sex-related patterns in the unit of perception. *Personality and Social Psychology Bulletin,* 297–300.

Dewey, J. (1933). *How we think.* Lexington, MA: D. C. Heath.

Garcia, J., & Koelling, R. A. (1966). Relation of cue to consequence in avoidance learning. *Psychonomic Science, 4,* 123–124.

Gibson, J. J. (1966). *The senses considered as perceptual systems.* Boston: Houghton–Mifflin.

Gibson, J. J. (1979). *The ecological approach to visual perception.* Boston: Houghton–Mifflin.

Jenkins, J. (1977). Remember that old theory of memory? Well forget it! In R. Shaw & J. Bransford (Eds.), *Perceiving, acting, and knowing.* Hillsdale, NJ: Lawrence Erlbaum Associates.

Kail, R. V., & Levine, L. E. (1976). Encoding processes and sex-role preferences. *Journal of Experimental Child Psychology, 21,* 256–263.

Koffka, K. (1935). *Principles of Gestalt psychology.* New York: Harcourt Brace Jovanovich.

Kucera, H., & Francis, W. N. (1967). *Computational analysis of present day American English.* Providence, RI: Brown University Press.

Lack, D. (1943). *The life of the robin.* London: Penguin.

Lawick-Goodall, J. van. (1968). The behavior of tree living chimpanzees in the Gombe Stream area. *Animal Behavior Monographs, 1,* 161–311.

Lippa, L. S., & Signorella, M. L. (in press). Gender-related schemata and constructive memory in children. *Child Development.*

Mace, W. W. (1977). James J. Gibson's strategy for perceiving: Ask not what's inside your head, but what your head's inside of. In R. Shaw & J. Bransford (Eds.), *Perceiving, acting, and knowing.* Hillsdale, NJ: Lawrence Erlbaum Associates.

McArthur, L. Z., & Post, D. (1977). Figural emphasis and person perception. *Journal of Experimental Social Psychology, 13,* 520–535.

McCabe, V. (1982). Invariants and affordances: An analysis of species-typical information. *Ethology and Sociobiology, 3,* 79–92.

McCabe, V. (1984). Abstract perceptual information for age level: A risk factor for maltreatment? *Child Development, 55.*

Miller, N. E. (1951). Learnable drives and rewards. In S. S. Stevens (Ed.), *Handbook of experimental psychology* (pp. 435–472). New York: Wiley.

Neisser, U. (1976). *Cognition and reality: Principles and implications of cognitive psychology.* San Francisco: W. H. Freeman.

Osgood, C. E. (1964). A behaviorist analysis of perception and language as cognitive phenomena. In R. Harper, C. Anderson, C. Christensen, & S. Hunka (Eds.), *The cognitive processes.* Englewood Cliffs, NJ: Prentice Hall.

Osgood, C. E., Suci, G. J., & Tannenbaum, P. H. (1957). *The measurement of meaning.* Urbana: University of Illinois Press.

Shaw, R., & Bransford, J. D. (1977). Introduction. In R. Shaw & J. Bransford (Eds.) *Perceiving, acting, and knowing.* Hillsdale, NJ: Lawrence Erlbaum Associates.

Skinner, B. F. (1957). *Verbal behavior.* New York: Appleton.

Taylor, S. E., & Fiske, S. T. (1978). Salience, attention, and attribution; Top of the head phenomena. In L. Berkowitz (Ed.), *Advances in experimental social psychology* (Vol. II). New York: Academic Press.

Tinbergen, N. (1951). *The study of instinct.* New York: Oxford University Press.

Turvey, M. T., & Shaw, R. (1979). The primacy of perceiving: An ecological reformulation of perception for understanding memory. In L. Nilsson (Ed.), *Perspectives on memory research: Essays in honor of Uppsala University's 500th anniversary.* Hillsdale, NJ: Lawrence Erlbaum Associates.

Tversky, A., & Kahneman, D. (1973). Availability: A heuristic for judging frequency and probability. *Cognitive Psychology, 5,* 207–232.

Weimer, W. B. (1973). Psycholinguistics and Plato's paradox of the Meno. *American Psychologist, 28,* 15–33.

Verbrugge, R. R. (1980). Transformations in knowing: A realist view of metaphor. In R. R. Honeck & R. R. Hoffman (Eds.), *Cognition and figurative language.* Hillsdale, NJ: Lawrence Erlbaum Associates.

Watson, J. B. (1920). Is thinking merely the action of language mechanisms? *British Journal of Psychology, 11,* 87–104.

Whitehead, A. (1948). *Essays in science and philosophy.* London: Rider.

V

MUSICAL EVENTS

In 1938 a paper of considerable importance for psychology was published in the French *Journal de Psychologie* by the philosopher Ernst Cassirer. The paper appeared in translation for English-speaking audiences in 1944, not in any psychology journal but in *Philosophy and Phenomenological Research* (Cassirer, 1938/1944), a journal little read by psychologists of the day. In "The Concept of Group and the Theory of Perception," Cassirer identified mathematical groups as the source of fundamental connection between scientific knowledge in its purest form, on the one hand, and knowledge of the world gained through the process of perception, on the other. Common to both, according to Cassirer, are the ideas of invariance and transformation, and these same ideas play a pivotal role in group theory. It is of some interest that Cassirer credits Helmholtz as being the first to attempt an application of the group concept to certain problems of perception. According to Cassirer, Helmholtz was in part led to an investigation of the axioms of geometry in the late 1860s as a consequence of his perceptual studies. "To be sure," Cassirer (1938/1944) writes, "Helmholtz was not able to see the new problem which he had raised with complete precision and to realize its full importance" (p. 1). Though Cassirer and Helmholtz differed widely in their philosophies, they were both concerned at several points in their respective careers with expressing the epistemological connection, the linking concept, between the "brute" acts of knowledge acquisition manifested in everyday acts of perceiving on the one hand and the pursuit of scientific knowledge on the other. Helmholtz, as almost every psychologist knows today, found his link in the concept of *inference*, his model of perception being one of unconscious inferences from the data of sense, analogous to inductive inferences in science. Cassirer, as only a few psychologists know today, found his link in the concept of *group*.

Certainly, the group concept was not nearly as well developed in Helmholtz's time as it had become by 1938. Hermann Weyl's account of quantum mechanics in terms of group theory, an evident source of inspiration for Cassirer, was first published in 1928. The 60-year period between Helmholtz's first geometric essay and Weyl's book saw groups as the focus of a tremendous amount of mathematical study. In fact, one of the most important applications of the group concept in history was being made during the very years of Helmholtz's geometric writings, an application often said to have brought about the unification of all of geometry: Felix Klein's *Erlanger Programme*, introduced in 1872. Briefly, Klein showed that the subject-matter of any particular branch of geometry was determined by an associated group of transformations. The theorems of a branch of geometry addressed only those properties of objects that were left invariant, or unaffected, by the transformations in the associated group. By this simple formula all of geometry from Euclidean metric geometry to topology could be comprehended.

For Cassirer, too, the *Erlanger Programme* was a fruitful model, and Cassirer applied it in a most insightful way to the perceptual constancies. For what is a constancy, asks Cassirer, if not an invariance preserved under a group of transformations? What often goes under the name of lightness constancy, for example, may be recast in these terms: The totality of possible illumination levels defines a group of transformations (illumination changes) under which object properties (like "lightness") and their corresponding manifestations in the flux of stimulation remain invariant. What this group formulation does, among other things, is to highlight the perceiver's ability to keep separate illumination from that which is illuminated. In a similar fashion one may speak of melodic constancy as an invariance of form over a group of transformations. "A melody," says Cassirer (1945/1979, pg. 286), "is a certain invariant." Cassirer's conclusion (1938/1944) could have almost come out of the writings of J. Gibson: "Such an analysis reveals that the 'possibility of the object' depends upon the formation of certain invariants in the flux of sense impressions" (p. 21).

Chapters 10 and 11 follow up on Cassirer's musical insight. **Jones and Hahn** are concerned with a description of music that is continuous with a description of nonmusical auditory events. In Chapter 10 they use the logarithmic spiral as a universal to capture basic invariants in the acoustic realm. The spiral may be generated by two independent motions, translation and rotation, giving rise to a view of pitch that contrasts sharply with one-dimensional psychophysical scales.

Chapter 11, on the other hand, is concerned not with the connection of music and other audible events, but with the uniqueness of music itself. **Balzano** shows how the basic pitch structures of Western music are built into the geometry implied by the underlying group structure of the music. His experiments demonstrate that constraints arising from the group structures made available in both pitch and rhythmic domains of music can be detected even by musically untrained listeners. In both of these chapters a new view of what is perceivable in music lays a firmer groundwork for musical cognition than has heretofore been possible.

REFERENCES

Cassirer, E. (1944). The concept of group and the theory of perception. *Philosophy and Phenomenological Research, 5,* 1–36. (Original work published 1938)

Cassirer, E. (1979). Reflections on the concept of group and the theory of perception. In D. P. Verene (Ed.), *Symbol, myth, and culture: Essays and lectures of Ernst Cassirer, 1935–1945.* New Haven: Yale University Press. (Original unpublished work 1945)

10 Invariants in Sound

Mari Riess Jones
June Hahn
Ohio State University

CONTENTS

The tradition of ecological optics established by J. J. Gibson (1966, 1979) places great emphasis upon identification of transformations and invariants in the environment. For Gibson it was the visible environment that was most fascinating. His approach tells us of the importance of describing higher order relationships in the optic array. Ecological optics is a relatively new approach to visual perception but it has nonetheless attracted much attention. This cannot be said of ecological approaches to the auditory environment; if ecological optics is in its infancy, ecological acoustics is yet to be born.

The birth of ecological acoustics requires that we begin to identify higher order transformations and invariants in sound patterns, invariants that have specific meanings for an organism. This chapter is addressed to such a task. It is a beginning. We suggest a way of describing frequency and frequency relationships that illuminates many higher order sound invariants. This description exploits the dynamic symmetries of a natural pattern. It is a description that is rich enough to support the complexity of most sound patterns and yet simple enough to outline the more powerful invariants that have meaning in music.

Broadly speaking, ecological acoustics must come to grips with sound invariants that figure in a multitude of environmental events. These include noises associated with natural occurrences, animal song, and human speech. In this chapter we focus upon what may seem to be a narrow segment of this domain,

197

namely human song and musical invariants therein. We contend that this is not really a narrow focus for two reasons. In the first place, although we illustrate a new means of specifying sound invariants through examples that are largely musical, the invariant symmetries that are involved are nonetheless quite general. Secondly, it is probably misleading to categorize musical patterns as unrepresentative of world sounds. They may, in fact, be exquisite examples of everyday sound patterns. After all, music is conceived and created by living things; and frequently it is even used to mimic naturally occurring sounds. In a real sense, musical art may highlight prototypical invariants that are buried within our complex auditory environment. As such music becomes a showcase of important sound invariants.

This chapter, therefore, attempts to extend the tradition of ecological psychology to sonic environments and particularly to musical patterns. This undertaking has implications for research in both music perception and psychophysical scaling.

SEARCH FOR INVARIANTS: SOME IMPLICATIONS FOR MUSIC PERCEPTION AND PSYCHOPHYSICAL SCALING

In music perception it is well known that invariant frequency ratios figure importantly in musical scales, chords, and melodic themes. Harmonic ratios are integral to musical art. They support familiar melodies played on different instruments, in different keys, and generally transformed over a range of sound frequencies. With the discovery of a parsimonious means of describing these invariants in terms of symmetries, there is support for recent approaches to music perception that assume that listeners learn to attend to and pick up higher order pitch invariants, such as harmonic ratios. According to Jones' theory, for example, these ratios are detected more or less adequately as a function of transformations suggested by the surrounding musical context (Jones, 1976, 1981, 1982).

Identification of sound invariants also has implications for psychophysical scaling. Questions surrounding the relationship between the frequency of a pure sine tone and its reported pitch have a long and controversial history in psychology (Attneave & Olson, 1971; Boring, 1942; Shepard, 1964; Stevens & Volkmann, 1940; Stevens, Volkmann, & Newman, 1937; Ward, 1954, 1970). And a means of identifying higher order relationships between sine tones that clarifies pitch components has implications for this continuing debate. Typically the controversy has flared over the validity of the mel scale as a subjective scale of musical pitch. This scale, derived by Stevens and his colleagues (Stevens & Volkman, 1940), relates pitch judgments from fractionation tasks to frequency in a fashion that suggests that musical intervals, measured in mels, "become subjectively larger as frequencies increase up to about the fourth octave above middle C" (p. 346).

These and other psychoacoustic studies typically present listeners with isolated pairs of tones to judge. The resulting scale has been roundly criticized by musicians (e.g., Ward, 1970), largely because it fails to portray significant musical relationships found in more realistically "musical" contexts. According to the mel scale, pitch has a one-dimensional character. There's the problem. Many have argued that pitch should not be conceived as a one-dimensional "ribbon" stretching from low-frequency tones to high-frequency ones (Jones, 1976; Ruckmick, 1929; Shepard, 1964; Ward, 1970). In addition to a tone height quality, many have persuasively argued that there is also an aspect of pitch that reflects a tone's unique location within an octave, i.e., a "chroma" dimension. The chroma dimension has been proposed to capture the recurrent similarity of tones within successive octaves, and in musical sound patterns it comes to serve very important functions. In a nutshell, then, the mel scale does not capture the significant musical invariant that uniquely identify a tone's location within an octave.

There is, by now, plenty of support for the psychological reality of a chroma dimension. For example, people often confuse corresponding notes in different octaves (e.g., Bachem, 1954; Baird, 1917; Humphreys, 1939; Kallman & Massaro, 1979). Furthermore, Shepard, using a special set of computer-generated complex tones that effectively collapsed "tone height" across adjacent octaves, illustrated the impact of a circular "tone chroma" dimension upon listeners' judgments of relative pitch. And in a striking illustration of the limitations of a one-dimensional mel scale, Attneave and Olson (1971) showed that even musically untutored people transposed a simple, well-learned melody according to a musical scale. Their subjects, when asked to create a new pattern that sounded like the original sequence, did so in such a way that the musical intervals of the original sequence were preserved. This would not have been the case if they were transposing according to the mel scale.

In the wake of this, multidimensional scaling (MDS), with its potential for capturing multiple pitch dimensions, has made steady inroads on territories once claimed by traditional psychophysics (Krumhansl, 1979; Levelt, van de Geer, & Plomp, 1966; Shepard, 1964, 1974). Recently, for example, Krumhansl (1979) found evidence supporting a three-dimensional pitch space. Her study, like that of Attneave and Olson, also involved a more explicitly musical context. She asked subjects to judge the similarity of two tones immediately after they (the subjects) had heard all eight tones of a particular diatonic scale. The solution indicated that within a given octave people made their judgments based upon tone height and tone chroma information, and, in addition, they distinguished salient relationships involving familiar musical scales (e.g., clusters reflecting diatonic scale versus nondiatonic scale tones emerged in the solution). Graphically, the solution suggested a conical representation of pitch. This sort of finding reinforces the general scaling result that there exists an inherently circular aspect to chromatic relationships. Along these same lines, Shepard (1979) recently described data that he argues support a five-dimensional subjective configuration of tonal relationships. These and related MDS data (e.g., Balzano, 1977; Hahn, 1980; Levelt, van de Geer, & Plomp, 1966) converge upon a common conclusion, namely that regardless of the number of pitch dimensions that emerge from perceptual reports, their nature suggests that a circular component is present.

It is important for this discussion to emphasize that both the mel scale and MDS techniques aim to portray perceptually valid representations of sine-wave relationships. But the mel scale appears to be more directly linked to aspects of the physical frequency dimension than the MDS solutions are. Indeed, implicit in attacks upon the mel scale has been an assumption that its shortcomings stem from its direct linkage to physical frequency, which is, in turn, assumed to be one dimension. Shepard (1964) made explicit this idea: "The construction of one-dimensional psychological scales of pitch corresponding to the one-dimensional physical side of frequency for tones has been accomplished by Stevens, Volkmann, and Newman, and others" (p. 2346). In one sense, the ascendency of multidimensional representations of pitch seems to have broken the once tight psychophysical linkage between frequency and pitch. Perhaps this is because frequency itself continues to be conceived as a one-dimensional physical scale, a scale that is hard to reconcile with multidimensional configurations.

Consequently, researchers in this area have often appealed to a constructionist model to fill the gap between an impoverished physical frequency representation and a rich perceptual experience. Information in the sound pattern that might specify "circularity" in chromatically-based and musical-scale-based dimensions is ignored. Instead hypotheses proposing that people "create" or "add to" the impoverished one-dimensional picture of the stimulus have been common. This constructionistic approach tends to lead theorists, perhaps prematurely, away from careful analyses of potentially influential factors in the environment, the context, and the task that could explain (e.g.,) MDS solutions. Indeed, there is a whole history of constructionist approaches to pitch in psychology. Helical pitch configurations were envisioned by Ruckmick and Drobisch (cf. Ruckmick, 1929) that presumably reflected distortions of an objective frequency continuum by the listener (see also Révész, 1954). Adapting this line of reasoning to multidimensional scaling configurations, it is tempting to argue that even these must be "created" in the mind because they have little meaning in terms of the objective frequency scale.

There is an alternative view. And this alternative view is a direct spinoff of the ecological approach to sound description. It simply involves denial of the dictum that physical frequency is best conceived as one-dimensional. If we talk instead about physical frequency relationships, then it is possible to show that sound waves contain invariant information that specifies the lawful configurations found in many pitch judgment tasks. Physical frequency relationships are multidimensional. In this case, one is not forced to a constructionist position: Instead one fills the gap by identifying a richer description of physical frequency. In other words, if it is possible to identify higher-order transformations and invariants in sound patterns that systematically correspond to salient psychological dimensions, then the tempting hypothesis that people construct these subjective dimensions can be resisted. Instead we appeal to objectively specified frequency invariants that define the shape of these configurations.

THE LOGARITHMIC SPIRAL

How do we identify these higher-order sound invariants in a fashion that is rigorous and yet reestablishes a linkage between frequency and multiple pitch dimensions? In this chapter, we rely upon powerful mathematical tools that arise from group symmetries. Group symmetries specify higher-order transformations and invariants in many natural patterns. Here we introduce and use the symmetry group[1] of the logarithmic spiral (Jones, 1976) to identify sound invariants. As it turns out, this pattern captures the curvilinear aspects of pitch and also depicts the logarithmic relationship between frequency and common musical intervals. In short, it not only captures the circular component present in pitch but can also incorporate harmonic ratios.

A spiral analysis of the relationships between frequencies can illustrate some of the power that symmetry theory holds for identifying transformations and invariants in stimulus patterns. Symmetry theory is the mathematical language of invariances that is widely used in physics and biology to describe the form of natural patterns. It is a language that allows the specification of what remains invariant within a pattern during some transformation. In fact, a set of transformations that keeps something constant can form a symmetry group. Properly, symmetry groups are formed when a set of transformations (rules) meet certain requirements. First, when two rules are combined, the resulting rule must also be in the set (closure). Second, the combination of rules must be associative. Third, there must be one member that functions as an identity rule, the application of which leaves things unchanged. Finally, each rule must have an inverse in the set.

The clock array of Fig. 10.1 can illustrate these properties. Here is shown a finite set of rules for moving around the circular array. This movement can be expressed by either of two sets of rules: (1) Arc length rules, N^j ($j = \mp 0 \pm 1 \ldots \pm 12$), accomplish the movements by shifting through 12 equal arc lengths; (2) Rotation rules, $k\theta$ where $\theta = 30°$ and ($k = +1, \ldots, +12$), accomplish the movements by shifting through 12 equal polar angles. It can be easily shown that this set of angles along with an addition operation satisfies the

---

[1]The term symmetry group as used here emphasizes those groups that deal with transformations of geometric objects.

A CLOCK ARRAY

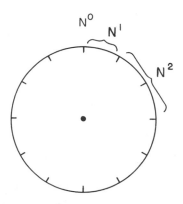

N^j are rotation rules

FIG. 10.1. A clock array illustrating rotation rules N^j. Not shown are corresponding polar angles, θ_j, that form a group under which the circular form is preserved.

required group properties. The combination, or addition, of any two angles in the set results in an angle which is also in the set ($10° + 20° = 30°$ or $30° + 60° = 90°$); the summation of two angles is associative; $360°$ serves as an identity rule because rotation through $360°$ leads back to the same point on the array. Finally each angle has an inverse: A rotation through $30°$ can be negated by a rotation through $330°$.

Together these rules form a particular symmetry group, often referred to as the cyclic group with modulus 12 or simply C_{12}. It has many applications in nature (Weyl, 1952). More recently it has been used to describe certain musical invariants that arise from the chromatic scale (Balzano, 1978, 1980, and this volume; Budden, 1972).

These mathematics are useful not only because they permit identification of certain compelling regularities within natural patterns, but also because they allow concise summaries of these regularities. The summaries are given by *generators* of a symmetry group. Often the entire set of transformations can be summarized by one or two rules, called the group's generators. In the clock array, for example, a generator rule is simply $\theta = 30°$. All other rules are $k\theta$ where k is an integer.

The symmetry group of Fig. 10.1 is a finite group of rotations. Now imagine transforming this group to an infinite group by allowing for infinitely small rotations. Also imagine that with each rotation, whatever its extent, there's a

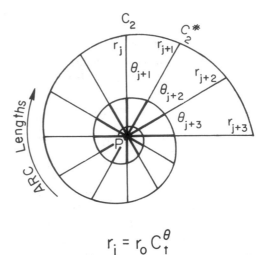

FIG. 10.2. A logarithmic spiral with equal polar angles, θ_j, and corresponding radii, r_j, that increase in length (note line thickness) as spiral unwinds.

$$r_j = r_0 C_\uparrow^\theta$$

proportional expansion of the circle so that the circle gradually widens in diameter as rotations increase. These motions in your imagination have created a logarithmic spiral! It is shown in Fig. 10.2. This pattern has intrigued mathematicians since its discovery by Descartes in 1638 (cf. Hambidge, 1920).

A logarithmic spiral actually arises from two sorts of transformations applied to the motion of a point with respect to a fixed reference point. One kind of transformation is a rotation about the fixed point, as found in the clock array, this transformation will create a circular path. The other transformation is a continuous length expansion of the radius of this circular path. (This involves a ratio expansion or a dilation transformation.) If a continuous rotation about a center point of a circle with initial radius, r_0, is combined with a regular dilation, the logarithmic spiral results.

THE SPIRAL AND FREQUENCY RELATIONSHIPS

The spiral pattern has special meaning for understanding transformations of sounds and sound invariants. One way of conceiving of the pattern, in fact, serves to highlight some potential parallels between ecological optics and ecological acoustics. Recall that the spiral shape is actually created by sets of *motions*. In this respect it suggests a basis for conceiving of sound transformations and invariants in terms of motions in much the way relative motion patterns in the flow fields of ecological optics have been conceived. Transformations of optic flow and higher-order motion ratios are critical in ecological optics. It is possible that some parallels to these distinctions operate in the acoustic domain.

A tempting candidate for summarizing such acoustic features is the spiral set of transformations and invariants. With respect to sound patterns, consider the simplest case of two harmonic (sine) tones. It is well known that each tone can be described conventionally as having a circular motion with uniform angular velocity, ω_i. This harmonic motion for a tone of frequency f_i has angular velocity given by the standard formula: $\omega_i = 2\pi f_i$. A relative motion pattern is created whenever two (or more) tones are considered. If we consider simply a pair of tones, for example, their difference in harmonic motions, $\omega_i - \omega_j$, is also expressible as a frequency difference: $2\pi(f_i - f_j)$. The point is, however, that the periodicities commonly associated with tonal frequency differences do arise from harmonic motions.

Motion differences between pairs of sounds, however, are essentially one dimensional; that is, they emphasize the additive or subtractive qualities associated with transforming one frequency into another along a single continuum defined by harmonic motion. Thus, the motion difference between a pair of tones can, from one perspective, be seen as a basis for describing frequency in terms of a unidimensional continuum, the description essentially underlying the mel scale.

There is a different perspective one can take even on the simple differences between harmonic motions. This perspective casts linear changes as motion transformations that carry one sine tone into another relative to some fixed reference point. In other words, the motion difference reflects only part of the important information available to a listener: the transforming part. This perspective is encouraged by the spiral analyses wherein tonal differences are conceived as change and tonal ratios as nonchange. Thus, there exists transformational information that specifies linear frequency change and there exists invariant information that specifies ratio-invariant information.

Motion ratios between sounds, as portrayed by the spiral, ultimately (we show) lead to rich partitionings of frequency relationships that underlie musical patterns and multidimensional analyses of pitch. It should be evident, moreover, that the ratio of two sine motions (relative to a common zero point) is also a frequency ratio: $\omega_i/\omega_j = 2\pi f_i/2\pi f_j = f_i/f_j$. These ratios function as salient invariants across transformations of tonal pairs of different linear extents, according to the spiral.

The major point then is that the spiral reconciles both the linear transformation of a harmonic motion as change and frequency ratios as nonchange. Furthermore, it is important to note from this discussion that there are interesting parallels between the way in which transformation and invariant information is conceived in ecological optics and the underlying rationale expressed for sound patterns by the spiral. The nature of the spiral permits us to describe sine tone relationships either as motions or as frequencies. The more common practice has been to refer to a tone's frequency, and we shall conform to this convention in discussing musical pitch relationships expressed by the spiral.

The spiral pattern of relative motions that springs from a given center (fixed reference point) can be aptly expressed in terms of rotations and expansions. In fact, it is useful to note that there are two limiting cases of the spiral: (1) When the dilation transformation has a ratio equal to one, then the spiral reduces to a circle. This case, we see shortly, describes purely chromatic information between two frequencies; and (2) when the rotation transformation is set to zero, the spiral collapses into a straight line with expansions along the line corresponding to the dilation (i.e., magnification) ratio. This case reflects largely the tone height information between a pair of tones.

In order to illustrate just how the relationship between frequencies contains this wealth of information, it is important to be more specific about the logarithmic spiral itself (Hahn & Jones, 1981; Weyl, 1952). This spiral is a pattern that can be described by the group of transformations that leave the shape of the pattern invariant (Weyl, 1952). This group involves rotations and dilations that can be summarized by a single compound generator.[2] This group generator is $c_t^{j\theta}$ and it consists of two important parameters, namely θ and c_t. The θ parameter represents the generative component arising from rotations, and the c_t parameter represents the generative component arising from dilations. The standard formula for a logarithmic spiral incorporates these two generators of, respectively, rotation groups and dilation groups as parameters in a single compound generator as:

$$r_j = r_0 c_t^{j\theta} \tag{1}$$

where r_j represents the radius once a dilative rotation has transformed some point associated with radius r_0 through a total angle $j\theta$. For example, let c_t denote the dilation ratio corresponding to a rotation through 1 radian (cf. e.g., Coxeter, 1969; Yates, 1947). Then, if $j\theta = 2$ radian, c_t^2 is the ratio for an angle generated by two rotations of the basic angle θ; similarly c_t^3 represents the ratio for an angle of three radians.

The logarithmic spiral is a geometrical shape in two dimensions. In the most general case, the spiral, as it is summarized in Equation 1, can describe the relationship between any two arbitrarily selected sine components, relative to the origin, in terms of two generative parameters. This permits a highly economical description of potentially salient invariances in any sound pattern. The usefulness of this description is illustrated here for the special case of the equally tempered musical scale. However, it can be generalized to virtually any other musical

---

[2]The group that leaves the spiral pattern invariant is also called the "free group." It has a single generator in which the two terms θ and c_t are parameters. Hahn and Jones (1981), however, originally referred to these parameters as group generators. Technically speaking, when combined to form the compound generator of the "free group," they are no longer separate generators but function instead as parameters.

tuning system and to other sound relations (for a more detailed discussion, see Hahn & Jones, 1981).

Consider the case of the equally tempered musical scale, for this set of frequency relationships most simply illustrates some of the important features of the spiral analysis. According to this tuning system, the musical pitch of a tone bears a logarithmic relation to its frequency. Through the range of pure sine components (or fundamental frequencies of complex tones) from about 16.3 Hz (i.e., C_0 in the lowest octave) to at least 4,186 Hz (i.e., C_8 in the ninth octave) similar musical intervals exist if equivalent frequency ratios obtain. Octaves, which are the basic unit of the equally tempered scale, are fixed throughout by their 2/1 frequency ratio; within the octave 12 subjectively equal pitch intervals (semitones) were historically fixed, each defined by the frequency ratio of 1.0594. These basic semitone intervals sound much the same between two low tones (e.g., between C_0 and $C\#_0$) as between two corresponding higher tones (e.g., between C_4 and $C\#_4$). In general, for a semitone (ST), the change in frequencies, Δf, forms a constant ratio: $\Delta f/f = .05946 \ldots$. For any musical interval between two tones, the constant frequency ratio is automatically cast in terms of constant logarithmic intervals.

Underlying this logarithmic relationship of frequency to musical scales are the fundamental relationships given by *frequency differences* and *frequency ratios*. Both differences and ratios are meaningfully represented by the logarithmic spiral. To show this, let us assume (for simplicity) that sine frequencies are referenced from 0 Hz and that 0 Hz corresponds to the origin of the spiral. (In certain contexts, it is useful to consider other frequencies as functional tonal referents.) Then, a frequency *difference* between any two tones then is directly proportional to the arc length difference along the spiral's circumference. This arc-length difference depicts transformational distance in terms of frequency shape. A frequency *ratio* is also obtainable and is expressed in the spiral directly as a ratio of arc lengths. This ratio functions as a spiral invariant for it can remain the same despite magnification or minification of the particular arc lengths involved. Finally, this interpretation of frequency relations makes it simple to write the expression for frequency ratios of a given musical interval in terms of the group generator of the spiral pattern.

The mathematical properties of the logarithmic spiral that allow this simplification follow from considering various sets of equal polar rotations, θ, about a fixed center point, P, of the curve (Hambidge, 1920; Yates, 1947). Figure 10.2 shows those polar angles identified by radii r_j extending from the center point, P. An important property of the logarithmic spiral involves ratios of these radii and their relation, in turn, to arc-length ratios. Originally Descartes showed that if polar angles are equal, then lengths of successive radii will always be lawfully related in that their ratios will be constant. It can be shown for adjacent radii, r_j and r_{j+1}, that the ratio of radii is expressible in terms of the spiral's parameters:

$$r_{j+1}/r_j = c_t^\theta \qquad\qquad (2)$$

This sort of relationship is the stepping stone to identifying harmonic ratios as invariant aspects of a spiral representation of auditory frequency. The trick is this: The frequency difference between a pair of tones corresponds to arc length difference and ultimately arc length can be substituted for radii.

Figures 10.2 and 10.3 show how this works. In these representations of the spiral, we have designated equal polar angles outlined by radii leading to the 12 notes of the chromatic scale (e.g., C_0, $C\#_0$, D_0, etc. $\cdots$ in the first octave and so

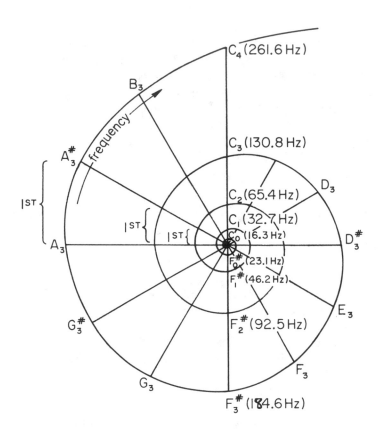

Pitch Spiral

FIG. 10.3.   The logarithmic spiral applied to musical pitch relationships. Frequency is shown as arc length; tone chroma relates to the circular dimensions; and tone height to the linearly expanding radii.

forth). The center point in both (p in Fig. 10.2) is the fixed reference point of the curve. Arc length is defined from P to any point X_j on the curve and is denoted PX_j.

For a logarithmic spiral, this arc length depends in part on a constant angle that the radius, r_j, forms with a line tangent to X_j. Ultimately, because this angle is constant, a property of the spiral is that the ratio of arc lengths between any two points on the curve, X_j and X_{j+m}, from a reference point, is the same as the ratio of corresponding radii:

$$\frac{PX_{j+m}}{PX_j} = \frac{r_{j+m}}{r_j} \tag{3}$$

The points X_j and X_{j+m} function, of course, to identify different frequencies relative to 0 Hz. For example, PC_2 and $PC\#_2$ correspond to two different arc lengths that identify tones in the second octave with respect to a fixed point, P. Finally, however, we seek an expression that relates frequencies in terms of the spiral's generators. This simply involves combining Equation 3 with Equation 1:

$$\frac{PX_{j+m}}{PX_j} = \frac{r_0 c_t^{(j+m)\theta}}{r_0 c_t^{j\theta}} \tag{4}$$

$$\frac{PX_{j+m}}{PX_j} = c_t^{m\theta} \tag{5}$$

This shows that the ratio of arc lengths is strictly a function of the dilation parameter raised to some multiple of the rotation parameter, where the multiple pertains to the difference in angles involved (i.e., to $m\theta$). For a given value of c_t and θ, ratios of arc lengths are fixed whenever the difference angle, m, is constant. Thus, though the total angles involved $(j+m)\theta$, $j\theta$ (in Equation 4) may involve several complete revolutions and so be greater than 360°, the ratios formed by pairs of obstensibly different frequencies will be equivalent whenever the m value involved in each ratio is the same.

Finally, we can determine the actual value of c_t for the equally tempered musical scale. The identification of a semitone with one of 12 equal polar angles yields $\theta = 360°/12 = 30°$, which is .52359 radians. Because the ratio of two tones a semitone apart is 1.05946, we can solve Equation 5 for c_t. This yields a c_t value of $c_t = 1.1166$.

What all of this means is that the spiral pattern expresses higher-order relationships between sine tones in two ways. In the first place, the simple difference between any pair of tones is expressed as an arc length difference (e.g., point X_j is carried into point X_{j+m} on the curve). In the second place, there is a basis for expressing the ratio relationship between the same two points directly in terms of the generator of the logarithmic spiral (i.e., as $c_t^{m\theta}$). The parameters c_t and θ of this generator reflect the spiral's dilations and rotations, respectively. They summarize the nature of invariant information that contributes to the ratio property.

In particular, they reflect invariant information about tone height and tone chroma. Thus, they address different dimensions entering into pitch.

To further illustrate the applicability of the spiral, let PX_j be the frequency of tone C_4 (261.6 Hz) and let PX_{j+m} be that of the tone an octave above, namely C_5 (523.09 Hz). The resulting harmonic ratio, of course, is 2.00. However, we can show that the generator value of $c_t = 1.1166$ of the spiral when combined with $\theta = 6.2831$ for an angle of 360° will also yield the desired frequency ratio. This is given by Equation 5:

$$\frac{523.09}{261.6} = 1.1166^{(6.2831)} = 2.00$$

This adaptation of the spiral pattern suggests that the ratio generator, c_t, is itself a frequency ratio. And because frequency is the reciprocal of a time period, the c_t value may be considered a ratio of time periods of two sinusoids, hence the subscript, t (cf. Jones, 1976). It is useful to exmphasize that the ratio generator is also readily expressible as a time ratio for it highlights the fact that harmonic intervals may be considered as microrhythmic constancies.

It should be clear that the mathematics of the logarithmic spiral do indeed summarize frequency relationships between pairs of pure tones. In particular, Equation 5 tells us some important things about the spiral and its adaptability to higher-order invariants in sound. In the first place, Equation 5 identifies harmonic ratios as invariants that are preserved under spiral transformations. In other words, it expresses the fact that the relationship between $C\sharp_0$ and C_0 will be the same as that between $G\sharp_0$ and G_0 or between $C\sharp_5$ and C_5. Furthermore, Equation 5 indicates that the constancy underlying these invariances depends on the two group parameters, c_t and θ.

Let's consider these two components of the group generator a bit further. They reflect an underlying bidimensionality in the frequency ratio between two tones. The dilation parameter, c_t, reflects the contribution of tone height; and the rotation parameter, θ, reflects the chroma component. The underlying bidimensionality of the spiral pattern is also evident in Fig. 10.3. Radii expand in length as they identify higher-pitched members of a given octave class; holding tone chroma constant, for example, C_0, C_1, C_2, etc. are identified. These frequencies mark off ever-increasing radial segments from the spiral's still center point. The polar angle parameter, which underlies chroma, is also apparent in Fig. 10.3. It is shown for an angle of 30° here but it may take on other values. In this case, the generating angle traces out the tones comprising the equally tempered musical scale. In short, Fig. 10.3, along with Equations 1 through 5, suggests that spiral symmetries capture several fundamental aspects of pitch: harmonic ratios, tone height, and tone chroma.

These applications of the spiral emphasize its value in describing sound invariants that have special meaning in music. They only scratch the surface of the potential of the spiral for capturing important invariants in various sound patterns. Even in musical sound patterns there is much more to be said about applications of the spiral. In a more extended treatment of this topic, Hahn and Jones (1981) have shown that analysis of the full group of spiral motions leads to parsimonious ways of identifying different musical tuning systems, various microtonal scales, and salient harmonic relationships. In fact, this analysis also bears upon an important musical controversy between adherents of just musical ratios (i.e., frequency ratios based on simple integers) and those proposing equally tempered ratios (cf. Backus, 1969). It turns out that the spiral pattern itself supplies the basis for this controversy in that it contains higher order invariants specific to both kinds of tuning systems. For example, the simple "just" ratios of just scales conform to proportions of the golden rectangles tangent to a logarithmic spiral, whereas the ratios of equally tempered scales exploit the spiral's equiangular properties.

Another important topic, also considered in greater detail by Hahn and Jones (1981), involves discontinuous subgroups[3] that are embedded within the larger continuous set of spiral transformations. Briefly, a discontinuous subgroup of the spiral is one in which the sets of spiral transformations are based upon iteration of a particular angle (i.e., subgroups are defined respectively by $\theta = 30°$, or $60°$, or $110°$, etc.). Table 10.1 summarizes the results of this sort of analysis. It shows that all the common musical intervals of the (in this case) equally tempered musical scale can be derived from the spiral's ratio generator ($c_t = 1.1166$) with application of the appropriate rotation generator, θ. Each of these intervals identifies a subgroup based upon particular invariant ratio values. Hence, we find groups of thirds, fourths, fifths, etc., very simply specified according to spiral parameters. Also, in this context, it may be possible to consider the meaning of different reference points or origins of the spiral for these may have special meaning for understanding tonal musical relationships.

Finally, because we have chosen here to illustrate applications of the spiral largely in terms of musical relationships, and, in particular, with respect to the equally tempered tuning system, a word is in order about the thesis that musical scales are purely arbitrary conventions. This is a commonly held thesis, although it is by no means universally accepted. To be sure, scales are conventions imposed by fashion (among other things). But they are not arbitrary. The decision to build a tuning system or a musical scale is never unrelated to perceivable sound invariants. Hahn and Jones (1981) have suggested that controversies about musical scales have arisen over when and how to use these invariants, not over whether they exist. The description arising from the logarithmic spiral is an infinitely rich one that offers an array of higher-order invariants from which to derive musical scales. It therefore provides the basis for the many heated controversies over musical scales that have dotted the musical literature.

---

[3]A subgroup is a set of transformations within the larger set that itself satisfies group properties. Within the infinite group of transformations, subgroups are also infinite.

TABLE 10.1
Harmonic Ratios Generated by a Spiral Analysis
General Expression: $r_j = r_0\, c_t^{\theta}$

Musical Interval	N^j	Polar Angle, θ		Equal Tempered Harmonic Ratios Equation 5 $c_t^{\theta} = 1.1166^{\theta}$
		deg.	rad.	
Unison	N^0	0°	0	1.000^a
Octave	N^{11}	360°	6.28319	2.000^a
Semitone	N^1	30°	.52359	1.0594
Whole Tone	N^2	60°	1.04719	1.1224
Perfect fifth	N^7	210°	3.66519	1.4981^a
Diminished fifth	N^6	180°	3.14159	1.4140
Perfect fourth	N^5	150°	2.61799	1.3347^b
Major third	N^4	120°	2.09439	1.2598^b
Minor third	N^3	90°	1.57079	1.1891^b
Major sixth	N^9	270°	4.71238	1.6815^a
Minor sixth	N^8	240°	4.18879	1.5872^a
Minor seventh	N^{10}	300°	5.23598	1.7815
Major seventh	N^{11}	330°	5.75958	1.8875

[a] Approximations to members of the Fibonacci sequence.
[b] Approximate octave inversions to members of the Fibonacci sequence.

CONCLUSION

The logarithmic spiral is a motion pattern that yields a rich, yet precise, description of sound relationships. It portrays various transformations of one harmonic motion into another and permits definition of special invariant frequency ratios that hold across different sound transformations. An important feature of this analysis is that the parameters of the spiral pattern not only summarize its ratio-invariant properties, they also capture psychologically salient aspects of musical pitch. These parameters, through contributing to the generator of the spiral, thus capture, among other things, chromatic and tone height information that exists in relation between tones.

The advantages that accompany this new approach are sufficient to encourage some reconsideration of habitual modes of description. Indeed, at the highest level, this approach raises epistemological questions that are worth reexamining from time to time; that is, "Do stimuli that we have routinely conceived of in one, perhaps limited, way actually reflect definable natural patterns when viewed from a different angle?" A thorough discussion of such a question inevitably evokes a long-standing philosophical debate between schools of realism and idealism. Realism assumes there is a world independent of the perceiver, a view that Garner (1974), in a good discussion of these issues, indicates is compatible with Gibson's theory (1966) and to some extent his own. Idealism lends itself to a constructionist view in which reality is invented in the mind of the perceiver. To the extent that a stimulus description is devoid of information that can explain responding, one is forced to a constructionist position.

Emerging evidence, particularly from multidimensional scaling analysis, indicates that behavior is indeed lawfully influenced by information about tone height, chroma, and diatonic relationships. To accommodate these data, theory builders are faced with a familiar dilemma. Does performance reflect the pickup of invariants in sound patterns or does it reflect one's invention of subjective dimensions? So long as tools for describing the stimulus mask the fact that information relevant to such behavior exists in the sound pattern, then a constructionist position that emphasizes invention becomes the only tenable one. In this regard, habitual modes of stimulus descriptions yield tools, such as linear or simple logarithmic frequency algorithms, that both reflect and encourage a philosophy of idealism in theory building. If the position of realism in theory building is to be explored at all, then psychologists require new tools, tools that can illuminate both transformations and higher order invariants in sound patterns. The group of spiral transformations is such a tool.

The spiral analysis bears significant implications for understanding not only psychological scaling but also for placing the results of MDS into a larger theoretical context that includes perceptual learning; that is, if this stimulus description is correct, then sound patterns supply an infinite array of ratio invariants that are configured in special ways. A listener's skill in attending to one or another subgroup of relationships will depend on perceptual learning as well as on the way a particular task instructs one to "listen for" certain things; that is, it is possible that people first learn to attend to or "listen for" simple frequency differences and/or to tone height. This may lead people to differentiate initially between instruments or sound sources on the basis of their different frequency ranges, or to attend initially to high- and low-pitch changes involving tone height within a melody. Perhaps it is only later in learning that people learn to detect the various and specific ratio invariants that specify chroma differences and properties of musical scales. Certainly there is evidence that naive listeners give relatively more weight to tone height information than to chroma and diatonicity whereas sophisticated listeners give more weight to chroma and diatonicity. Perceptual learning may thus reflect gradual attunement to certain more subtle spiral parameters.

Clearly, the information that influences pitch judgments does change in amount and nature with learning. Ultimately, this means that scaling solutions may give us time slices of a dynamic learning process: They tell us to what information a listener is currently attending. Furthermore, this general argument suggests that scaling solutions of musical stimuli are not limited to merely two, or three, or even five psychological dimensions. The number and kind of invariances attended will depend on a listener's acquired attunement and the task posed.

It is also true that scaling techniques, both traditional and modern, may tell us more about how a particular psychophysical task "instructs" one to attend to one or another invariant at a particular stage of learning than they tell us about purely mental inventions. If this is so, then perhaps some unresolved controversies in the scaling tradition can be profitably evaluated from this perspective. For example, is it possible that the fractionation tasks which have given us the mel scale "instruct" the listener to attend largely to simple frequency differences between tones? And is it possible that the impoverished contexts of other psychoacoustic tasks force attention to (e.g.,) summation and difference tones of sine components because these contexts lack multiple sound changes that focus attention on the ratio-invariant features of sounds? Conversely, is it the case in pairwise judgment tasks within a tonal context of several frequencies that attending is more likely to focus upon the musical ratios preserved over these changes? These are questions that illustrate the need to contemplate the functional specificities of transformational information and invariant information for different tasks and contexts.

Finally, we should stress that in advocating the use of spiral symmetries as tools for stimulus descriptions in various tasks we are not claiming that people pick up these spiral invariants in an "error-free" fashion. Indeed, we know they do not. In octave judgment tasks, subjective octave ratios are often greater than the physical, 2/1 ratio particularly with higher frequencies (i.e., octave "stretch"; Hahn, 1980; see also Dowling, 1978, for a good discussion). And musical intervals themselves may be categorically perceived in certain contexts (e.g., Burns & Ward, 1978; Siegel & Siegel, 1977). Furthermore, people vary greatly in their ability to respond to different invariant features of world patterns both as a result of natural limitations and cultural acclimatization. One cannot deny that what individuals perceive rarely distills perfectly the available invariances.

In summary, by outlining a description of physical frequency relationships that parsimoniously embeds a variety of information about tonal relations, we have established a basis for new interpretations of psychophysical scales as well as for understanding the acquisition of skilled musical percepts. Configurations revealed by scaling experiments need not be considered mental inventions. Instead they may reflect the way training and task guides attention to lawful invariants embedded within a natural pattern.

REFERENCES

Attneave, F., & Olson, R. K. (1971). Pitch as a medium: A new approach to psychophysical scaling. *American Journal of Psychology, 84,* 147–165.

Bachem, A. (1954). Time factors in relative and absolute pitch determination. *Journal of the Acoustical Society of America, 26,* 751–753.

Backus, J. (1969). *The acoustical foundations of music.* New York: Norton.

Baird, J. W. (1917). Memory for absolute pitch: Studies in psychology. In *Titchener commemorative volume,* Worcester.

Balzano, G. (1977). On the basis of similarity of musical intervals: A chronometric analysis. *Journal of the Acoustical Society of America, 61,* 551.

Balzano, G. J. (1978, April). The structural uniqueness of the diatonic order. In R. N. Shepard (Chair), *Cognitive atructure of musical pitch.* Symposium presented at the annual meeting of the Western Psychological Association, San Francisco.

Balzano, G. J. (1980). The group theoretic description of twelvefold and microtonal pitch systems. *Computer Music Journal, 4*(4), 66–84.

Boring, E. G. (1942). *Sensation and perception in the history of experimental psychology.* New York: Appleton–Century.

Budden, F. J. (1972). *The fascination of groups.* London: Cambridge University Press.

Burns, E. M., & Ward, W. D. (1978). Categorical perception—phenomenon or epiphenomenon: Evidence from experiments in the perception of melodic musical intervals. *Journal of the Acoustical Society of America, 53,* 456–468.

Coxeter, H. S. M. (1969). Introduction to geometry, (2nd ed.). New York: Wiley.

Dowling, W. J. (1978). Scale and contour: Two components of a theory of memory for melodies. *Psychological Review, 85,* 351–354.

Garner, W. R. (1974). *The processing of information and structure.* Potomac, MD: Lawrence Erlbaum Associates.

Gibson, J. J. (1966). *The senses considered as perceptual systems.* Boston: Houghton–Mifflin.

Gibson, J. J. (1979). *The ecological approach to visual perception.* Boston: Houghton Mifflin.

Hahn, J. (1980). *A subjective representation of frequency and octave stretch.* Unpublished Ph.D. Dissertation, Ohio State University.

Hahn, J., & Jones, M. R. (1981). Invariants in auditory frequency relations. *Scandinavian Journal of Psychology, 22,* 129–144.

Hambidge, J. (1920). *Dynamic symmetry.* New Haven, CT: Yale University Press.

Humphreys, L. F. (1939). Generalization as a function of method of reinforcement. *Journal of Experimental Psychology, 25,* 361–372.

Jones, M. R. (1976). Time, our lost dimension: Toward a new theory of perception, attention, and memory. *Psychological Review, 83,* 323–355.

Jones, M. R. (1981). Music as a stimulus for psychological motion: Part I. Some determinants of expectancies. *Psychomusicology, 1,* 34–51.

Jones, M. R. (1982). Music as a stimulus for psychological motion: Part II. An expectancy model. *Psychomusicology, 2,* 1–13.

Kallman, H. J., & Massaro, D. W. (1979). Tone chroma is functional in melody recognition. *Perception & Psychophysics, 26,* 32–36.

Krumhansl, C. L. (1979). The psychological representation of musical pitch in a tonal context. *Cognitive Psychology, 11,* 346–374.

Levelt, W. J. M., van de Geer, J. P., & Plomp, R. (1966). Triadic comparisons of musical intervals. *British Journal of Mathematical and Statistical Psychology, 19,* 163–179.

Révész, G. (1954). *Introduction to the psychology of music.* Norman, OK: University of Oklahoma Press.

Ruckmick, C. A. (1929). A new classification of tonal qualities. *Psychological Review, 36,* 172–180.

Shepard, R. N. (1964). Circularity in judgments of relative pitch. *Journal of the Acoustical Society of America, 36,* 2346–2353.

Shepard, R. N. (1974). Representation of structure in similarity data: Problems and prospects. *Psychometrika, 39,* 373–422.

Shepard, R. N. (1979). Psychophysical complementarity. In M. Kubovy & J. R. Pomerantz (Eds.), *Perceptual organization.* Hillsdale, NJ: Lawrence Erlbaum Associates.

Siegel, J. A., & Siegel, W. (1977). Categorical perception of tonal intervals: Musicians can't *sharp* from *falt. Perception & Psychophysics, 21,* 399–407.

Stevens, S. S., & Volkmann, J. (1940). The relation of pitch to frequency: A revised scale. *American Journal of Psychology, 53,* 329–353.

Stevens, S. S., Volkmann, J., & Newman, E. B. (1937). A scale for the measurement of the psychological magnitude pitch. *Journal of the Acoustical Society of America, 8,* 185–190.

Ward, W. D. (1954). Subjective musical pitch. *Journal of the Acoustical Society of America, 26,* 369–380.

Ward, W. D. (1970). Musical perception. In J. V. Tobias (Ed.), *Foundations of modern auditory theory* (Vol. 1). New York: Academic Press.

Weyl, H. (1952). *Symmetry.* Princeton, NJ: Princeton University Press.

Yates, R. C. (1947). *A handbook of curves and their properties.* Ann Arbor, MI: Edwards Brothers.

Music Perception as Detection Of Pitch–Time Constraints

Gerald J. Balzano
University of California, San Diego

CONTENTS

Introduction: Group Theory and Musical Pitch and Time
Experiments on the Detection of Pitch and Time Constraints
Realism and Musical Perception
Epilog: Music Perception or Cognition?

INTRODUCTION: GROUP THEORY AND MUSICAL PITCH AND TIME

The theory and experiments to be presented in this chapter are consequences of a view of music as *constrained pitch–time structure*. Perceiving music is regarded as a process of detecting constraints; more properly, a process of detecting the structures created, or made perceptually available, by the presence of such constraints. I begin by sketching the theoretical approach to music taken here, for it departs from traditional approaches in many important ways. After the theory I describe some experiments using random "pseudomelodies," pitch–time arrays if you will, with varying kinds and degrees of constraint. The primary question posed in these experiments is, is the presence of such constraints detectable by listeners? The listeners here are primarily unschooled in music. None of the 60-odd listeners employed in the experiments were music majors, no screening of subjects for musical ability took place, and no subject's data was thrown out. After the description of the experiments, which I feel are really just a first step, I try to elaborate the general view of music and music perception a little further.

To begin with a question: What makes music a unique stimulus? Alternately, what is distinctive about musical information? To be sure, music is usually accompanied by the presence of all sorts of sound-producing instruments that do not generally appear in nonmusical settings. But music can also be created—indeed, was probably *first* created, both in the life of the species and the life of the individual—by an unaccompanied human voice. Recognizing this, we are led to ask, what distinguishes music from human speech? It cannot be mere verbal content, because music with lyrics has that. Our answer, it seems to me, must lie in the presence of certain rather specific constraints in the global selection of pitch and time values. A spoken sentence will be delivered with an "intonation contour" and "rhythm" that may be at least superficially likened to the pitch and time variation that is characteristic of melody. The difference is that in speech, pitch and time values may vary continuously, whereas in music only a small number of determinately related pitch and time values may occur. There are two points here: the reduction from an infinite to an (in principle) finite number of values, and the presence of specific relationships among these values. Call the first the *quantal* property of musical pitch and time, and call the second the *generative* property. Foreshadowing briefly, the first experiment examines quantal and generative properties of musical pitch and time.

Figure 11.1 illustrates these properties, using idealized long-term frequency distributions of pitch occurrences (pitch plotted as log frequency), although the graph could be adapted to make the same point about time and temporal structure in music. The first distribution is meant to be unconstrained; perhaps the result of 10 minutes' worth of 10 people talking. The second is more like 10 minutes' worth of 10 people singing. In the second distribution we find within an octave

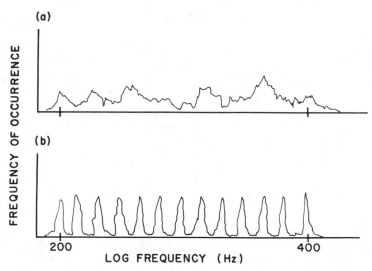

FIG. 11.1. Schematic frequency distributions for one octave of pitch (log frequency); (a) No constraints on pitch, (b) Pitches constrained to be interrelated by transformations of the group C_{12}, with the octave as an equivalence relation.

12 specific peaks of pitch activity, more or less equally spaced. This corresponds to the musical division of the octave into 12 pitch places, characteristic of Western music and any music playable on instruments like clarinets, pianos, and trumpets. There is nothing controversial or even contestable about these constraints; as I have said, clear evidence of their existence can be found in the very design of musical instruments. Some instruments achieve these pitch places through the operation of a small-integer frequency ratio principle, others through a principle of equal log-frequency division. What seems clear is that a general theory should have to encompass both.

This last point is important, for it seems to mandate against the classic Pythagorean, Helmholtzian manner of viewing pitch relationships (Helmholtz, 1885/1954). According to that view, the fundamental pitch relationships—the musical intervals—are viewed primarily as *ratios* of small integers, mathematical objects of the form $2^p 3^q 5^r$, with the perfect 5th, classically defined as a 3:2 ratio, being $2^{-1}3^1$, for example. There have been endless discussions and heated arguments about what is wrong with this formal approach, but from the present point of view its main problem is that it is insufficiently general. For at the level of frequency ratios, we must regard the pitch system realized on a piano as different from that realized on a guitar; more abstractly, we must regard the three classic intonation schemes, Just, Pythagorean, and Equal Temperament (cf. Barbour, 1953), as different. But because guitars and pianos can and do play music together, and because one can generally play a piano melody on a guitar and vice versa, I would say that from the standpoint of a pitch system, we are more concerned with the sense in which Pythagorean, Just, and ET are the *same*—different tuning schemes, but for the same pitch system. Given that the ratios used in the tuning schemes are different, they cannot address the level of this fundamental commonality; small-number ratios do not capture the invariances we are interested in.

The essential, invariant property of our pitch system that I focus on is its approximately symmetrical twelvefold division of the octave. Formally, the pitch manifold may be generated from two relations, an *order relation* and an *equivalence relation*. The order relation is the asymmetric transitive relation of higher than/lower than, and gives rise to the so-called "dimension of tone height." When men and women sing a tune together, the women's voices are generally "higher" in just the sense meant here; the pitches sung by the two sexes differ on the height dimension. The equivalence relation is the octave, which sorts the values of tone height into a cyclic arrangement of *pitch classes* constituting the so-called "dimension of tone chroma" (Revesz, 1954; Shepard, 1964; see also Chapter 10, this volume). Because men and women naturally sing a tune an octave apart, they generally do *not* differ on the chroma dimension. If they did, one would say they are singing the tune "in different keys." Were it not for chroma, musical instruments with nonoverlapping (height) ranges could never play the "same" melody together.

As I have suggested, the pitch manifold is not yet in its properly musical form until it has been generatively quantized. This amounts to defining a "unit" interval, some specific log-frequency difference, and literally generating points by iterated application of the unit transformation. Reflection of the (octave) equivalence relation in the system is accomplished by choosing the unit interval such that it divides the octave evenly and thus arrives at the same pitch-class points in each octave. The content of the system may then be characterized by a finite number of pitch classes—alternatively, a finite (and equal) number of pitch-class transformations, "musical intervals," that are mathematically dual to the set of pitch classes. This set of points/transformations constitutes what is known as a *group*. In the particular case of the Western/European pitch system, the generating interval is the semitone, a logarithmic $1/12$ of an octave, and the associated group is the cyclic group of order 12, or C_{12}. A picture of the space of group element relations is shown in Fig. 11.2. The elements, which should be considered, dually, to be *either* the 12 pitch classes or the 12 musical intervals, are arranged in a simple chroma-like ordering.

To go into the full justification and derivation of the group structure for our pitch system is not possible here (cf. Balzano, 1978; Balzano, 1982; and particularly Balzano, 1980). I, however, illustrate some striking characteristics of the isomorphisms of C_{12} vis-a-vis the structure of music as it has evolved in the

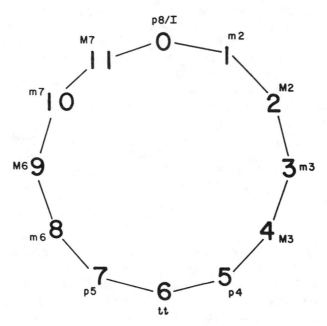

FIG. 11.2.   First isomorphism of C_{12}, generated by the semitone or the interval minor 2nd (m2, "1"). A space of melodic relations.

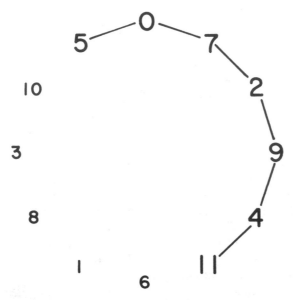

FIG. 11.3. Second isomorphism of C_{12}, generated by the perfect 5th (p^5, "7") interval; a "circle of fifths." A space of scale/key relations. A diatonic scale {0, 2, 4, 5, 7, 9, 11} is represented by the connected elements. When this scale (region) is transposed (translated) up a perfect 5th (30° clockwise), the resulting scale (region) is of the same form and shares six of seven elements.

Western world. The essential story these isomorphisms have to tell is that the arrangement in Fig. 11.2 is only one of three structurally identical (isomorphic = "same structure") arrangements, none of which has any inherently privileged status over the others. And most Western music calling itself "tonal" makes available information intrinsic to all three arrangements.

The first isomorphism, then, is represented in Fig. 11.2. The second isomorphism, shown in Fig. 11.3, is a space with the same outward appearance as the first, but a different ordering of elements, and thereby a different definition of "closeness." This is none other than the cycle of fifths, familiar to most musicians. When music is based on diatonic scales, size-7 pitch sets dating back several thousand years and still overwhelmingly used today, the cycle of fifths becomes a space of key relations, such that "close" keys are represented by close locations on the cycle. It is no coincidence that diatonic scales are *directly constituted* from the order given in this space. As Fig. 11.3 shows, a diatonic scale is a size-7 subregion of the fifth-generated "cycle of fifths" space, and this design principle insures that any two C_{12}-related transformations of a diatonic scale—in everyday musical parlance, any two transpositions—will display an overlap of pitch class content that is a function of transformational distance in fifths. There is no mere convention involved here: The diatonic scale is the only size-7 pitch set that exhibits such highly differentiated and orderly overlap relations, and the cycle of fifths is the only arrangement (besides our original "cycle of semitones," Fig. 11.2) that permits such a complete ordering.

The third isomorphism gives rise to a space that has a very different superficial appearance from the first two, because it is a Cartesian product of two smaller cycles rather than one large cycle. A product of two cycles gives, not a sphere, but a torus, shown in Fig. 11.4a. Relationships on the torus are a little hard to see, so a common technique is to cut and unroll the torus, representing the cyclical aspect by periodic repetition of identical elements, representable on a plane like a "normal" Cartesian product space, shown in Fig. 11.4b. Once again there is a critically important musical pitch construct that is linked to the construction of the space, even though the latter is based on purely mathematical concerns. The construct here is that of the *triad,* particularly the pitch sets we call the major and minor triads, the building blocks of musical harmony. These triads can be seen as the primitive space-filling triangular shapes in this space, and are related to one another by 180° rotation. Moreover, if we lay such triangles alternately end to end in a manner that will span both axes of this *major-3rd × minor-3rd* product space, we return to our original point after generating, once again, precisely the seven pitches of a diatonic scale. Thus the diatonic scale is strongly implicated in the structure of both the "fifths space" of the second isomorphism and the "thirds space" of the third isomorphism.

How do these spaces operate in real music? My approach to this question has been to link up the three spaces with three different kinds or levels of constraint in tonal music. The space of *semitones* supplies a constraint that appears in even the simplest of music, guiding local note-to-note transitions and acting as the basic criterion for "smooth" or (more formally) "conjunct" melodic motion. Somewhat less locally, individual notes are constrained by membership in triads; the pitches of a melody may change although the underlying triad remains invariant. The triads themselves change more slowly in a piece of music, and here the space of *thirds* is the basis for triadic motion; in particular, major and minor triads that are third related (share an edge in thirds' space) are often treated as substitutable for one another, a relation not shared by more distant pairs of triads. Diatonic scales serve as an even more global context of constraint for triads, which may change but still leave the underlying scale or key invariant. Analogously, scales may change in the course of a musical piece but will do so even more slowly than triads, and much more slowly than single notes. When they do, it is the space of *fifths* that provides the basis for "near" and "far" movement. And, of course, underlying all three spaces, all three levels, and common to every one is the "globally invariant" constraint on pitch selection provided by the parent system C_{12}, which *never* changes in the course of a musical composition. To change the system would lead us into the world of microtonality, a fascinating subject into which I believe the group-theoretic approach provides some insights (Balzano, 1980), but into which we cannot delve here. The empirical research I describe looks for evidence that human

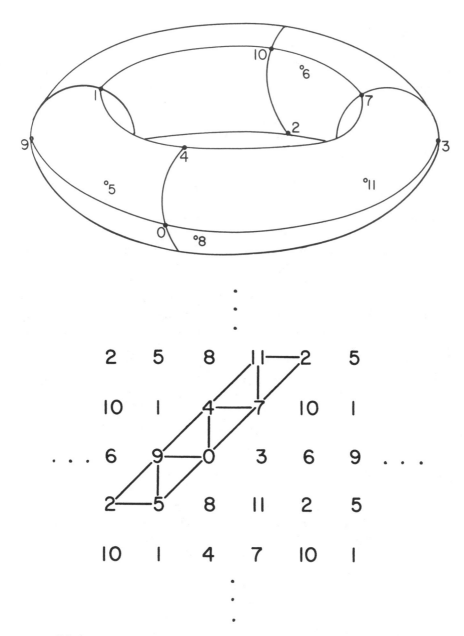

FIG. 11.4. Third isomorphism of C_{12}. Dual generators of this product space $C_3 \times C_4$ are the major 3rd (M3, "4") and the minor 3rd (m3, "3"). A space of chord relations. (Top) (a) Cyclic representation; two orthogonal cycles yield the shape of a torus. Unfilled circles represent points occluded by the surface of the torus as seen from this point of observation. (b) Rectilinear representation; con- nected elements constitute a diatonic scale {0, 2, 4, 5, 7, 9, 11} (compare Fig. 11.3), and triangles constitute major (e.g., {0, 4, 7}) and minor (e.g., {9, 0, 4}) triads. This is an "unwrapped" version of (a); every point with the same label (e.g., "10") should be considered the same point.

listeners have become perceptually attuned to the presence of C_{12} structure in pitch–time arrays, and to the additional constraint provided by restricting pitch selection according to closeness in fifths space. More than merely providing constraints, the structure of these spaces actually plays a significant role in determining how music fashioned from them *sounds* to a listener.

We now sketch briefly how this group-based approach handles time structure in music. Perhaps surprisingly, it is again finite cyclic groups that are at the core. Thus again we have an *order relation* and an *equivalence relation*. The order relation for time is simply that of earlier than/later than, but what is less obvious is that the musical *barline* induces an equivalence relation on time in much the same way as the octave does for pitch. Corresponding time points in each measure created by the barline are rendered equivalent; in particular, there is the distinctive timepoint, the initial one of each measure, called the "downbeat." In "Oh say can you see," the opening lyrics of *The Star-Spangled Banner*, "say" occurs earlier than "see" (order relation), but they each occur on beat #1 (the downbeat) of their respective measures. Metrical distinctions in music such as "strong beat" versus "weak beat" and "onbeat" versus "offbeat" are left invariant by this equivalence relation in much the same way as pitch classes like "C sharp" and "B flat" are left invariant by the octave relation.

Because of the arbitrary time length of a measure (in contrast to the apparently nonarbitrary size of the pitch modulus, the octave), the only reasonable way of quantizing time generatively is by using unit time intervals that evenly divide the measure. Indeed, the only way the time length called the measure can be created in a real musical event is by the presence of longer periodicities in a sequence of generated time points. Because the choice of number of time divisions need not become a fixed feature of a musical instrument (in contrast to the way 12 pitch divisions are ingrained in the structure of pianos and guitars), this number can also be varied freely, but musical usage in the West has seen primarily metrical divisions of two and three, and their powers and products. Thus we have duple, triple, and quadruple (2^2) meters. The pulses created by these divisions of a measure are themselves further subdivided by two or three, giving rise to the distinction between simple and compound meters. This process of subdividing time intervals (usually by two) can go on to create as many as four or even five levels of subdivision within a piece of music. Meters based not on two- or three-fold time divisions but on five- or seven-fold division of the measure do occur in Western music, but much less frequently. In contrast to pitch, it is not difficult to find rhythmic traditions in other cultures (e.g., African) that use more complex systems of time division more frequently than Westeners do. Interestingly enough, such cultures tend to use simpler pitch structures, as if in compensation for the temporal complexities. In Western music, uniform tendencies toward even divisions of time have rendered the mathematical concept of *subgroup* more important than the concept of *isomorphism* for understanding musical time. Isomorphisms point to multiplicities; in our culture we tend to see these as rhythmical *ambiguities*. More rhythmically adventurous cultures do indeed display rhythmic tendencies that are analogous to our Western pitch tendencies. As a striking example, there are a number of African drumming traditions (Pressing, 1980) that use both a twelvefold division of a "measure" and a basic 7-element rhythm pattern that is a strict time-analogue to a diatonic scale! Though the topic is of considerable interest, space limitations mandate a hasty move to the experiments themselves, which deal with only the simplest constraints on time structure.

EXPERIMENTS ON THE DETECTION OF PITCH AND TIME CONSTRAINTS

Two studies were done, with 31 subjects in the first and 34 in the second, all participating to fulfill course credit in the U. C. San Diego Psychology Department. Subjects were tested in groups of 8–15 in sessions lasting approximately 50 minutes. They heard 38 pairs of pseudomelodies, of which the first two were for practice and were not used in data analysis. The remaining 36 were divided up equally to test pitch constraints and time constraints, with pitch pairs and time pairs alternating from trial to trial. On a pitch pair, the two pseudomelodies used the identical rhythm (time structure) and differed only in type of pitch constraint; subjects were informed of this and told that they should base their judgment on pitch content only. The time pairs were analogous with the roles of the two variables reversed; for these, subjects were instructed to ignore pitch and base their judgments on the rhythm. As for the judgments themselves, they were reasonably straightforward. Subjects, after being made aware that all pseudomelodies were "composed" by computer, were asked to choose the pseudomelody out of each pair that was "more musical" or more reminiscent of real music. The phrases "in tune" and "in time" were also used to describe musically desirable aspects of the pseudomelodies. No subjects had any problem with these instructions, and none asked for further clarification at any point during the experiment.

For the first experiment, 70-note pseudomelodies were used. Tone durations varied from .14 to .475 sec, and the pitch range was the two-octave range from A3 (220 Hz) to A5 (880 Hz), close to the range of a good female vocalist. What varied among the different conditions of the experiment was how these pitch and time ranges were partitioned. In the low-constraint condition, pitch and time values were continuously distributed throughout their range, with any pitch or time value being possible. The medium- and high-constraint conditions both employed a small *quantized* set of pitch or time values, the difference being the presence (high) or absence (medium) of a determinate, *generative* relation among the quantized values. For pitch, both medium and high conditions used 12 notes per octave, but the high-constraint condition had equal log-frequency differences between adjacent places and the medium-constraint condition did not.

The medium-constraint places did not deviate more than .4 semitone from corresponding equally spaced places. For time, both the medium- and high-constraint conditions used three distinct time values, .17, .265, and .465 for the former and .15, .30, and .45 for the latter. As in the case for pitch, there is a group-generative relation in the quantized places of the high-constraint condition but not in the medium-constraint condition. All three constraint conditions were designed to give equal mean and variance of pitch and time values. To make all the pseudomelodies sound more musical in a constant way, no adjacent tones were permitted to differ by more than 7 semitones. No adjacent tones were within .8 semitone of one another. All of this information is summarized in Table 11.1. In short, the high-constraint condition exhibited both quantal and generative constraints, medium conditions exhibited quantal constraints only, and low conditions exhibited neither.

TABLE 11.1
Summary of Conditions and Results for Experiment 1

PITCH

Low constraint — Random selection from a (continuous) rectangular distribution in the interval 220 Hz - 880 Hz. .8 semitone< adjacent pitch separation<7 semitones.

Medium constraint— Selection from fixed 24-pitch array given in log frequencies below with 0 = 220 Hz and 24 = 880 Hz. Adjacent pitches: none repeated, none more than 7 semitones apart. (0.0 0.8 1.7 3.1 3.9 4.7 6.2 7.4 8.2 9.4 10.3 11.1 11.9 12.7 14.0 15.3 16.3 17.1 17.9 19.2 20.3 21.1 22.4 23.4)

High constraint — Selection from fixed 24-pitch array conforming to two octaves of equal-tempered semitones. Range and adjacent-pitch constraints same as medium condition. (0 1 2 3 4 5 6 7 8 9 10 11 12 13 14 15 16 17 18 19 20 21 22 23)

Results (proportion of times each type chosen as the more musical):

Low Constraint	Medium Constraint	High Constraint
.448	.433	.619

TIME

Low constraint — Random selection from a (continuous) normal distribution of time values with mean = .3 sec, standard deviation = .122 sec. Minimum value used = .14 sec, maximum value used = .475 sec.

Medium constraint — Selection from fixed 3-time array (.17 .265 .465), mean and standard deviation equal to Low condition.

High constraint — Selection from fixed 3-time array (.15 .30 .45), mean and standard deviation equal to Low and Medium conditions.

Results:

Low Constraint	Medium Constraint	High Constraint
.438	.479	.583

There were three types of pitch (and time) pairs, low versus medium, low versus high, and medium versus high constraint. One pair was generated for each order (e.g., medium first, low first) for each constraint level of the unattended time (pitch) dimension, making $3 \times 2 \times 3 = 18$ pitch (time) pairs, and 36 pairs in all. The variables were Type (of pair), Order, and Level (of unattended dimension). Pitch and time trials were analyzed separately. Although the data analysis was carried out on pairs, I have found that the results are more simply understood when presented as a function of constraint type rather than pair type.

Table 11.1 shows the proportion of times each constraint type was chosen as the more musical. If the medium-constraint condition is exactly midway between the low and high conditions, its mean value should be .500. If overall performance is at chance, all three constraint conditions should be around .500. The latter did not occur; there was a significant effect of Type for both pitch and time pairs. But both medium-constraint conditions show scores of under .500, and in neither case are they reliably different from the low conditions. Thus quantizing pitch or time in and of itself does not lead to more musical-sounding pseudomelodies. The reduction from a potentially infinite number of pitch and time places must be a principled reduction. When the quantized pitch or time places are generatively related, the further constraint does appear to make a difference in the sound of the music. The superiority of the high-constraint over the medium-constraint condition is especially apparent in the pitch domain (see Table 11.1).

These results cannot be comprehended from a simple information-theoretic uncertainty/redundancy perspective. From this point of view, both the medium and high-constraint differed from the low-constraint conditions in the same way. In the low condition, any one of an infinite number of pitches could occur, a maximum-uncertainty situation. The medium and high conditions, in contrast, both had only 24 pitches, each of which occurred (approximately) $\frac{1}{24}$th of the time. The same was true for time, except that the medium and high conditions represented an even greater reduction in uncertainty, from an infinite number of potential time intervals to only three. Yet this (quantizing) change in pitch and time structure was not nearly as easy to detect as one that changed not statistical uncertainty but *generative relationship*.

One might suppose that the present results can be accounted for by supposing that subjects voted for melodies that sounded "more familiar" somehow. This notion will not work; even the most highly constrained pseudomelodies were strongly "atonal" in their pitch structure and exhibited no longer-range temporal periodicities of the sort that permit measures (barlines) to arise. In both of these respects, the pseudomelodies were grossly *unfamiliar* to subjects. And if one says that the melodies were differentially familiar to the extent that they possessed quantal and generative pitch and time constraints, that is obviously an entirely question-begging way of saying that human listeners are sensitive to the joint presence of two kinds of pitch–time constraints, which is exactly what this experiment set out to show.

The second experiment differed from the first in the use of longer time values and a reduction of the length of the pseudomelodies from 70 to 40 notes. There were 34 subjects. Because the results for time constraints in Experiment 1 were not as strong as one might have hoped, the time conditions in Experiment 2 were set up to be qualitatively identical to the first experiment, the main difference being that the mean tone duration was .5 second instead of .3 second. The high-constraint time values were .25, .5, .75, and the medium-constraint values, again equated for variance, were .22, .58, and .7. Low-constraint time values were continuously normally distributed with appropriate mean and variance.

Results of the time conditions were nearly identical to the first experiment, as Table 11.2 shows. Once again, the judged musicalness of the medium-constraint condition was slightly, but not quite significantly, higher than that of the low-

TABLE 11.2
Summary of Conditions and Results for Experiment 2

PITCH

Low constraint—Selection from fixed 14-pitch array, diatonic
    scale with pitches mistuned up to .4 semitones.
    (0.0 1.6 4.4 5.4 6.7 8.6 11.3
    12.0 13.6 16.4 17.4 18.7 20.6 23.3)

Medium constraint—Selection from fixed 14-pitch array, two
    different diatonic scales, one in lower octave, one in
    upper octave.
    (0 2 4 5 7 9 11
    13 15 17 18 20 22 24)

High constraint—Selection from fixed 14-pitch array, two octaves
    of a diatonic scale.
    (0 2 4 5 7 9 11
    12 14 16 17 19 21 23)

Results (proportion of times each type chosen as the more musical):

Low Constraint	Medium Constraint	High Constraint
.306	.515	.679

TIME

Low constraint—Random selection from a (continuous) normal distri-
    bution of time values with mean = .5 sec, standard deviation =
    .204 sec. Minimum value used = .21 sec, maximum value used =
    .76 sec.

Medium constraint—Selection from fixed 3-time array (.22 .58 .70),
    mean and standard deviation equal to Low condition.

High constraint—Selection from fixed 3-time array (.25 .50 .75),
    mean and standard deviation equal to Low and Medium conditions.

Results:

Low Constraint	Medium Constraint	High Constraint
.431	.485	.584

constraint condition. So the effect of quantizing time to a mere three recurring time values has only weak implications for musical outcomes. And once again, the high-constraint condition, with both quantal and generative time constraints, is clearly heard as most music–like. An overall analysis of variance combining time–pair data from both experiments yielded a significant effect of Type (of constraint–pair), no effect of Experiment, and no Experiment-by-Type interaction.

The pitch arrays in Experiment 2 used variations of diatonic scales as constraints. All arrays contained two octaves worth of notes and contained seven notes in each octave. The low-constraint sequences used haphazardly chosen (but fixed) deviations from a diatonic scale of up to .4 semitones; the exact elements can be found in Table 11.2. The medium-constraint sequences used pitch places generated by C_{12}, unperturbed, but violated octave equivalence by using the elements of a *different* diatonic scale in the upper octave than in the lower octave. The two scales were a semitone apart, a distance that is "small" in pitch height terms but large in terms of fifths space. The high-constraint pseudomelodies used genuine diatonic scale arrays that abided by C_{12} constraints *and* octave equivalence.

First of all, the results showed considerably greater differentiation of the three constraint conditions than we have seen previously. Given that these pitch arrays are much closer approximations to real music in the kind and number of constraints exhibited, perhaps this is not surprising. The three means in Table 11.2 can be seen to be in the expected order, with approximately .200 separating low from medium, and medium from high conditions. Each higher level of constraint is heard as significantly more music like than the one below it. The poor showing of the low-constraint condition shows that, in the absence of strong generative constraints linking the pitches to one another, even approximations to diatonic scales that observe octave equivalence sound relatively unmusical. That octave equivalence and its key-defining ability is itself important is shown by the difference between the medium and high conditions. Both sets of pseudomelodies used generatively related pitches, but only the high-constraint pseudomelodies exhibited octave equivalence. This was a sufficient difference to make the high-constraint pseudomelodies sound significantly more musical.

It is worth noting that current thinking about *categorical perceiving*, especially as something humans are liable to do under high-uncertainty conditions (Burns & Ward, 1982), cannot deal effectively with the results of either of these experiments, especially Experiment 2. To the extent that the familiar diatonic-scale categories (to which the low and medium conditions provided approximations) were prepotent in determining perception, subjects should have been correspondingly unable to distinguish any level of constraint from any other. The present results cast strong doubt on the adequacy of any theory of music perception where listeners must assimilate musical information to templates or schemas in order to make sense of it.

REALISM AND MUSICAL PERCEPTION

In this section, I should like to make a few general theoretical remarks about the present approach to music perception. In particular, it differs from many currently fashionable views by reflecting a philosophy of *realism* as opposed to *phenomenalism*.

In taking a realist view, I treat the structures being described as present in stimulation, to be detected by a perceiver, and not something to be invented or constructed by a perceiver. As a consequence, I end up talking about *what* is being perceived rather than *what* is being constructed, or *what* are the contents of a particular mental construction. It seems to me that theories of the latter must always ultimately refer back to the former (else we would at least have to ask how such constructions originate), and once we can say that something has been perceived, it's not clear what additional benefit we gain by saying that some internal representation has been constructed. Of course, if it is held that the perceiving of something automatically entails the having of an internal representation, then we have a tautology and it is clear that nothing useful has been purchased. I would prefer to think that the perceiving of something does not necessarily imply the having of an internal representation; in particular, certain customarily taken implications of having an internal representation, such as the ability to classify the represented elements, are inappropriate for musical perception and behavior.

The present view may be taken in contrast with a view originally associated with Jerome Bruner, that perception is essentially a categorizing or classifying process (Bruner, 1957). I would hold instead that perceiving can *lead* to categorizing, and when verbal materials or pictures of well-known objects are the focus of study, this categorizing may follow so quickly and so naturally upon the perceiving as to be hard to disentangle from it. But where things like music are concerned, I feel we must disentangle perceiving from categorizing, to render sensible remarks to the effect that one can hear (read *perceive*) a piece of music, even enjoy what one is hearing, without knowing anything about (read *categorizing*) what one is hearing. As a skilled musical perceiver, I can usually tell you quite a bit about a piece of music I am hearing; I can "sort" the "inputs" into a variety of musically acceptable "categories." The proof of the pudding is that I can write down, in staff notation, pitch and time values that will symbolize for a reader/performer a correct specification of the tune I heard. This perceptual-cum-categorical skill, which goes under the name of "ear-training," is difficult to acquire, but I repeat, it is sensible to say that persons without such skill (i.e., most of us) are able to *perceive* music.

The metaphor I prefer for talking about perceiving renders is more like a process of *tracking*. Consider a standard pursuit-rotor task, or, perhaps better, the task of following the movement of a bird in flight. All that I must do to discharge these tasks effectively is to keep the tracking organ (eye, hand) reasonably close to the (moving) object of the tracking. No categories, no concepts enter in here; if they did they would likely interfere with the successful performance of the task. Yet it is difficult to deny that perceiving, perhaps even a paradigm case of perceiving, has taken place. Similarly, I would want to say that perceiving a melody is a matter of tracking its trajectories. To the question of what the appropriate "spaces" are for representing the trajectories, I would reply that the mathematical group (C_{12}) associated with the global structure of the trajectories provides the space with respect to which the trajectories may be represented, and, by hypothesis, detected. This state of affairs is not circular, but rather self-determinative: In the words of Shaw and Pittenger (1977), "the structure of perceptual space may at any given time conform to the geometry of the stimuli being perceived" (p. 105).

The experiments I have reported here are admittedly programmatic in form and content. Perhaps a reasonable attempt could be made to account for them from a very different perspective. I would suggest, however, that mechanisms that look at too superficial or local information, and mechanisms that are designed to make too many inferences on the basis of inadequate information will deal with results like the present ones only in a forced and cumbersome way. The failure of traditional acoustical measurements to come to grips with musical structure in the large must not be misconstrued as evidence for the subjectivity of musical perception, but rather the uniqueness of the human perceiver as a measurer of musical information.

EPILOG: MUSIC PERCEPTION OR COGNITION?

How are judgments of musical value made? There is a skeptical school of thought proposing that we become indoctrinated through an almost conditioning-like procedure by being told "This is fine music" in the presence of, say, Mozart's 40th Symphony. Such a perspective either implicitly begs the question of how the specific musical choices arise or explicitly declares the choices arbitrary. The skeptical point of view has the apparent advantage of being more explicit than a more idealistic point of view, which would hold that there really is something to musical excellence, even if we cannot specify what it is. In any case, it is clear that judging musical excellence is a *cognitive* achievement, in the customary sense of that term.

Or is it? One might argue that it is "cognitive" in that persons who are expert in music doubtless make such judgments more ably and consistently than those who are not (or at least we believe so unless we are the most hardened of skeptics). Alternatively one might argue that the judgment is "cognitive" in the sense that one would be very surprised if a chicken should prove able to make such a judgment, or even behave "as if" it had made such a judgment (Reed, 1981). Even if someone were to insist that, say, plants respond differentially to different kinds of music, we might be reluctant to grant them (the plants) sensitivity to higher-order properties of the musical flux. But "sensitivity to higher order properties of the flux of stimulation" sounds like a description of *perception* (Gibson, 1966), not cognition.

The pseudomusic our subjects heard in these experiments does not even begin to approach anything remotely like musical excellence (and I understate my point here). Yet the kind of judgments subjects were making, viz. "which one of these melodies sounds more musical/like real music?" does not seem very different from the kind of judgment we are talking about. The stimuli, to be sure, are near the opposite end of the continuum from the likes of Mozart's 40th. They are not yet music and yet not so unlike music that listeners cannot reliably—and lawfully—distinguish among them when considering them *as* music. How are they accomplishing this task?

A "cognitive" attempt to answer the question might go as follows. A pseudomelody has features that remind us of, or "retrieve," certain other melodies that we have heard. To the extent that the pseudomelody does this, or to the extent that it does so with melodies that are already stored as high in musicality, we give the pseudomelody a high musicality score. The hidden perceptual variable in this familiar-sounding account is cloistered away in the basis for retrieval—what is that basis? We haven't said. One way to say without saying is to use the word "similarity," as in "we retrieve melodies that are *similar* to the pseudomelody." But what constitutes similarity? However we think similarity to be "computed," we must still specify *properties of the stimulus information* upon which the computation is based, and we must take those properties as given in perception. So we are back to what Gibson (1966, 1979) called our attention to as our first task: to specify what is perceived.

Until we do this, there is no in-principle, *a priori* way of distinguishing a perceptual task from a cognitive one (Runeson, 1977; cf. Chapter 13, this volume). Just because someone can become more expert at a judgment does not make it a cognitive judgment. And there are perceptual abilities unique to humanity; the fact that no other (i.e., "lower") species can make a particular judgment does not render it cognitive either. What we have done in this chapter, then, is to take a phenomenon that received thinking, would classify as cognitive, and show that it has a rather direct perceptual basis in the presence of certain group-structural properties in stimulation. Rather than posit retrieval of past melodies from memory, a process that in any case requires attunement to a particular property or constraint, we consider that same attunement, direct it first to the stimulus, and say instead that listeners are sensitive to the presence of that constraint in what they are hearing. As I have argued, to place the constraint in the listener's head as something to which stimuli are to be assimilated (Piaget, 1961/1969) misses the point that assimilation does *not* occur in these experiments. Melodies that obey fewer constraints are not willy-nilly assimilated but are distinguished and heard as different. With the present experiments and theory

I have argued that people can—without musical training—pick up structural constraints of the sort that distinguish music from nonmusic. Attaining more articulated degrees of attunement to these underlying structures as revealed in a wide variety of ways by real music, we can come to make more musical judgments, not by developing more internal categories, but by *hearing* more of the music.

REFERENCES

Balzano, G. J. (1978, April). The structural uniqueness of the diatonic order. In R. N. Shepard (Chair), *Cognitive structure of musical pitch.* Symposium presented at the meeting of the Western Psychological Association, San Francisco.

Balzano, G. J. (1980). The group-theoretic description of 12-fold and microtonal pitch systems. *Computer Music Journal, 4*(4), 66–84.

Balzano, G. J. (1982). The pitch set as a level of description for studying musical pitch perception. In M. Clynes (Ed.), *Music, mind, and brain: The neuropsychology of music.* New York: Plenum.

Barbour, J. M. (1953). *Tuning and temperament: A historical survey* (2nd ed.). East Lansing: Michigan State College Press.

Bruner, J. (1957). On perceptual readiness. *Psychological Review, 64,* 123–152.

Burns, E. M., & Ward, W. D. (1982). Intervals, scales, and tuning. In D. Deutsch (Ed.), *The psychology of music.* New York: Academic Press.

Gibson, J. J. (1966). *The senses considered as perceptual systems.* Boston: Houghton–Mifflin.

Gibson, J. J. (1979). *The ecological approach to visual perception.* Boston: Houghton–Mifflin.

Helmholtz, H. von. (1954). *On the sensations of tone as a physiological basis for the theory of music* (A. J. Ellis, Ed. & Trans.). New York: Dover. (Original work published 1885)

Piaget, J. (1969). *The mechanisms of perception* (G. N. Seagrim, Trans.). New York: Basic Books. (Original work published 1961)

Pressing, J. (1980). *Cognitive isomorphisms in pitch and rhythm in world musics:* West Africa, the Balkans, Thailand, and Western tonality. Unpublished manuscript, La Trobe University, Bundoora, Australia.

Reed, E. S. (1981). Can mental representations cause behavior? *Behavioral and Brain Sciences, 4,* 635–637.

Revesz, G. (1954). *Introduction to the psychology of music.* Norman: University of Oklahoma Press.

Runeson, S. (1977). On the possibility of "smart" perceptual mechanisms. *Scandinavian Journal of Psychology, 18,* 172–179.

Shaw, R. E., & Pittenger, J. (1977). Perceiving the face of change in changing faces: Implications for a theory of object perception. In R. E. Shaw & J. Bransford (Eds.), *Perceiving, acting, and knowing.* Hillsdale, NJ: Lawrence Erlbaum Associates.

Shepard, R. N. (1964). Circularity in judgments of relative pitch. *Journal of the Acoustical Society of America, 36,* 2346–2353.

VI SOCIAL EVENTS

The social world of children, friends, and lovers is a world of affordances, real-world specifications of reciprocal fit that support important human relationships. The notion of an affordance as an objectively specifiable and meaningful property of an environment measured relative to a perceiving and acting organism is uniquely J. J. Gibson's. But with the advantage of hindsight, we can see protean versions of the idea in the thought of the ethologist J. von Uexkull and the Gestalt psychologist K. Koffka, more than 50 years ago.

As an ethologist, von Uexkull (1934/1957) immediately appreciated the need to understand the environment from the point of view of the particular species under study—to do otherwise and talk of "the world" as described by human science was to be guilty of anthrocentrism. Von Uexkull filled this need with his concept of *Umwelt*, or "surrounding world." In his monograph, "A Stroll through the Worlds of Animals and Men," he sketched the diverse and different Umwelten of the sea urchin, the tick, the migratory bird, and the dog, to name but a few. Von Uexkull explicitly recognized that organisms can possess sensitivity to stimulation of a highly complex nature. He emphasized the mutuality and complementarity of perceiving and acting, organism and environment, but most important for von Uexkull was the selectivity embodied in organism/environment loops: Von Uexkull (1934/1957) stated, "As the spider spins its threads, every subject spins his relations to certain characters of the things around him, and weaves them into a firm web which carries his existence" (p. 14). But Von Uexkull was misled by his fundamental allegiance to the doctrine of specific nerve energies; his theory of perception was a cue theory built up from "local signs" in the "receptor mosaic." The topology of space was equated with the topology of receptive units, the structure of time with receptor latencies. To the extent that receptor topologies and latencies are unequal across sense modalities, we are given not a unitary world, but multiple discoordinated worlds. Von Uexkull's ethology thus had a constructivist, Kantian flavor; space and time are "given by the subject to the things in his Umwelt, and [do] not exist in his environment" (p. 19). Nonetheless the Umwelt was fundamentally—if intermittently—an attempt to describe species-specific affordances of an environment, the *niche* as both a place to live and a way of life. Ironically, although Von Uexkull criticized his colleagues for denying the reality of Umwelten, his Kantianism eventually led him to deny it too.

Koffka (1935) brushed up against the notion of an affordance in two places in his classic *Principles of Gestalt Psychology.* The first was his concept of a *behavioral environment,* not unlike von Uexkull's *Umwelt* except that Koffka was concerned not with differences in the niches of different species but with differences in situations, and perhaps individuals, within a species. A favorite example (p. 31) involves two apes separately brought into a cage where a box lies on the floor and a banana dangles from the ceiling. One ape (in a flash of "insight") runs to the box, carries it to a point under the banana, and gets a meal. The other jumps at the banana unsuccessfully awhile, then goes and sits dejectedly on the box. The behavioral environment of the first ape contains a *stool,* said Koffka, whereas the behavioral environment of the second ape houses only a *seat.* Behavioral environments thus consist of affordances, or so it seems. But Koffka was troubled about the ontological status of the behavioral environment, and he was unable to disentangle the relation between the behavioral and geographical environment from that between "appearance" and "reality." He treated the behavioral environment as a "mediator," and in a revealing diagram (p. 40 of the *Principles*), Koffka ultimately placed the behavioral environment *inside* the organism.

Much later in the book, Koffka approached the affordance concept even more closely, albeit from a different direction, with his idea of "physiognomic characters" (pp. 359*ff*). Here he used the example of Kohler's chimpanzees fleeing their playground in fright when Kohler enters wearing a cardboard version of a Singhalese demon mask; this illustrates the character "threatening." Physiognomic characters are not simple functions of physical variables, according to Koffka (1935), but they are nonetheless "apt to exert a powerful influence on our behavior" (p. 359). They are, he says, "more primitive and more elementary contents of perception" than sensations, which from this point of view appear "no longer as the raw material out of which all consciousness is built"

(p. 360). But Koffka stopped well short of admitting the reality of his physiognomic characters, although he implied it when he said that they arise when an organism is "less separated from the [geographical] environment" (p. 361). Koffka remained puzzled about the origin of physiognomic characters, failing to consider that they might be complex but nonetheless determinate functions of physical variables, and he eventually sentenced them to inhabit the behavioral environment.

The next two chapters build on von Uexkull, Koffka, and Gibson by actually specifying invariant biomorphic properties that afford support for social events involving age and gender. In Chapter 12, **Alley** looks at evolutionary and ecological constraints on social cognition revealed through caregiving relationships between primate adults and their offspring. An analysis is done of the age-related information available in both fast events and slow events to which caregiving adults are sensitive. Alley also presents some experimental evidence showing that adult humans dispense protection as a lawful function of age-specific transformational invariants in children's craniofacial and bodily forms.

Chapter 13 presents the impressive work of **Runeson and Frykholm** demonstrating the existence of, and perceivers' sensitivity to, abstract information in changing point–light arrays specifying the gender and the intention of actors. By the principle of Kinematic Specification of Dynamics (KSD), patterns of movements reveal underlying forces, and the latter cannot be concealed by deceptive intentions on the part of an actor. Rather, the movement pattern of one who wishes to deceive an observer about gender reveals *both* the true gender and the deceptive intention.

REFERENCES

Koffka, K. (1935). *Principles of Gestalt psychology*. New York: Harcourt Brace World.
von Uexkull, J. (1957). A stroll through the worlds of animals and men. In C. H. Schiller (Ed. & Trans.), *Instinctive behavior*. New York: International University Press. (Original work published 1934)

12

An Ecological Analysis of the Protection of Primate Infants

Thomas R. Alley
Clemson University

CONTENTS

My main concern in this chapter is the basis for the general tendency in adults of most primate species to protect infant conspecifics. This protection appears to be grounded in age-differentiation, a phenomenon seen in the social interactions of many animal species, including all primates. The developmental events that specify age level are thus important modifiers of social relations and social cognition. These events alter the capacities and potential of a developing organism and are commonly accompanied by changes in the way the organism influences others.

The most widespread and obvious form of age-differentiation, at least among mammals, is the special treatment of infants by adult caretakers. Successful caretaker-young interactions of species bearing dependent offspring must be regulated by reciprocally exchanged stimuli if the young are to receive proper care (Alley, 198 2; Bell & Harper, 1977). Both the slow events of aging and the fast events used in behavioral signaling (e.g., vocalizations) play important but

239

often distinct roles in governing infant care and other forms of age-differentiation. The special treatment of infants by adult primates provides a rich source of
examples of ways in which evolution and ecology constrain social cognition. The
role of evolutionary and ecological constraints in determining the significance of
biotic events is highlighted by both the consideration of infant care in evolutionary perspective and by a review of the role of physical appearance in eliciting
adult protection.

I begin the discussion with an overview of some evolutionary constraints on
the role of age-related events in mammalian infant care. This is followed by a
review of some empirical evidence that age-related events are linked to infant
protection in both human and nonhuman primates. After I present some of my
own research, I close by using the analysis of infant protection to make some
more general comments on event cognition and intraspecies communication.

EVOLUTION AND INFANT CARE

Event cognition and infant care, like other animal functions, have been shaped
by evolutionary selection. Infant caretaking has been channeled by natural selection toward a maximum genetic representation of (individual) caregivers in future generations; evolutionary selection will favor those whose patterns of infant
care most successfully produce individuals carrying genes in common with the
caregiver. In general, selection ensures that infant caretaking and other vital
social interactions are maintained and regulated through a reciprocal exchange of
signals, organism-based structural or transformational invariants that provide
significant information for other organisms. Such evolutionary attunement is
especially likely in social species, such as most primates, for conspecifics are a
relatively constant, important, and stable feature of their surroundings. When a
specific style of interaction between two classes of conspecifics tends to increase
the reproductive success of *both* parties (as does parental care of mammalian
offspring), this constancy should increase the selection pressure for mutually
adapted signaling systems. In this manner, certain infantile characteristics can
"demand" or "invite" appropriate caretaking behaviors of a perceiving adult;
that is, characteristically infantile patterns of stimulation will not only permit
recognition of the infancy of an animal but will also tend to elicit appropriate
forms of caregiving. This implies cognitive attunement affecting the significance
of such signals, and perceptual attunement influencing their reception. In the
remainder of this section I consider some factors that may influence the emergence of such evolutionary attunement.

Protection and other forms of infant care are often displayed by members of
primate groups besides the parents. Such "alloparental" care (Wilson, 1975) is
not surprising from an evolutionary perspective because natural selection should
tend to favor child-oriented, altruistic behavior by some process such as kin

selection in ancestrally (i.e., genetically) related societies (Clutton-Brock & Harvey, 1976; Crook, 1971; West Eberhard, 1975; Wilson, 1975). By behaving so as to increase the chances of survival of a genetically related individual (e.g., by protecting them), an adult may increase its ("inclusive") fitness. Thus, the protection of an infant of similar genetic composition may foster selection of that behavioral trait (cf. Gifford, 1967).

Although primate mothers are typically the primary infant caretakers, male primates are often larger—sometimes twice as large as females in baboons, macaques, gorillas and some other species (Simonds, 1974)—and better equipped (e.g., with large canines) to protect infants. Besides increasing the survival rate of infants by augmenting the protection provided by females, protection by males may increase the "social rank" of the protected infants, thereby increasing the infants' access to food and water and decreasing the chance of attack or injury by other group members (Gifford, 1967; Luft & Altmann, 1982; Weisbard & Goy, 1976). The additional vigilance and protection of males may also permit mothers to devote more time and attention to other forms of caregiving, such as feeding and grooming. Adaptive advantages also accrue to caregiving by primate females other than the mother (see Clutton-Brock & Harvey, 1976; Hrdy, 1976; Horwich & Manski, 1975; Lancaster, 1972; Quiatt, 1979; West Eberhard, 1975), so that they too may be expected to show special responses to infants of other mothers, as in so-called "aunt-behavior" (see Alley, 1980; Hrdy, 1976; Rowell, 1972).

Infantile physical characteristics are especially likely to serve as elicitors of caretaking behavior. Any readily detectable physical characteristic will suffice as the stimulus for a genetically "programmed" response as long as two conditions are met: (1) The characteristic should *reliably* appear in the "target" objects (in our case, immature conspecifics) and, (2) if false positives (provision of care to inappropriate recipients) are costly, the characteristic should also be *specific* to members of the target class. Scalar, textural, or morphological characteristics could all serve as the basis for the age-specific responses of primates as long as they met these requirements.

In the case of caregiving responses, false positives *are* usually costly. Parental caregiving generally utilizes limited resources, an obvious case being the provision of nourishment to neonates by mammalian mothers. The provision of protection is potentially costly in that it may endanger the protector. Hence, parental care should be given only to dependent conspecifics (unless a system of reciprocal altruism is operative). Moreover, in primates and other species in which offspring vulnerability and dependency decrease with increasing age, parents should respond more positively to offsprings' signals of need the younger the offspring are. In other words, the likelihood of eliciting protection, nourishment, or other forms of care from older conspecifics should decrease after a "point of diminishing returns" (Irons, 1979) on caregiving investment is reached, assuming the changes in maturational level can be perceived. More generally, in species capable of distinguishing age-classes, selection will favor a tendency to change the likelihood that members of each age-group will behave altruistically towards individuals of other age-groups (Emlen, 1970; Gadgil, 1982). Likewise, selection should favor age discrimination in primates and other species that can increase their fitness through age-differentiated behavior.

In sum, from an evolutionary perspective it is to be expected that caregiving will be attuned to the needs of infants. At least some members of all mammalian species can be expected to detect the stimulation that specifies infancy and the vulnerability and nurturance requirements of the immature. Reciprocally, infants may be expected to detect information specifying parenthood (or adulthood) and the nurturing and protective capacity of adults. A cost-benefit analysis with respect to the probable genetic contribution to later generations is required in order to fully understand the social cognition involved in age-differentiation (see Gadgil, 1982). Moreover, as shown earlier, factors like kinship, competence, and the ratio of potential risk to potential benefit can influence attention, cognition, and responsiveness to socially significant events.

PROTECTION OF NONHUMAN PRIMATE INFANTS

Infant primates typically elicit a high degree of interest and protection from at least some older conspecifics. For example, adult male chimpanzees are tolerant and protective of infant chimps, and older female siblings show intense interest and ''maternal protective behavior'' towards infants (Lawick-Goodall, 1968). Besides tolerance, protection appears to be the most common category of paternalistic behavior among primates (see Bales, 1980). Attacks in defense of infants have been found to be a major source of aggression within groups of several primate species (Hall & Mayer, 1967; Nagel & Kummer, 1974). Kummer (1967) argues that maternal protection of the infant is the first and most basic tripartite relation in a primate's life. Indeed, a ''closely protective and nurturing mother–infant relationship seems to be one of the more universal features of primate societies'' (van den Berghe, 1973, p. 31).

A number of observations attest to the importance of infant protection in primate societies. Infants in all primate species are especially dependent on parental protection for they are reared in close contact to the mother rather than hidden away in a den or nest (Lancaster & Whitten, 1980; Lozoff & Brittenham, 1979; Simonds, 1974). The tree shrews (*Tupaia*) are an (alleged) exception which, however, proves the rule. Tree shrews cache their young in a nest and show no protective parental responses, presumably relying instead on the protection provided by being hidden (Doyle, 1974). Such parental ''absenteeism'' is seen in no other primate families (Wilson, 1975). Indeed, the minimal parental care of tree shrews and other aspects of their reproductive behavior and anatomy indicate that they should not be classified as primates (Martin, 1982).

Protection is probably the male's most important contribution to infant survival in those primate species in which the male remains in proximity to the mother–infant pair (Horwich & Manski, 1975; Hrdy, 1976), especially in species that have a high degree of sexual dimorphism (mentioned earlier). Infant protection is about the only form of caregiving shown by adult males of some primate species, including *Colobus* monkeys (Horwich & Manski, 1975), gorillas (Veit, 1982), Nilgiri langurs, and rhesus and stumptail macaques (Gifford, 1967; Redican, 1976; Roonwal & Mohnot, 1977). (Such limited male care is especially likely in polygynous species, where greater aggression-related sex differences and less paternal care are to be expected (Clutton-Brock & Harvey, 1976; Redicon, 1976)). The protection of infants has even been deemed an appropriate operational definition of "paternal care" for macaques (Itani, 1963).

Infantile Coloration and Infant Protection

There is evidence that distinctively infantile physical characteristics can elicit caregiving in many bird and mammal species (Eibl-Eibesfeldt, 1975; Portmann, 1967; Tinbergen, 1964), including nonhuman primates. The infants of many primate species possess distinctively colored coats or flesh (Alley, 1980). For example, gray langurs have brown infants, red spider monkeys have black infants, and silver leaf monkeys have bright orange infants. Many observations on both captive and feral primates indicate that infantile coloration is at least partially responsible for eliciting special protection and other forms of caretaking from older conspecifics in some species (Alley, 1980; Rowell, 1972). Jay (1963) and Poirier (1968; 1973) have gone further and suggested that the natal coat of langurs and some *Cercopithecus* monkeys may be "essential" in releasing females' maternal behavior. They both argue that it is almost certainly more than just a coincidence that the period of coat color difference coincides with the period of dependency during which the infant most needs protection and care from older conspecifics.

Other more specific observations support the notion that distinctive coloration in nonhuman primate young is associated with their protection. For instance, the change in coat characteristics of Gibraltar macaques seems to be a "critical biological development" of later infancy which "inaugurates qualitatively different interactions, characterized by increasing independence of the infant" (Burton, 1972, p. 42). More specifically, Burton noticed that the change with age in infants' coats (increasing their resemblance to adults) was associated with less and slower protective interference by older conspecifics. Others have suggested that changes in coloration may also play a role in the termination of protection of immature macaques (Rosenblum, 1971; Simonds, 1974) and vervets (Lancaster, 1972).

In general, cross-species comparisons of the varying lengths of maternal attachment, tolerance, and protection of infants support this view (Alley, 1980;

Rowell, 1972). For example, spider monkey mothers show "strong signs of maternal attachment and protection" for several months longer than howler mothers, and infant spider monkeys do indeed retain their distinctive infantile coloration for several months longer than infant howlers (Simonds, 1974). A comparison of *Cercopithecus* species that display a conspicuous natal coat with those in which a distinctive natal coat does not appear suggests that conspicuously distinctive natal coats appear in those species whose infants are more vulnerable to environmental dangers (Gartlan, 1969). Similarly, among "social" primates the differentiation between infantile and adult coloration "tends to be marked in species characterized by the threat of aggression" (Simonds, 1974, p. 113). These observations suggest that more distinctive infantile coloration is found in primate species whose young generally have a greater need for protection (cf. Hrdy, 1976).

Booth (1962) found that the sight of the natal coat of an infant in a situation that is seen as dangerous will elicit a "rescuing reaction" in all adults of its kind. The sight of her carrying either an infant in its natal coat or a stuffed but moving natal coat skin produced strikingly bold threatening and aggressive behavior from adult monkeys. Vocalizations were not needed to evoke this protective response. In contrast, these same adults showed neither aggression nor any inclination towards rescuing young monkeys after the natal coat was lost. Comparable displays of exceptional aggression to protect infants have been reported for lutong (Bernstein, 1968), baboons (DeVore, 1963), rhesus (Altmann, 1962) and Japanese (Itani, 1963) macaques, patas (Hall & Mayer, 1967) and *Colobus* (Booth, 1962; Horwich & Manski, 1975; Wooldridge, 1971) monkeys, and Hanuman langurs (McCann, 1933; Sugiyama, 1965).

Visual Perception and Protection

It would be surprising if *visually* perceived characteristics were not prominent among the factors that influence caregiving and protection, for easily discriminable, age-specific visual stimuli are readily available. Furthermore, primates are typically very reliant on their characteristically good vision. Within groups of primates, visual "elements" are apparently "supremely important in maintaining the differential spacing within the group that correlates with sex, age, and dominance status" (Marler, 1968, p. 434). Visual communication seems to be especially well suited for governing the intricate structure of primate societies because it allows several complex signals to be sent or received simultaneously (Gautier & Gautier, 1977; Rowell, 1972). Also, vision is unsurpassed as a means of locating objects at a distance (Gautier & Gautier, 1977; Gibson, 1966, 1979). Thus, "when the mode of life and the environment permit it", vision is likely to be the means of communication where (as in infant caretaking) precise localization over distance is important (Marler, 1965, p. 547). Through vision, the location, age-class, immediate surroundings, and protective needs of an infant may be simultaneously perceived by adult primates. A cross-species comparison of social organization suggests that good eyes and a reliance on vision may even be required for the evolution of complex social organization: "Perhaps only the instantaneous recognition of other individuals by visual cues, and communication by visually perceived gestures, permits the development of complex, permanent societies" (Rowell, 1972, p. 24). In any case, whenever vision is available, optical signals are "paramount in the identification of . . . the status of individuals within dominance systems" (Wilson, 1975, p. 239).

Summary: Physical Appearance and the Protection of Nonhuman Primates

Although it is almost certainly more than just coincidence that the natal coat is present when the infant is most dependent on its mother and other older conspecifics for nourishment, transportation, and protection, it cannot be concluded with certainty that natal coat characteristics are essential for the elicitation of these responses in any primate species (Alley, 1980). Natal coloration is not necessary to evoke adult male protection in some species (e.g., chacma baboons) in which protection may continue unabated after the natal coat is lost. Nonetheless, there is strong evidence that some distinctive physical characteristic(s) of primate young can evoke protection, attention, and caregiving from at least some conspecifics. Primate infants are protected from both environmental dangers and intraspecies aggression. They attract a disproportionate amount of attention (DeVore, 1963; Spencer-Booth, 1970), and this tends to increase the effectiveness of their protection (Alley, 1980; DeVore, 1963; Weisbard & Goy, 1976).

Despite ambiguity regarding the most important stimuli involved in the differential treatment of immature primates, it is abundantly clear that the special treatment of infants has immense adaptive value (Alley, 1980). Indeed, special responses to infants are required for the survival of all primates. Man is similar enough to other higher primates for comparable age-differentiated treatment of conspecifics (i.e., with regard to protection, attention, attraction, etc.) to have the same general types of adaptive value. Ontogenetic *dis*similarities, however, indicate that the adaptive value of appropriate infant caretaking should be even greater for humans than for our primate relatives.

INFANT CARE IN NEOTENOUS APES (HUMANS)

An examination of the ontogeny of the various primate species reveals a progressive increase in the length of infant and juvenile periods from prosimian to monkey to ape to human (Schultz, 1960; Wilson, 1975). Indeed, the prolongation of the periods of development is a distinctive hominid characteristic (Gould, 1977; Schultz, 1960); humans are *neotenous* animals with "absolutely the most protracted period of infancy, childhood and juvenility of all forms of life" (Krogman, 1972, p. 2). Our prolonged postnatal dependency entails a longer period during which some infantile characteristic(s) could increase the safety and nurturance of the infant by eliciting protection and caregiving. In fact, this "relatively prolonged state of immaturity in the human young is made possible . . . by strongly developed 'parenting' behavior in the adults" (Freedman, 1974, p. 23).

Our retarded maturation also results in the human neonate being "about as dependent a creature as we find among placental mammalian infants" (Gould, 1977, p. 400). Furthermore, due to the physical constraints of the birth canal, we are born with a marked biological prematurity as compared to all other primates (Gould, 1977; Kovacs, 1960; Simonds, 1974) and, hence, require an unusually high level of parental caregiving. Finally, as Morris (1977) and others have noted, compared to most other primates (and probably as a result of neoteny), human neonates have a disadvantage with regard to ensuring close maternal contact: We cannot cling to our mother's fur. As a result, the "achievement of consistent and regular proximity and contact is dependent essentially upon adequate motivation of the mother to keep near to her infant" and to provide the various kinds of essential stimulation (Ambrose, 1966, p. 361) and protection.

Endogenous protective responses to endangered immature offspring would certainly have adaptive value for parents in terms of increased chances of survival for their progeny and may even have been a prerequisite for the survival of primates in a relatively dangerous environment (e.g., a savanna) despite a long period of development and dependency. Due to the reduced threat of predation, arboreal species should, in general, have less need for infant protection than semiterrestrial and terrestrial species (including members of the primate genera *Homo, Macaca, Mandrillus, Papio, Pan,* and *Theropithecus*). Eimerl and De-Vore (1974) came to this conclusion in discussing the dependence of female and infant baboons on adult males for protection.

> In the course of their adaptation to life on the ground, baboon males have acquired a tendency to feel affection or at least a strong protective urge towards all infants; and it is this urge that, in an emergency, will give males a motive to defend them. . . . the urge to protect their babies must also have evolved in men before they could successfully adapt to life on the ground. (p. 94)

Many primiparous mothers of neonates do feel "a sense of 'protectiveness' toward their infants" (Robson & Moss, 1970, p. 978).

The slow, neotenic maturation of humans should have tended to increase the selection pressure for a linkage of some distinctive characteristic(s) of our young with caretaking and protective responses in older conspecifics. Moreover, at least for a large part of human evolutionary history, man has been characterized by most of the other aforementioned factors that increase selection pressures for infant care and protection: Our hominid ancestors were terrestrial, savanna-dwelling, uniparous, large, carried their young, and had relatively long intervals between births. Defense and protection of infants constitutes one of the basic caregiving requirements of human parenthood. It can be expected that natural selection will have ensured that relatively defenseless human young are usually provided with the requisite protection. In sum, the qualitatively and quantitatively increased dependency of our young, human socioecology, and the evidence for its presence in our closest relatives, the higher primates, together provide a sound basis for expecting some youthful characteristics of endangered human infants to tend to elicit protective responses in adults. The next section reviews empirical evidence relevant to this expectation.

ADULT RESPONSES TO INFANTILE APPEARANCE

A fairly large and fast-growing literature supports the theory that infants receive special treatment from human adults due to the adults' perception of their infantile status or behavior (Alley, 1982; Bell, 1974; Bell & Harper, 1977; Harper, 1981). One especially pertinent study observed visual scanning prior to crossing a dangerous street, finding that both male and female adult pedestrians are more likely to display this protective behavior when they are accompanied by children (Barash, 1977). Several studies have reported a greater preference for, or attractiveness of, infant over adult photographs (Beier, Izard, Smock, & Tougas, 1957; Cann, 1953 (reported in Hess, 1975); Fullard & Reiling, 1976), and attractive individuals are often given preferential treatment (Berscheid & Walster, 1974; Hildebrandt, 1982). Hildebrandt and Fitzgerald (1978) monitored the facial muscle activity of adults while viewing photographs of infants, adults, and a variety of other subjects. They found a rather specific association of a pattern of muscle activity corresponding to a happy facial expression with the perception of the infant photographs. Comparable evidence of a positive affective response to infants has been reported in other studies using photographs (Harlow, 1971) or schematic drawings of faces (Alley, 1981; Hess, 1975; Sternglanz, Gray, & Murakami, 1977), and cephalic profiles (Alley, 1981; Huckstedt, 1965).

From an evolutionary perspective it may be expected that human females, being the primary and chief providers of parental care (Lozoff & Brittenham, 1979), will tend to be more sensitive and responsive to the needs of young for protection as a function of the latter's maturational status. Females in most primate species exhibit more positive responses to younger conspecifics and expend more time and energy caring for individual offspring than do males (Hrdy, 1976; Lancaster, 1972; Mitchell & Brandt, 1972; Rowell, 1972). Likewise, human adult females apparently are more likely than males to react with positive responses to infants (Berman, 1980; Goldberg, Blumberg, & Kriger, 1982; Huckstedt, 1965).

In the remainder of this section, I present some of my own experimental evidence that developmental changes in human morphological characteristics alter the likelihood of receiving protection from adults. In these experiments, head and body shape were specifically examined as possible sources of information about maturational status. From an evolutionary perspective, one would expect that the perception of another's need for care is based on properties that are reliable indices of maturational status; that is, "parental" caregiving should be based on the detection of attributes that are distinctive of and present in all normal infants and that change reliably with age. Cephalic shape is a variable which meets these requirements, for the shape of the head changes in a perceptible and more or less predictable manner during the early years of life (Lowrey, 1973; Todd, Mark, Shaw, & Pittenger, 1980). Likewise, there is a readily perceived pattern of change in body proportions across the growth period (Jackson, 1928; Medawar, 1944). Size, of course, is also highly correlated with age and (therefore) may also influence protection and other forms of care. Size changes, however, do not provide information on maturational status as reliably as do variations in morphology (Tanner, 1974).

The experiments I have conducted are based on the general hypothesis that some age-specific physical characteristics of human young can alter the likelihood of receiving adult protection. In particular, I expected the willingness of adults to dispense protection or caregiving to be inversely related to the maturational level reflected in human morphology, as measured by head and body shape indices. Simply put, the tendency to protect other humans was expected to be positively correlated with the "babyishness" of their shape. I also expected that females, being the primary caretakers of infants, would be more influenced by babyishness than are males (mentioned earlier).

The general method followed in the experiments was to present adults with visual displays (drawings) of humans varying only in "babyishness," asking them to respond "according to how compelled you would feel to intervene if someone were striking the human depicted." This dependent variable of "defense provokingness" was intended to be a more direct measure of an affordance of human infants for adults than measures such as cuteness, pupil dilation, or attractiveness used in previous studies of adult responses to infantile appearance.

In one set of experiments (Alley, 1983b), young adults were shown line drawings from four series depicting human heads varying in morphological age level. The "babyishness" of the drawings in three of these series was varied through differential application of a cardioidal "growth transformation" developed as a model of the growth of the human head (Pittenger & Shaw, 1975; Shaw, McIntyre, & Mace, 1974; Shaw & Pittenger, 1977). This transformation provides a good means for varying the babyishness of cephalic form, for it mimics the changes in head shape that actually occur during growth and very effectively alters the perception of relative age in frontal and profile drawings (Pittenger & Shaw, 1975; Pittenger, Shaw, & Mark, 1979; Shaw & Pittenger,

1977; Todd et al., 1980), as well as in three-dimensional computer-sculpted busts (Todd et al., 1980).

This cardioidal transformation was applied to one frontal and two profile drawings to create three series. Each series consisted of the original drawing, two more babyish drawings, and two more elderly drawings. The two original profiles were traced from the soft tissue outlines in X-rays of two 4-year-old boys selected at random from the files of the Denver Research Council's longitudinal growth study. The drawing used to create the frontal series was borrowed from a study (Sternglanz, Gray, Murakami, 1977; Figure 7) which provided evidence that it portrayed exceptionally attractive or cute facial features. The facial features of this frontal drawing were not transformed. Note that although (mathematically) equal intervals of cardioidal strain separated ordinally adjacent items in all three transformational series, the intervals do not reflect equal periods of time because growth and morphological change are not a linear function of age (Gould, 1977; Lowrey, 1973). The effect of the transformation can be seen in Fig. 12.1 and 12.2. The variation within these series is most apparent in the relatively large cranial vault of the more babyish heads.

In one experimental task, 25 undergraduates were asked to select the more defense provoking of the humans depicted in 10 pairs of profiles selected from each of the two computer-generated profile series. As predicted, they tended to select the more youthful profiles as more defense provoking, a tendency that was stronger in females than males and in subjects who had younger siblings. Similarly, in a second, related task, these subjects tended to rank-order the five drawings in each of the three computer-generated series from youngest to oldest when asked to rank them from most to least defense provoking (see Fig. 12.3). As before, the tendency to favor the more youthful was stronger in females and those with younger siblings.

FIG. 12.1. Two of the pairs of cephalic profiles from the computer-generated series. These two pairs were derived from two different Profile Series, each based on the profile outline of a different 4-year-old boy. (From "Infantile head shape as an elicitor of adult protection" by T. R. Alley, *Merrill–Palmer Quarterly*, 1983, Fig. 1. Copyright 1983 by Wayne State University Press. Reproduced by permission.)

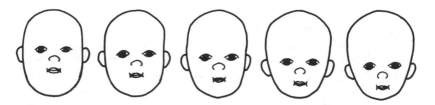

FIG. 12.2.   The Frontal Series. The original, untransformed drawing appears in the center. (From ''Adult preferences for infantile facial features: An ethological approach'' by S. H. Sternglanz, J. L. Gray, & M. Murakami, *Animal Behaviour,* 1977, Fig. 7. Copyright 1977 by Bailliere Tindall. Reproduced by permission.) Two more infantile transformational variants appear on the right, and two more elderly variants on the left.

In a third experimental task, two matched groups of 40 undergraduates were asked to rate four profile outlines of a girl on a 9-point scale of defense provokingness. One of these groups viewed a randomly ordered set of tracings of the cephalic profile as captured in a longitudinal series of lateral X-rays of a girl at the ages of 3 months, 57 months, 8.7 years, and 15 years. The other group was shown the set of four computer-transformed profiles used in the preceding experiment. The results (see Alley, 1983b) again indicated that defense provokingness decreases as cephalic morphology changes due to growth. Moreover, these

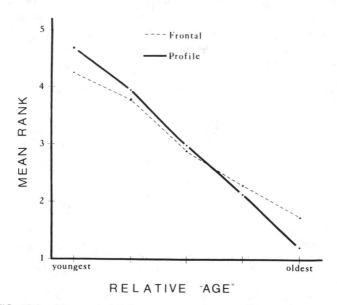

FIG. 12.3.   Mean ranked defense provokingness of the frontal and profile series. The results from two trials and both profile series have been combined because there were no significant effects due to profile series or trial.

results cannot be explained as an artifact of the cardioidal transformation used in the first two tasks; nor are they merely a consequence of using readily seriable sets of drawings.

Thus, the hypothesis that the perceived "defense provokingness" of humans is inversely related to the relative maturity of their head shape is supported by these results. All three tasks indicate that the likelihood of receiving protection may decrease as the head changes shape during growth. Some preliminary indication of the *relative* importance of head shape in determining our inclination to protect conspecifics is provided by the lack of significant differences between the responses to the drawings based on different individuals. This lack of significant differences indicates that idiosyncratic variation in cephalic profile characteristics has little, if any, effect on defense provokingness compared to babyishness of cephalic shape. This same pattern of results was also found when subjects were asked to judge the "cuteness" of drawings used in these experiments, indicating that the protective tendencies elicited by babyish cephalic characteristics are accompanied by a positive affective response (Alley, 1981; see also Huckstedt, 1965.)

Like head shape, the proportions of the main body parts change in a perceptible and fairly predictable manner during growth (Jackson, 1928; Medawar, 1944). Two experiments were conducted to test the ethological hypothesis that individuals with more youthful bodily proportions are more likely to be recipients of adult protection (Alley, 1983a). Two groups of 40 university students were asked, respectively, to rate or select from pairs of outline drawings depicting the typical body proportions of a male at birth, 2, 6, 12, and 25 years of age. Their judgments of defense provokingness again reflected a negative correlation between portrayed (and perceived) age and the relative urge to protect the depicted individual. A sex effect, comparable to that obtained with variations in head shape (Alley, 1983b), was also found: there was a higher negative correlation between portrayed age and rated defense provokingness for females than for males (Alley, 1983a). Similar sex effects have been reported in several earlier studies employing infantile stimuli and human subjects (see Alley, 1982; Berman, 1980). For instance, there are reports that females show a significantly greater preference for photographs of infants (Cann, 1953; reported in Hess, 1975; Fullard & Reiling, 1976) and toddlers (Beier et al., 1957) over adults. Huckstedt's (1965) investigation of the effects of cranial shape variations in schematic profile drawings revealed a significantly greater preference shown by females than by males to more infantile profiles.

In summary, morphologically more babyish or youthful line drawings of faces, cephalic profiles, and entire human bodies were judged (in ranking or rating tasks) to be more defense provoking and were more likely to be selected (in paired-comparisons) as "most defense provoking". It may not be safe to generalize from these results to actual human caregiving, for my experiments recorded self-reports (rather than actual behavior) of responses to grossly simplified depictions of individuals of various ages. Nonetheless, these results and the additional data reviewed herein are quite compatible with the ethological theory that the perception of babyish characteristics promotes adult caregiving.

EVENTS AND INTRASPECIES COMMUNICATION

So far we have focused on the role of morphology and color in modifying protective responses, but infants undoubtedly use many means to signal their dependency and needs. In this final section, I examine a broader set of infantile characteristics that may influence adult caregiving. The discussion begins from the perspective of slow versus fast events, then moves to the perspective of richness or redundancy in social communication.

The Information in Slow versus Fast Events

In addition to their distinctive body proportions and head shape, infants' rounded or pudgy body forms and limbs (Lorenz, 1971), and soft, warm skin (Bell & Harper, 1977; Poirier, 1973), as well as such dynamic or behavioral characteristics as infants' clumsy movements (Lorenz, 1971), "cooing" (Freedman, 1974), crying (Bell & Ainsworth, 1972; Bell & Harper, 1977; Freedman, 1974; Murray, 1979), and smiling (Bell & Harper, 1977; Freedman, 1974; Stern, 1977) have also been thought of as elicitors of human parental caregiving. Nearly all primate infants can use vocalizations to evoke protective responses from congeners (Gautier & Gautier, 1977). Of these infantile characteristics, it is the behavioral characteristics, particularly crying and smiling (cf. Bell & Ainsworth, 1972; Bell & Harper, 1977; Freedman, 1974; Murray, 1979; Stern, 1977), to which most previous research concerning child effects on adults has been devoted. Such *fast events* can be considered as a different kind of information source for behavioral guidance than *slow events* such as morphological development. Although morphology is a source of information for maturational status just because it changes with age, it is nonetheless a relatively stable and constant characteristic of individuals as compared to brief, dynamic patterns of stimulation (fast events) such as vocalizations and facial expressions. Although such fast events can provide good sources of information about relatively momentary needs, desires or states, slow events probably provide a more effective and efficient means of informing older conspecifics about relatively constant or continual needs, such as primate infants' need for protection.

Slow and fast events can be further distinguished by examining some fairly general relationships in intraspecies communication between types of signals, the kinds of information they convey, and the context in which communication occurs. For example, there are at least three reasons why fast events are probably inherently inferior to slow events as a means of signaling some of an infant's needs, particularly the need for protection. First, fast events (such as sounds or movements) may be more likely to increase the peril of an infant by attracting the attention of predators than are slow events such as static visual simuli (cf. Tinbergen, 1964). This is illustrated by evidence that the ease of localizing the vocal calls of some infant rodent and bird species is correlated with the infants' vulnerability to predation (Marler, 1959). Second, the use of fast events to communicate one's needs to others requires, at some level, an awareness of the need, yet infants are usually the class that is least likely to spot or recognize dangers. This is particularly true of the higher primates and other species that rely heavily on learning. Third, if elicitation of caregiving required a dynamic type of display, then the needs of infants would seldom be met whenever the infant was asleep, weakened, sick, or injured. The slow events of physical development allow the cognitive burden of recognizing infants' needs to rest on their more competent elders.

Slowly changing morphological characteristics of infants, on the other hand, cannot provide information with which caretaking interactions can be specifically attuned to the momentary requirements of infants. Structure that persists across a given time span cannot specify an affordance that prevails for a much shorter duration; the temporal span of an event (or cycle of events) that provides a particular affordance for an organism should be more or less equal to the duration of time during which the affordance is adaptive. In some cases, an event of much shorter duration than a corresponding organismic condition may be an appropriate structure to signify an affordance due to the "cost" of the display (e.g., in terms of attracting predators or expenditure of energy). But events lasting longer than a condition for an adaptive affordance will not serve as good signals, especially when the "invited" behavior is costly under inappropriate conditions. Consequently, both fast and slow events can be expected to play a part in the elicitation of caregiving.

Some basic forms of intragroup communication can be expected to rely more on continually available information (as in slow events) than on brief displays (fast events), because the former are a more efficient means of communicating information about relatively long-term states. For example, intragroup communication of age- and sex-class is vital to the maintenance of social structure in most primate species. We can expect such species to use persisting structures or events, which are slow enough to constitute more or less continual signals (such as coloration or morphology) to keep conspecifics informed about their age and sex. Although a fast event such as sexual "presentation" may be used to signal more specific information about, say, sexual receptivity, continual signals can be expected to be employed to keep others informed about one's sex class.

Redundancy in Information for Caregiving

It would be surprising not to find at least several infantile attributes that influence adult caregiving, for appropriate responses from adults are required for the survival of infants and (therefore) the successful reproduction of adults. Bell and Harper (1977) state:

A margin of error develops in behavior patterns possessing high adaptive value; in other words, the behavior pattern is "buffered." Evidence from several mammalian species indicates that the young provide a variety of stimuli to which caregivers are sensitive. Parental responses may be elicited by stimulation of any one of several sensory systems. Impairment of one or more sources of input often does not prevent functionally adequate caregiving, although it may be quantitatively diminished. (p. 155)

That is, redundancy in signals will increase the reliability of the communication process. If, for example, patterns of both light and sound are capable of signaling the infancy and dependency of primate young, then adults may be able to detect a pattern of stimulation specifying infants' needs for care even when the infants are out of sight. Although different sensory systems are capable of detecting some of the same information (Gibson, 1966), each sensory system is sensitive to different patterns or ranges of stimulation, and each system will vary in relative effectiveness under different environmental conditions. In an environment with dense vegetation, for example, the optic array does not carry information over distance as well as the acoustic array: It is much easier to hear an infant behind a patch of thick undergrowth crying than to see that it is in distress. Thus, the social stimulation that is provided by dependent offspring to signal their vital needs can be expected to be directed at, and detectable by, more than one sensory system in order to ensure that it is detected by potential caregivers.

Multimodal signals are typically used by primates to communicate at close range. Moreover, because visual contact provides species identification and is usually available at close range, their signaling can be variable and graded (Gautier & Gautier, 1977; Marler, 1965).

Following the ethological "Law of Heterogenous Summation" (see Eibl-Eibesfeldt, 1975), Morris (1977) has claimed that other infantile signals must be added to the distinctive anatomical attributes of an infant's face "to step up the appeal and ensure greater parental devotion" (p. 256). According to Morris, the most important of these are crying, smiling, and laughing. As noted earlier, these and other fast events are likely to reflect specific states of the infant and to elicit specific types of caregiving attuned to these states. For example, crying may tend to motivate maternal contact (Murray, 1979).

In summary, more than one signal is likely to be used to communicate information about vital needs. The use of multiple signals increases the probability that one of them will be compatible with the perceptual capacities of potential caregivers under a variety of conditions, and that the signals will be sufficiently "powerful" to evoke the necessary responses. The empirical work reported herein primarily has provided evidence that adults are more likely to protect individuals with more infantile morphology. Other sources of information about maturational status still need to be examined with respect to their influence on caregiving. Ideally, future research should investigate the association between a multitude of caregiving behaviors and all perceptible and reliable sources of information concerning maturational status and dependency. More generally, research on social-event cognition should be done with an eye to the relationship between type of stimulus event and type of need to which responses are devoted. In this way we may fruitfully expand our picture of the informational basis for caregiving and protection, an important variety of social event cognition.

ACKNOWLEDGMENTS

The author gratefully acknowledges the helpful comments on an earlier draft of this chapter by Irwin S. Bernstein, Dian Fossey, Bill Mace, Gary Mitchell, and John Oates.

REFERENCES

Alley, T. R. (1980). Infantile colouration as an elicitor of caretaking behaviour in Old World primates. *Primates, 21,* 416–429.

Alley, T. R. (1981). Head shape and the perception of cuteness. *Developmental Psychology, 17,* 650–654.

Alley, T. R. (1982). *Caregiving and the perception of maturational status.* Doctoral dissertation, University of Connecticut. (*Dissertation Abstracts International, 42,* 3452-B).

Alley, T. R. (1983a). Growth-produced changes in body shape and size as determinants of perceived age and adult caregiving. *Child Development, 54,* 241–248.

Alley, T. R. (1983b). Infantile held shape as an elicitor of adult protection. *Merrill–Palmer Quarterly, 29,* 411–427.

Altmann, S. A. (1962). A field study of the sociobiology of rhesus monkeys, *Macaca mulatta. Annals of the New York Academy of Sciences, 102,* 338–435.

Ambrose, J. A. (1966). Ritualization in the human infant–mother bond. *Transactions of the Royal Society of London, 251* (B), 359–362.

Bales, K. B. (1980). Cumulative scaling of paternalistic behavior in primates. *American Naturalist, 116,* 454–461.

Barash, D. P. (1977). Human ethology: Exchanging cheetahs for Chevrolets? *Environment and Behavior, 9,* 487–490.

Beier, E. G., Izard, C. E., Smock, C. D., & Tougas, R. R. (1957). Response to the human face as a standard stimulus: A re-examination. *Journal of Counseling Psychology, 2,* 165–170.

Bell, R. Q. (1974). Contributions of human infants to caregiving and social interaction. In M. Lewis & L. A. Rosenblum (Eds.), *Origins of fear.* New York: Wiley.

Bell, R. Q., & Harper, L. V. (1977). *Child effects on adults.* Hillsdale, NJ: Lawrence Erlbaum Associates.

Bell, S. M., & Ainsworth, M. D. S. (1972). Infant crying and maternal responsiveness. *Child Development, 43,* 1171–1190.

Berman, P. W. (1980). Are women more responsive than men to the young? A review of developmental and situational variables. *Psychological Bulletin, 88,* 668–695.

Bernstein, I. S. (1968). The lutong of Kuala Selangor. *Behaviour, 32,* 1–16.

Berscheid, E., & Walster, E. (1974). Physical attractiveness. *Advances in Experimental Social Psychology, 7,* 157–215.

Booth, C. (1962). Some observations on behavior of *Cercopithecus* monkeys. *Annals of the New York Academy of Sciences, 102,* 477–487.

Burton, F. D. (1972). The integration of biology and behavior in the socialization of *Macaca sylvana* of Gilbraltar. In F. E. Poirier (Ed.), *Primate socialization*. New York: Random House.

Clutton-Brock, T. H., & Harvey, P. H. (1976). Evolutionary rules and primate societies. In P. P. G. Bateson & R. A. Hinde (Eds.), *Growing points in ethology*. Cambridge: Cambridge University Press.

Crook, J. H. (1971). Sources of cooperation in animals and man. In J. F. Eisenberg & W. S. Dillon (Eds.), *Man and beast: Comparative social behavior*. Washington, DC: Smithsonian Institute Press.

DeVore, I. (1963). Mother–infant relations in free-ranging baboons. In H. L. Rheingold (Ed.), *Maternal behavior in mammals*. New York: Wiley.

Doyle, G. A. (1974). Behavior of prosimians. In A. M. Schrier & F. Stollnitz (Eds.), *Behavior of nonhuman primates* (Vol. 5). New York: Academic Press.

Eibl-Eibesfeldt, I. (1975). *Ethology: The biology of behavior* (2nd ed.). New York: Holt, Rinehart, & Winston.

Eimerl, S., & DeVore, I. (1974). *The primates.* Alexandria, VA: Time–Life Books.

Emlen, J. M. (1970). Age specificity and ecological theory. *Ecology, 51,* 588–601.

Freedman, D. G. (1974). *Human infancy: An evolutionary perspective*. Hillsdale, NJ: Lawrence Erlbaum Associates.

Fullard, W., & Reiling, A. M. (1976). An investigation of Lorenz's "Babyness." *Child Development, 47,* 1191–1193.

Gadgil, M. (1982). Changes with age in the strategy of social behavior. In P. P. G. Bateson & P. H. Klopfer (Eds.), *Perspectives in ethology* (Vol. 5). New York: Plenum Press.

Gartlan, J. S. (1969). Sexual and maternal behavior of the Vervet Monkey, *Cercopithecus aethiops. Journal of Reproduction and Fertility,* (Suppl. 6), 137–150.

Gautier, J-P., & Gautier, A. (1977). Communication in Old World monkeys. In T. A. Sebeok (Ed.), *How animals communicate*. Bloomington: Indiana University Press.

Gibson, J. J. (1966). *The senses considered as perceptual systems*. Boston: Houghton Mifflin.

Gibson, J. J. (1979). *The ecological approach to visual perception*. Boston: Houghton Mifflin.

Gifford, D. P. (1967). The expression of male interest in the infant in five species of macaque. *Kroeber Anthropological Society Papers,* (No. 36), 32–40.

Goldberg, S., Blumberg, S. L., & Kriger, A. (1982). Menarche and interest in infants: Biological and social influences. *Child Development, 53,* 1544–1550.

Gould, S. J. (1977). *Ontogeny and phylogeny*. Cambridge: Harvard University Press.

Hall, K. R. L., & Mayer, B. (1967). Social interactions in a group of patas monkeys (*Erythrocebus patas*). *Folia Primatalogica, 5,* 213–236.

Harlow, H. F. (1971). *Learning to love*. San Francisco: Albion.

Harper, L. V. (1981). Offspring effects upon parents. In D. J. Gubernick & P. H. Klopfer (Eds.), *Parental care in mammals*. New York: Plenum.

Hess, E. H. (1975). *The tell-tale eye*. New York: Van Nostrand Reinhold.

Hildebrandt, K. A. (1982). The role of physical appearance in infant and child development. In H. E. Fitzgerald, B. M. Lester, & M. W. Yogman (Eds.), *Theory and research in behavioral pediatrics* (Vol. 1). New York: Plenum Press.

Hildebrandt, K. A., & Fitzgerald, H. E. (1978). Adults' responses to infants varying in perceived cuteness. *Behavioural Processes, 3,* 159–172.

Horwich, R. H., & Manski, D. (1975). Maternal care and infant transfer in two species of *Colobus* monkeys. *Primates, 16,* 49–73.

Hrdy, S. B. (1976). Care and exploitation of nonhuman primate infants by conspecifics other than the mother. In J. Rosenblatt, R. Hinde, C. Beer, & E. Shaw (Eds.), *Advances in the study of behavior* (Vol. 6). New York: Academic Press.

Huckstedt, B. (1965). Experimentelle untersuchungen zum "Kindchenschema." *Zeitschrift fur Experimentelle und Angewandte Psychologie, 12,* 421–450.

Irons, W. (1979). Natural selection, adaptation, and human social behavior. In N. A. Chagnon & W. Irons (Eds.), *Evolutionary biology and human social behavior: An anthropological perspective.* North Scituate, MA: Duxbury Press, 1979.

Itani, J. (1963). Paternal care in the wild Japanese monkey, *Macaca fuscata.* In C. H. Southwick (Ed.), *Primate social behavior.* Princeton, NJ: Van Nostrand.

Jackson, C. M. (1928). Some aspects of form and growth. In W. J. Robbins, S. Brody, A. G. Hogan, C. M. Jackson, & C. W. Greene, *Growth.* New Haven: Yale University Press.

Jay, P. (1963). Mother–infant relations in langurs. In H. L. Rheingold (Ed.), *Maternal behavior in mammals.* New York: Wiley.

Kovacs, F. (1960). Biological interpretation of the nine months duration of human pregnancy. *Acta Biologica Academiae Scientiarum Hungaricae, 10,* 331–361.

Krogman, W. M. (1967). *Child growth.* Ann Arbor: University of Michigan Press.

Kummer, H. (1967). Tripartite relations in hamadryas baboons. In S. A. Altmann (Ed.), *Social communication among primates.* Chicago: University of Chicago Press.

Lancaster, J. B. (1972). Play-mothering: The relations between juvenile females and young infants among free-ranging vervet monkeys. In F. E. Poirier (Ed.), *Primate socialization.* New York: Random House.

Lancaster, J. B., & Whitten, P. (1980). Family matters. *Sciences, 20*(1), 10–15.

Lawick-Goodall, J. van. (1968). The behavior of free-living chimpanzees in the Gombe Stream area. *Animal Behavior Monographs, 1,* 161–311.

Lorenz, K. (1971). Part and parcel in animal and human societies. In K. Lorenz, *Studies in animal and human behavior* (Vol. II). Cambridge: Harvard University Press.

Lowrey, G. H. (1973). *Growth and development of children* (6th ed.). Chicago: Year Book Medical Publishers.

Lozoff, B., & Brittenham, G. (1979). Infant care: Cache or carry? *Journal of Pediatrics, 95,* 478–483.

Luft, J., & Altmann, J. (1982). Mother baboon. *Natural History, 91*(9), 30–39.

Marler, P. (1959). Developments in the study of animal communication. In P. R. Bell (Ed.), *Darwin's biological work: Some aspects reconsidered.* London: Cambridge University Press.

Marler, P. (1965). Communication in monkeys and apes. In I. DeVore (Ed.), *Primate behavior.* New York: Holt, Rinehart, & Winston.

Marler, P. (1968). Aggregation and dispersal: Two functions in primate communication. In P. C. Jay (Ed.), *Primates: Studies in adaptation and variability.* New York: Holt, Rinehart, & Winston.

Martin, R. D. (1982). *Et tu,* tree shrew? *Natural History, 91*(8), 26–33.

McCann, C. (1933). Observations on some of the Indian langurs. *Journal of the Bombay Natural History Society, 36,* 618–628.

Medawar, P. B. (1944). The shape of the human being as a function of time. *Proceedings of the Royal Society of London, 132*(B), 133–141.

Mitchell, G., & Brandt, E. M. (1972). Paternal behavior in primates. In F. E. Poirier (Ed.), *Primate socialization.* New York: Random House.

Morris, D. (1977). *Manwatching: A field guide to human behavior.* New York: Abrams.

Murray, A. D. (1979). Infant crying as an elicitor of parental behavior: An examination of two models. *Psychological Bulletin, 86,* 191–215.

Nagel, U., & Kummer, H. (1974). Variation in Cercopithecoid behavior. In R. L. Holloway (Ed.), *Primate aggression, territorility, and xenophobia.* New York: Academic Press.

Pittenger, J. B., & Shaw, R. E. (1975). Aging faces as viscal-elastic events: Implications for a theory of nonrigid shape perception. *Journal of Experimental Psychology: Human Perception and Performance, 1,* 374–382.

Pittenger, J. B., Shaw, R. E., & Mark, L. S. (1979). Perceptual information for the age-level of faces as a higher-order invariant of growth. *Journal of Experimental Psychology: Human Perception and Performance, 5,* 478–493.

Poirier, F. E. (1968). The Nilgiri langur (*Presbytis johnii*) mother–infant dyad. *Primates, 9,* 45–68.

Poirier, F. E. (1973). Socialization and learning among nonhuman primates. In S. T. Kimball & J. H. Burnett (Eds.), *Learning and culture.* Seattle: University of Washington Press.

Portmann, A. (1967). *Animal forms and patterns.* New York: Schocken.

Quiatt, D. (1979). Aunts and mothers: Adaptive implications of allomaternal behavior of nonhuman primates. *American Anthropologist, 81,* 310–319.

Redicon, W. K. (1976). Adult man-infant interaction in adult primates. In M. E. Lamlo (Ed.). *The role of the father in child development.* New York: John Wiley.

Robson, K. S., & Moss, H. A. (1970). Patterns and determinants of maternal attachment. *Journal of Pediatrics, 77,* 976–985.

Rosenblum, L. A. (1971). The ontogeny of mother–infant relations in macaques. In H. Moltz (Ed.), *The ontogeny of vertebrate behavior.* New York: Academic Press.

Rowell, T. (1972). *The social behaviour of monkeys.* Baltimore: Penguin Books.

Schultz, A. H. (1960). Age changes in primates and their modification in man. In J. M. Tanner (Ed.), *Human growth.* London: Pergamon Press.

Shaw, R., McIntyre, M., & Mace, W. (1974). The role of symmetry theory in event perception. In R. MacLeod & H. Pick, Jr. (Eds.), *Perception: Essays in honor of James J. Gibson.* Ithaca, NY: Cornell University Press.

Shaw, R., & Pittenger, J. (1977). Perceiving the face of change in changing faces: Implications for a theory of object perception. In R. Shaw & J. Bransford (Eds.), *Perceiving, acting, and knowing: Toward an ecological psychology.* Hillsdale, NJ: Lawrence Erlbaum Associates.

Simonds, P. E. (1974). *The social primates.* New York, Harper & Row.

Spencer-Booth, Y. (1970). The relationships between mammalian young and conspecifics other than mothers and peers: A review. In D. S. Lehrman, R. A. Hinde, & E. Shaw (Eds.), *Advances in the study of behavior* (Vol. 3). New York: Academic Press.

Stern, D. (1977). *The first relationship: Mother and infant.* Cambridge: Harvard University Press.

Sternglanz, S. H., Gray, J. L., & Murakami, M. (1977). Adult preferences for infantile facial features: An ethological approach. *Animal Behaviour, 25,* 108–115.

Sugiyama, Y. (1965). Behavioral development and social structure in two troops of Hanuman langurs (*Presbytis entellus*). *Primates, 6,* 213–247.

Tanner, J. M. (1974). Variability of growth and maturity in newborn infants. In M. Lewis & L. A. Rosenblum (Eds.), *The effect of the infant on its caregiver.* New York: Wiley.

Tinbergen, N. (1964). *Social behaviour in animals.* London: Chapman & Hall.

Todd, J. T., Mark, L., Shaw, R. & Pittenger, J. (1980). The perception of growth. *Scientific American, 242*(2), 132–144.

van den Berghe, P. L. (1973). *Age and sex in human societies: A biosocial perspective.* Belmont, CA: Wadsworth.

Veit, P. G. (1982). Gorilla society. *Natural History, 91*(3), 48–59.

Weisbard, C., & Goy, R. W. (1976). Effect of parturition and group composition on competitive drinking in Stumptail macaques (*Macaca arctoides*). *Folia Primatologica, 25,* 95–121.

West Eberhard, M. J. (1975). The evolution of social behavior by kin selection. *Quarterly Review of Biology, 50,* 1–33.

Wilson, E. O. (1975). *Sociobiology: The new synthesis.* Cambridge: Harvard University Press.

Wooldridge, F. L. (1971). *Colobus guereza:* Birth and development in captivity. *Animal Behavior, 19,* 481–485.

13 Kinematic Specification of Gender and Gender Expression

Sverker Runeson
Gunilla Frykholm
University of Uppsala

CONTENTS

The ability to identify the stable and transient characteristics of others as well as the meanings of their actions is of crucial importance for social interactions. Topics such as social knowing, social perception, person perception, nonverbal communication, and kinesics are all concerned with the process of acquiring information about the people around us. The mechanisms involved in acquiring such information are often assumed to be learned and thus specifications of characteristics such as gender, emotion, and intention are considered subject to cultural variation (Birdwhistell, 1973). In addition, the formation of social impressions is widely considered to be a constructive process of putting scanty pieces of information together from impoverished percepts with the aid of cognitively stored material (Anderson & Barrios, 1961; Hastorf, Schneider, & Polefka, 1970).

Recently, several authors have expressed dissatisfaction with this cognitive and learning-based approach to social knowing. They have pointed, for example, to the discrepancy between the speed and immediacy of normal social interaction and the slowness and formalness of cognitive inference processes (Baron, 1980,

1981; Knowles & Smith, 1982; McArthur & Baron, 1983). These authors suggest an alternate *ecological approach* to the field of social knowing (Gibson, 1950, 1966, 1979; Reed & Jones, 1982; Shaw, Turvey, & Mace, 1982).

My colleagues and I have presented some similar arguments and have specifically addressed the issue that constitutes the parting of the ways for the ecological and traditional approaches: The issue of the amount and quality of available information for knowing (Runeson, 1977, 1983; Runeson & Frykholm, 1981, 1983). In this chapter we analyze socially relevant information available from gender-specific properties to illustrate a general principle called Kinematic Specification of Dynamics. We maintain that the KSD principle governs the information available in observed events; this information is revealed in human movements. We then present some empirical studies on recognition of gender and gender-expressive intentions and conclude by discussing the import of this work for social psychology and the issue of perceptual versus cognitive modes of knowing.

TRADITIONAL VERSUS ECOLOGICAL PERSPECTIVES ON GENDER RECOGNITION

Nonverbal Communication

The assumption of learning as a basis for social perception suggests that expressive body movements are fakeable. It is generally accepted that bodily expressions "leak" true social information (Ekman & Friesen, 1969); on the other hand, because these expressions are considered manipulable, they can be used to conceal the truth. The following quotes from Argyle (1975) highlight this subtle inconsistency: "Human beings . . . can identify one another more easily by appearance—most of which is the object of deliberate manipulation" (p. 330), and "while these [age and sex] are communicated involuntarily, the cues concerned can also be manipulated. . . . It is possible to pass for the opposite sex" (p. 330). Argyle conceives social perception as a process requiring cognitive acts such as the weighing of cues and the making of inferences. Given a multitude of inconsistent research results, the prevailing assumption is that information about social properties is not to be found in the social stimulus as such. Rather, the implication is that the best place to search for the basis of such judgments is in people's minds.

We believe the reason for the general failure to identify reliable stimulus information for social perception is that the very existence of such information has not been considered a serious possibility. Examination of information available in people's movements is usually limited to *simply described* features (cues), which, quite naturally, are found to relate equivocally to meaningful properties of the person.

The Ecological Approach

In contrast, the ecological approach holds that perception involves the pickup of useful information through direct, noninferential processes. For visual perception, it is the detection of spatio-temporal invariants of the optic array that specify properties of the environment of direct relevance for an organism's activities. Thus, in the ecological view, it is reasonable to expect that humans have developed the capacity to pick up useful information available in their physical and social world. The crucial question, however, is whether relatively *firm* information about socially relevant aspects of people and their actions is available or not.

Kinematic Specification of Dynamics.   In treating human movements as unreliable information about the true properties of a person, traditional approaches to person perception have been congruent with traditional ideas about the motor system. Motor control has been compared to the action of piano playing, with each muscle, as it were, connected to a key of its own on the keyboard. Although a person might have some favorite songs and styles of playing, there would not be much to prevent him or her from learning other songs and playing them in the style of someone else. The implication is not only that we are free to move about any way we choose, but that our movements therefore reflect little except how we wish to move and (sometimes) what we wish to express through movement.

Contrary to this picture, recent developments in motor control theory have shown that our freedom to move is extensively constrained. One source of constraint is mechanical. Each part of our body has mass and for that reason is subject to the laws of motion. In order to maintain upright posture we must make movements that compensate for all horizontal impulses that occur, including reactive impulses from our own actions. Movements in general, and compensatory ones in particular, can therefore be expected to be characteristic of the anatomical makeup of the person.

A second source of constraint arises from the more than 100° of freedom of our bodies (Bernstein, 1967). It simply isn't possible for a central controller, brain, or computer, however large and sophisticated, to control such a complex system by computing point-for-point and moment-for-moment the desired motion at each joint, issuing appropriate commands, monitoring the progress, and modifying the commands accordingly. The only possibility is to limit the options at the "executive" level to relatively broad functional categories and leave it to lower levels to handle the details. These lower levels must fight the mechanical constraints as little as possible in order to economize on energy and control. The mechanical properties of the body, including geometrical dimensions, distribution of mass, and elasticity and damping characteristics of muscles and tendons, establish natural ballistic and oscillatory movement patterns. The task of the neural apparatus might be better understood as *harnessing* these "free" movements.

Rather than computing and producing body movements, then, the "executive" *sets up certain conditions* such as the linking of muscle groups together into functional units (Easton, 1972; Kelso & Saltzman, 1982) and setting their elasticity, damping, and resting length. The detailed kinematic shape of the movements then *unfolds* in a mass spring-like fashion without ever requiring internal representation. It follows that the anatomical makeup of a person not only constrains his or her movements in the sense of setting limits to what can be done but also is a crucial determinant of the shape of the movements.

These constraints and characteristics of the motor system provide a basis for subsuming animate motion under the principle of *Kinematic Specification of Dynamics* (henceforth abbreviated as "the KSD principle"; see Runeson & Frykholm, 1983, for a detailed account). The crucial claim is that the detailed spatio-temporal pattern of motion (the kinematics) *specifies* the underlying dynamics of an event. By "dynamics" we mean all those constraints that together determine the unfolding motion pattern. Stated simply, movements specify their causes. When applied to animate beings, the relevant dynamics are not only mechanical properties but also socially relevant internal properties such as intentions and emotions. The KSD principle therefore provides a new route to understanding the perception of social events.

The essential reason why different dynamic factors can be simultaneously yet separately specified in the kinematic pattern is that animate motion is *multidimensional* and *nonlinear;* this means that the effects of changing one dynamic factor cannot be substituted for or cancelled by a change in another. For example, an attempt to compensate for a change of mass of a limb by altering muscular action will not succeed, because both the mass change and the muscle change will alter the motion at several (in principle all) joints. Although their effects may sum to zero at one or a few joints they will not do so at the rest of the joints. An interesting case in point involves deceptive action; deceptive action can, at best, recreate *some* kinematic details, but there will be other aspects of the kinematic pattern that are altered in an inappropriate manner. It is therefore an entirely reasonable hypothesis that the kinematics of deceptive action reveal to an observer *both* the true conditions and the deceptive intention.

The notion of *nonsubstitutability* expressed earlier clashes with established beliefs that a person can successfully choose either to express or to conceal socially relevant properties. An analogous situation has been documented in the perception literature, where, for example, changes in an object's distance were thought of as interchangeable with changes in its size; this size-distance invariance and the related shape-slant invariance (a square at one angle of regard equals a trapezoid from another angle) are classical examples of substitutability (Runeson & Bingham, 1983). It was J. J. Gibson (1950) who realized that substitutability vanishes if the full multivariable optic array of a natural environment is considered, and we suggest that social events are equally subject to this insight.

Perception of Gender as a Dynamic Event.   Each gender has a different distribution of bodily proportions (Bernstein, 1967; Krogman, 1962), although there is some overlap between genders. Any person's set of proportions can be expected to give rise to a characteristic kinematic pattern, which thereby provides information about gender and the gender-typicality of that person. When, in what follows, we talk about information for "real gender" we are, strictly speaking, referring only to male and female *types* of anatomical constitution, and our arguments apply only to the (considerable) extent that people's anatomies are reasonably gender-typical.

Gender Deception.   As we have indicated, social psychologists generally assume that people can deceive others about their social characteristics. In fact, the validity of many experiments rests on this assumption. Gender, for instance, is thought to be signaled by certain properties such as voice, touch, facial expressions, verbal signals, and clothing, all of which are subject to conscious control and therefore amenable to manipulation. When deceptive signals are sent they are supposed to be just as efficient in steering the observer's perception as true expressions would have been. Although such an equivalence of true and false *expressions* seems inevitable, it is not so for the sort of information derivable by the KSD principle—anatomical proportions and the laws of mechanics are not to be manipulated.

In line with the KSD principle, we therefore suggest that a person's true gender and his or her intentions to express a certain gender, true or false, can be considered as *different dynamic factors,* both of which are specified in the kinematics of a person in action. Hence, it may well be the case that, although subjects can generally distinguish between true and false social information, in experimental settings they respond to that which they believe they are expected to attend, namely the expressions and not the concomitantly available information about true conditions. To tap the ability of perceivers to use the latter information in perceiving other people, we must instruct subjects to report both what is really there and what is superimposed or intended, as in "that person behaves like a male but I can see that she is really a female." We look at perceptual tasks that both do and do not extend this distinction-making opportunity to subjects, so that we may assess the capabilities of ordinary people to deceive and to "see through" deceptive intentions concerning gender.

SOME EMPIRICAL RESEARCH

Experiment 1

Gender Recognition of Actors in Varied Activities.   The first of our present experiments was a partial replication of the experiment of Kozlowski and Cutting (1977), except that our observers saw actors involved in more complex and energetic activities, and saw them for a longer time. We relaxed the requirement of matched actor heights, compensating for unmatched heights by having actors move substantially in depth, and we used a larger sample of actors, thereby hoping to achieve conditions more representative of normal perception.

We also used Johansson's (1973) point–light technique. Actors wore dark, tight-fitting clothes with 20mm-wide retroreflectant tape attached to the main joints and the forehead. The actors' performances were videotaped, using a spotlight adjacent to the camera in order to maximize contrast. All actors performed the same actions, including walking, running, jumping, climbing, sitting, lifting, and throwing; the program lasted approximately 50 seconds.

Twenty actors were videotaped, an equal number (five) of adults and children (11–12-years-old), males and females. Twelve adult observers participated in the experiment. They were tested in groups of two to four, viewing the actions on an 8″ video monitor in a normally lit room. The contrast was turned up and the intensity down on the monitor, rendering the action events as bright patches of light on a dark background.

The results showed that 75% of the gender judgments were correct and misidentifications were largely attributable to a few actors. One adult female was judged male by 10 out of 12 observers, and one boy was judged a girl by 8 out of 12 observers. Most of the actors' genders, however, were judged correctly by a majority of observers: three were judged correctly by all 12 observers, five by 11 of 12, and five more by 10 of 12. There was no overall difference in the percentage of correct identifications for children versus adult actors.

Conclusions.   The greater accuracy of gender recognition in the present experiment over Kozlowski and Cutting (1977), we suggest, is attributable to the greater variety and vigor of the activities used. In energetic movements the mechanical properties of the body have a more prominent role in shaping the kinematics because the greater accelerations lead to larger reactive impulses, requiring larger postural adjustments. Under such circumstances it is reasonable to expect gender differences in anatomical makeup to be more easily discernible. Our use of longer exposure times might also have contributed; however, our observers saw each actor only once whereas Kozlowski and Cutting (1977) let their observers judge each walker several times.

Gender information seems to be equally available from children and adults, even though most of the children were still prepubescent.

Experiment 2

Gender Recognition and Deceptive Intention.   An important question we raised near the beginning of this chapter was whether an actor is truly capable of deceiving an observer about his or her gender by faking body movements. A fair test of this question would require giving observers the opportunity to respond to an actor's real gender and intended (either real or false) gender separately; we therefore had both male and female actors perform while varying their intentions concerning gender appearance. We were interested in whether an actor's intention to portray a particular gender alters their kinematic pattern in a way that disguises their true gender, or if observers are able to pick up information about true gender independently of intended gender.

The actors in this experiment were recorded under three conditions: (1) neutral, i.e., actors were not made aware that gender was relevant, (2) emphasizing characteristics of their own sex, and (3) faking, i.e., pretending to be a person of the opposite sex. Five male and five female adults performed the same actions under each of the three conditions. Before the first recording, actors were told only that the purpose was to find out if their specific actions were recognizable in the form of moving point–light displays. This instruction was intended to focus actors' attention specifically on their actions; nothing was said about gender and we assume there was no particular self-awareness of gender informing actors' movements in this condition. Before the second recording, the actors were told that recognition of sex was in fact the primary focus of the experiment. They were instructed to pay attention to their movements insofar as those movements were typical of their gender, and to emphasize, but not exaggerate, the movements to help observers identify gender more easily. For the third recording, the actors were asked to perform like the opposite sex, the purpose stated as being to find out whether observers could be fooled about gender. The action program in this experiment included walking, sitting, jumping, lifting and carrying a chair, and balancing on a narrow beam. The program was rehearsed before each of the three recordings; in particular, the actors were given time to practice the *gender-expressive* conditions (2) and (3).

Ten male and 10 female adults participated as observers. They were told that an actor might either move naturally, emphasize his or her own sex, or fake the opposite sex. For each presentation (one actor performing the whole action program under one of the three intention conditions), the observer's task was to judge both the real and, where applicable, the intended sex of the actor. In other respects the experimental situation and procedure were like Experiment 1.

Correct identification of gender occurred in 85.5% of the cases where actors moved naturally. Presentations with same-sex emphasis were recognized only 67.5% of the time, while deceptive displays were actually better than this, with 75.5% correct judgments of true gender.

The figure obtained for gender recognition under the natural (non-expressive) condition (condition 1) is, to our knowledge, the highest obtained with natural (as opposed to computer-generated) point–light displays. When actions are performed with deceptive intent, recognition of true gender is only moderately degraded, remaining at a level comparable to our results from Experiment 1; the deception has almost no effect. The surprising result is the drop in the condition where the actors' own sex was emphasized, particularly for the female actors where it is down to 56%. Rather than facilitating recognition, the actors' attempts to emphasize their own sex seem to have confused the observers.

Overall, the occurrence of gender-expressive intentions was reported in 60% of the nonnatural scenes, whereas there were 45% of "false alarms" for the natural scenes (no gender-related intentions). Intentional acts, when identified as such, were correctly judged for which sex was intended in 76% of the cases. It seems therefore that the occurrence of deliberate deceptive or supportive gender intentions is somewhat harder to detect than the actual gender of an actor.

Conclusions: Perception of Real Gender.   The results of Experiment 2 demonstrate observers' ability to detect faking and see what is really behind the performance. Real gender is correctly identified a high proportion of the time, both for naturally performing persons and for persons performing with deliberate gender-expressive intentions. On the average, the gender of six out of seven persons is correctly recognized when they are performing without knowing that gender recognition is the purpose of the experiment. Contrary to a common belief that a credible impression of gender category can be intentionally created (regardless of real sex), our results show that efforts to express one's own sex degrades rather than enhances recognition, although deceptive expressions have only a marginal effect. The intention itself is frequently, but not always, picked up and identified. We conclude that true gender, as a dynamic factor behind unfolding movements, is discernible from gender-expressive intentions, even when the two are nominally in conflict with one another, as in the case of a male acting female.

Knowledge of the gender-recognition purpose of the experiment (and the ensuing self-awareness) could be considered a further dynamic (and complicating) factor influencing actors' movements. We note that the low (63%) gender recognition accuracy in Kozlowski and Cutting (1977) might also be partly attributable to their actors being informed about the purpose of the experiment.

In both of our experiments we found fairly large differences among actors. Kozlowski and Cutting (1977) also observed this; just as in our Experiment 1, one of their female actors was judged male by a substantial majority of observers. In the "emphasized own sex" condition of our second experiment, four out of 10 actors elicited reversed gender judgments, yet these actors (and all the others as well) were judged correctly by a majority of observers in both the natural and the deceptive conditions. Hence it is not the case that certain actors tend to be misjudged under all conditions, and reversed judgments are thus not adequately explained by deviant anatomical makeup. Instead, in the "emphasized own sex" condition, these actors are doing something to alter their kinematic patterns with the effect of reversing some observer judgments. This is a further indication that actor awareness of observers who will be attending to sex may constitute another dynamic factor shaping the kinematic pattern. On the whole, however, information about real gender is not concealed by the influence of this additional dynamic factor.

According to the KSD principle, adding a dynamic factor should not conceal information already present. The negative effects that occurred might be accommodated by noting that when dynamic factors are added, there will literally be *more* to see. The added factors could have higher attensity (Shaw & McIntyre, 1974) and therefore attract observers' attention away from true gender.

Conclusions: Perception of Gender-Expressive Intention.   By extension of the KSD principle as just invoked, recognition of real gender and detection of deliberate gender-expressive intentions should be independent of one another. In the conventional view, on the other hand, both true and intended gender would be signaled through the same sort of expressive movements and judgments should therefore be closely related. We have already seen that deceptive intentions do not infiltrate judgments of true gender, but a dependence would also be in evidence if there was a tendency for observers to prefer "convergent" judgments (e.g., male acting male) over "divergent" ones (female acting male). Instead, the results show that convergent judgments of true and intended gender are substantially *less* common than divergent judgments, so the observed dependence goes, if anything, in the opposite direction from the conventional prediction. Another way to assess this issue is to look at how the accuracy of the two types of responses—to real and intended gender—covary. Conventionally, one would expect accuracies to correlate positively because they would be supported by the same type of information. From the KSD principle one would instead predict statistical independence for the accuracies. In this respect, too, our results support the KSD view: there is no positive correlation between the accuracy of gender and gender-expressive judgments (see Runeson & Frykholm, 1983, for a detailed account).

Experiment 3

Gender Deception in a Conventional Deception Design.   The results of Experiment 2 were perhaps counterintuitive in demonstrating an almost complete lack of success in actors' attempts to deceive observers about their gender. Very similar results have also been obtained with attempts to fool observers about the weight of a lifted box (Runeson & Frykholm, 1983). However, our methods were unusual in that the observers were alerted to the possibility of deceptive action and given the dual task of judging both true and faked properties. Would the results have come out differently if a conventional design had been used, omitting any mention of the distinction between real and intended gender? This question was addressed in Experiment 3 by showing the recordings from Experiment 2 to a new set of observers and plainly asking them to judge "gender" after the presentation of each actor. Our hypothesis was that the results would indicate a successful deception effect. If so, however, we know from the contrast with Experiment 2 that such a result would not prove effective gender deception but would rather be an artifact of the method. What we were really testing, therefore, was the adequacy of a conventional design in the study of deception.

Nineteen observers participated in the experiment. To ensure a naive attitude, we recruited no observers having anything to do with psychology studies or teaching. Except as just noted, the experimental procedures were similar to the first two experiments.

Correct identification of gender was observed in 84.6% of the cases when the actors moved naturally, 84.2% when they emphasized their own sex. As expected, the deceptive condition led to substantially lower accuracy, 66.3%.

The result for the natural condition is very close to that obtained in Experiment 2, demonstrating the stability of gender recognition under different instructional sets when actors move naturally. Own-sex emphasis by the actors had essentially no effect in this experiment. We note that, although judgments under deceptive action were clearly less accurate than under the other two conditions, they were decidedly not reversed in the direction of the deceptive intention (i.e., recognition was still better than chance, 50%).

Conclusions.   When seen in the light of the previous experiment, the results fall nicely in line with the KSD view. Given the option of perceiving true gender and gender expression as distinct from one another, observers might choose to attend to either or both as they please but will mostly be influenced by the requirements of the situation. When the task is ambiguous concerning natural movements versus deliberate movements, the experimenter has, in effect, given up the possibility of drawing valid conclusions concerning the effects of deceptive and other expressive intentions. Some consequences of these observations for research in social psychology are developed later.

CONCLUDING DISCUSSION

The results support a reorientation of our thinking about the basis for social knowing in personal interaction. A far greater role must be given to meaningful perceptual information as the primary support for knowing about people in face-to-face situations.

Expressions or Anatomy?

The KSD principle implies that anatomical properties as determinants of movements, rather than learned gestures, are fundamental sources of information for gender recognition. Such a basis is neither arbitrary nor culturally determined, and its contribution cannot be manipulated. In addition, the KSD view compels the maintenance of a clear distinction between true gender and gender-expressive intentions. The latter might have little to do with the recognition of gender as such but rather serve a communicative function concerning matters that accrue to gender. For example, it may mean that the person expects to be treated according to sex-role demands. Minimizing sex-typical movements may communicate a wish not to be treated according to traditional roles. However, in situations where reality is more important than deliberate intentions, we as observers place greater weight on seeing the "face behind the mask." Thus the recognition of gender, on one hand, and the recognition of gender-expressive behavior, on the other hand, emerge as important but distinct phenomena to be studied. The distinction between perceiving true conditions and perceiving expressive intentions is applicable to all domains of social knowing. If we examine existing research from this perspective, we may find that the major part of it has relevance mainly for the expressive side.

Normally, gender expressions occur in concordance with true gender; that is, men usually express role characteristics of a male variety, and similarly, for women. As long as this concordance holds, correct recognition of gender can result from pickup of either kind of information. Therefore, the mere occurrence of high accuracy in gender recognition in point–light experiments offers no conclusive support for the KSD view over the traditional view.

However, when we consider the possibility of successful deception, different predictions emerge from the two views. If gender recognition is based on learned, arbitrary, and manipulable gestures and styles of moving, genuine deception should be possible; there would be no firm basis for distinguishing between concordant and discordant expressions, because they would all be of the same (learned) origin. If, on the other hand, gender recognition is based on anatomical properties, as faithfully specified in the kinematic pattern, then gender cannot be disguised. Our results support the latter view, because attempts to imitate the opposite sex did not succeed in reversing gender judgments.

Skilled Actors.   It might be objected that our actors (nonpsychology students with no theatrical or related experiences) were too amateurish to do credible imitations of the opposite sex, and that, for example, "drag-show" performers would have been more successful. We would maintain that for the understanding of normal social interaction, studies employing people without special talents or training are of more direct relevance. If special skills were to be brought in on the actor side, which no doubt would be of interest as such, one should note that a corresponding variation in skill occurs among observers. We might speculate that although trained actors might be more successful at deceiving the average person, they are likely to fail in front of seasoned observers, such as teachers or critics of theatrical acting, pantomime, or stuntsmanship. As we have discussed before (Runeson & Frykholm, 1983), the KSD view leads one to the observation that the purpose of the theatre or the pantomime is not to deceive the audience about what is really going on but instead to express, in the sense of communicate, imaginary events. A strongly experienced discrepancy between what's real and what's expressed might even be a crucial part of the thrill in some performances. This is not to slight the often remarkable effects achieved by mime actors and stuntmen. Indeed, the KSD principle leads instead to an interesting question concerning their skills: if genuine faking of movements is not possible, we cannot describe the behavior of mimes in terms of "straight" learning of false movements—so what is it that they do instead?

Studies With Simulated Human Action.   Further support for the importance of anatomical properties in gender recognition comes from Cutting (1978). He had observers judge the gender category of computer-generated point–light patterns that simulated walking human beings. The patterns were generated according to one anatomical property that differentiates males from females, namely the ratio of hip to shoulder width. Observer judgments were indeed a function of this ratio, with patterns having extreme values of the ratio leading to higher interobserver agreement about gender. These results illustrate how an anatomical difference between sexes can give rise to differences in movement patterns that are both (1) detectable and (2) seen as a variation of gender. But gender recognition in our experiments, and in natural situations, is more accurate than at Cutting's intermediate values of hip/shoulder ratio, suggesting that perceiving real human actors involves information beyond what is given by the hip/shoulder ratio. Interestingly, skeletons of prepubescent males and females are difficult to gender-classify on the basis of gross dimensions only (Krogman, 1962), yet our child actors in Experiment 1 were as accurately classified as the adults.

From the vantage point of the KSD principle, Cutting's (1978) study with computer-generated walker displays can be characterized as following a *kinematic approach* in that stimuli are generated by taking a geometrical configuration and *adding* specific motions (pure sinusoids) to its various parts; hence masses and forces are not involved. The alternative possibility is a *dynamic approach* in which motion is not added on; instead one starts the simulation with a model of a *dynamic* configuration (i.e., one whose parts have not only geometrical dimensions but also mass, elasticity, damping, power sources, etc.) and computes the motions as they would *ensue* according to the laws of mechanics applicable to the modeled system. Under a dynamic approach, one is working with properties of the system itself and not just properties of its movements. (See Runeson, 1977, 1983, for the development of the distinction between kinematic and dynamic approaches and its application to other cases of event perception.)

Consequences for Research in Social Psychology

Our experiments 2 and 3 used the same stimulus material and general procedure and differed only by the inclusion of the intention–judgment task and the alerting of observers to the possibility of gender-expressive intentions in Experiment 2. Nevertheless a clear reversal of the usual effects of emphatic (own-sex) and deceptive intentions occurred. Accordingly, the results obtained under the conventional design are seen as grossly misleading. Our findings indicate a need for a reconsideration of certain results and methodologies in the field of social psychology. Of direct concern are conventional studies of deception; One must now ask whether subjects are given adequate means for responding differentially to true and faked occurrences. Such considerations must be undertaken in light of the KSD principle and its growing body of supporting empirical evidence, according to which a firm and usable informational basis is indeed available for the distinguishing of true from faked conditions.

Similar objections can be raised against the even more common practice of using written descriptions of behavior or trait lists (instead of live accomplices). Rather than being given false or discordant perceptual information about persons they are supposed to "interact" with, the subjects are presented situations with no perceptual information available. In both cases the absence of normal conditions for person perception must be expected to constrain people's reactions in substantial and unknown ways (see Knowles & Smith, 1982, for a critical discussion).

Our development of the KSD principle has shown that information is available in people's movements that makes deceptive action potentially transparent to perception. It is of crucial importance to note, however, that the consequences of perception are not limited to conscious and reportable impressions. Much information picked up goes directly into the control of our actions. Because perception, in the ecological view, is an active information-seeking process, one may expect that it is subject to certain criteria for a *well-informed state,* in terms of the relevance, clarity, and internal consistency of the information picked up. When these criteria are not met, the activity of the perceiver is likely to be geared more to the seeking of further information than to outright action or interaction with the social (and nonsocial) environment.

In social psychological experiments with accomplices, several things can happen. The information about both true and faked conditions might be clearly picked up and distinguished by subjects who can then either (1) ignore the faking, and thus "spoil the experiment," or (2) ignore the truth and "play the game." Alternatively, subjects may not reach perceptual clarity about the situation, in which case they will be likely to act on the expressive signals because of the latter's higher saliency. In this case, however, we may expect the subjects to continue the search for perceptual clarity. Their overt actions (e.g., interaction with the accomplice) may be marked by an absence of what we have called the well-informed state, and hence may be more passive or inhibited. In none of these cases would there be any warrant for conclusions about social behavior in normal situations, barring perhaps encounters with naturally occurring fakers.

A Perceptual Mode of Knowing

A contribution of the ecological view in general and the KSD principle in particular is a revised notion of sensitivity that explains how direct apprehension of complex informational invariants is possible without computations and representations. We believe that psychological theorizing has been held in a deadlock by its adherence to an inappropriate ontology that declares meaningless physical elements as the only real entities (see Runeson, 1977; Runeson and Bingham, 1983; Wilcox and Edwards, 1982). Relative to these meaningless entities, useful or meaningful occurrences appear very complex and apprehendable only through a process of inference. A more appropriate ontology leads to a relaxing of the complexity constraint and permits us to think of knowing in terms of "smart mechanisms" (Runeson, 1977) that are specifically designed for pickup of relevant information, independent of its apparent complexity (see Chapter 11, this volume). As a matter of fact, smart mechanisms, or direct sensitivity to highly specific environmental conditions, are a normal occurrence in nature (Waters, 1983).

Specifically for the field of social knowing, the KSD principle rejects the assumption that certain person properties, especially the more interesting ones, are necessarily "hidden" and therefore only apprehendable through a process of first registering "behavior" and then attributing possible internal causes to it. We know now that in perceiving events *we do not see movements as such*. What we see instead is the dynamics underlying the movements, that is, the essential properties of the objects and/or beings involved.

The KSD principle implies that intentional aspects of actions, as well as "hidden" or dispositional properties of both objects and animate beings, are specified in the kinematic movement patterns of those events. The studies of gender recognition presented earlier, as well as several other studies of human action employing the point–light technique (see Chapter 8, this volume), provide strong evidence that such information is perceptually apprehended. Similarly, it has been shown that "hidden" properties such as mass and material damping in objects can be seen by observing the objects in a collision event (Runeson, 1977, 1983; Todd & Warren, 1982). It follows (cf. Runeson & Bingham, 1983) that when distinctions among modes of knowing are to be drawn, they cannot be done in the *aprioristic* way to which we have been accustomed. Rather, these will have to be empirical matters and our terminology may be in need of extensive revision.

REFERENCES

Anderson, N. H., & Barrios, A. A. (1961). Primary effects in personality impression formation. *Journal of Abnormal and Social Psychology, 63,* 346–350.

Argyle, M. (1975). *Bodily communication.* London: Methuen.

Baron, R. M. (1980). Contrasting approaches to social knowing: An ecological perspective. *Personality and Social Psychology Bulletin, 6,* 591–600.

Baron, R. M. (1981). Social knowing from an ecological event perspective: A consideration of the relative domains of power for cognitive and perceptual modes of knowing. In J. Harvey (Ed.), *Cognition, social behavior and the environment.* Hillsdale, NJ: Lawrence Erlbaum Associates.

Bernstein, N. (1967). *The co-ordination and regulation of movements.* Oxford, England: Pergamon Press.

Birdwhistell, R. L. (1973). *Kinesics and context*. Norwich: Penguin Books.

Cutting, J. E. (1978). Generation of synthetic male and female walkers through manipulation of a biomechanical invariant. *Perception, 7,* 393–405.

Easton, T. A. (1972). On the normal use of reflexes. *American Scientist, 60,* 591–599.

Ekman, P., & Friesen, W. V. (1969). Nonverbal leakage and clues to deception. *Psychiatry, 32,* 88–106.

Gibson, J. J. (1950). *The perception of the visual world*. Boston: Houghton Mifflin.

Gibson, J. J. (1966). *The senses considered as perceptual systems*. Boston: Houghton Mifflin.

Gibson, J. J. (1979). *The ecological approach to visual perception*. Boston: Houghton Mifflin.

Hastorf, A. H., Schneider, D. J., & Polefka, J. (1970). *Person perception*. Reading, MA: Addison–Wesley.

Johansson, G. (1973). Visual perception of biological motion and a model for its analysis. *Perception and Psychophysics, 14,* 201–211.

Kelso, J. A. S., & Saltzman, E. L. (1982). Motor control: Which themes do we orchestrate? *Behavioral and Brain Sciences, 5,* 554–557.

Knowles, P. L., & Smith, D. L. (1982). The ecological perspective applied to social perception: Revision of a working paper. *Journal for the Theory of Social Behaviour, 12,* 53–78.

Kozlowski, L. T., & Cutting, J. T. (1977). Recognizing the sex of a walker from a dynamic point-light display. *Perception and Psychophysics, 21,* 575–580.

Krogman, W. M. (1962). *The human skeleton in forensic medicine,* Springfield, Ill: Charles C. Thomas.

McArthur, L. Z., & Baron, R. M. (1983). Toward an ecological theory of social perception. *Psychological Review, 90,* 215–238.

Reed, E. S., & Jones, R. (1982). *Reasons for realism: Selected essays of James J. Gibson*. Hillsdale, NJ: Lawrence Erlbaum Associates.

Runeson, S. (1977). On the possibility of 'smart' perceptual mechanisms. *Scandinavian Journal of Psychology, 18,* 172–179.

Runeson, S. (1983). On visual perception of dynamic events. *Acta Universitatis Upsaliensis: Studia Psychologica Upsaliensia,* (Serial No. 9). (Originally published, 1977)

Runeson, S., & Bingham, G. (1983). Sight and insights: Contributions to the study of cognition from an ecological perspective on perception. *Uppsala Psychological Reports,* No. 364.

Runeson, S., & Frykholm, G. (1981). Visual perception of lifted weight. *Journal of Experimental Psychology: Human Perception and Performance, 7,* 733–740.

Runeson, S., & Frykholm, G. (1983). Kinematic specification of dynamics as an informational basis for person and action perception: Expectation, gender recognition, and deceptive intention. *Journal of Experimental Psychology: General, 112,* 580–610.

Shaw, R., & McIntyre, M. (1974). Algoristic foundations to cognitive psychology. In: W. B. Weimer & D. S. Palermo (Eds.), *Cognition and the symbolic processes*. Hillsdale, NJ: Lawrence Erlbaum Associates.

Shaw, R. E., Turvey, M. T., & Mace, W. M. (1982). Ecological psychology: The consequences of a committment to realism. In W. Weimer & D. Palermo (Eds.), *Cognition and the symbolic processes II*. Hillsdale, NJ: Lawrence Erlbaum Associates.

Todd, J. T., & Warren Jr. W. H. (1982). Visual perception of relative mass in dynamic events. *Perception, 11,* 325–335.

Waters, D. P. (1983). *The universal enzyme model of perception and action*. Paper presented at the Second International Conference on Event Perception, Vanderbilt University, Nashville, TN.

14

Epilogue: Cognition and Ethics

Viki McCabe
University of California, Los Angeles

Scientists typically claim that the scientific method is value free and that moral responsibility is not an issue in basic research. As scientists, cognitive theorists often hold similar views. Consequently, convention restricts scientific analyses to statements about *what* we know and cognitive theory to statements of *how* we know. It is left to ethics to tell us what to *do* about it.

But scientific principles and the cognitive theories that follow such principles may unintentionally contribute to ethical issues and dilemmas. The source of such contributions are central to the methodological restrictions science itself imposes by conforming to an atomistic world view. Atomism may suit certain types of scientific analysis (e.g., molecular biology) but contains two serious flaws for theories of cognition: First, it fails to characterize the breadth of our cognitive capacities and second, it provides the ground for arbitrary and biased mental constructions of the world. The atomistic view, however, is ubiquitous in Western thought, which makes it difficult to keep its assumptions in proper perspective; the normative status of this view tends to mask the difference between its assumptions about the world and the actual properties of the world itself. The conflation of atomism and actuality obscures the fact that the properties of the world can be examined on several different levels from several different perspectives, possibly using larger and more ecologically valid units of analysis.

Atomism places arbitrary limits on what constitutes scientific evidence by restricting the attribution of truth value to very small units of analysis. In adhering to this view, science implicitly agrees to and adopts both a set of metaphysical assumptions about what constitutes reality and a set of epistemological assumptions about what constitutes knowledge of that reality. In brief, the bulk of established scientific doctrine considers reality to be most available in small particles and considers knowledge to be about how these particles behave and combine. Such assumptions implicitly support a focus on parts and a view that parts are separate from and prior to the larger wholes or systems in which they participate. In assigning priority to parts and thereby requiring building-block explanations of origin and cause, the scientific enterprise has difficulty accounting for integral wholes and global relationships. Assigning parts such separate and prior status is both philosophically and ethically problematic.

Such an assignment leads easily to attributing special causal properties to particular (and possibly arbitrarily chosen) parts with respect to the whole that they constitute (for example, see the research on "healthy" traits outlined later). But even if particular parts could be considered to have special causal properties with respect to an integral whole, they first must be part of that whole. Yet such individual parts do not appear to have any mechanism that would allow them to change from their a priori separate state and aggregate into the wholes in which they can then be causal. Both the notion of privileged causal properties and the problem of aggregation are ethically problematic because, as we shall see, they can both lead to making scientific and cognitive judgments pawn to value judgments. One might consider that using apparently separate parts of patently integral wholes as appropriate units of analysis to study those wholes needs further examination.

For traditional scientific theories of cognition, small units of analysis easily translate into such items as features, attributes, or dimensions. The problem of aggregating such units into an integral whole leads inevitably to some form of the argument from design, that knowable order must be imposed on these separate features by a power extrinsic to themselves. The original source for the argument from design, a transcendent God (Paley, 1802), is not presently favored in scientific circles as either a material or a final cause. Thus, the job of supplying order falls to the current heir to this argument, the rational mind; traditional theory endows this mind with its own ordering capabilities in the form of entities such as internal schemas. In short, if one applies close scrutiny, traditional views of cognition imply that the mind surveys the world, selects the pertinent separate parts to aggregate, and then aggregates those parts according to its own internal logic.

The consequences of choosing separable parts as the primary unit of analysis and then using a mechanism external to those parts to create meaningful wholes opens the way to confusing the products of such mental processes with the world as it actually is. Claims that cognitive processes use incoming data from the real world, which is then matched to our internal schemas, will not correct the situation. Logical analysis predicts that such data would merely get caught and obscured in the mental net of the imposed design. The consequences of this solipsistic arrangement is that any attribute can be considered to have separate status and can thus be chosen as characteristic of any person or event. Indeed, the psychological literature is replete with mentally constructed lists of characteristics that serve as supports for judgmental evaluations of just about anything that moves (McCabe, 1973). What something might actually be can be completely confounded with hidden value judgments masquerading as its accurate attributes.

If we ignore our direct participation in the world as the most reliable source of our knowledge of the world, we open the gates to relying on our mental capability to abstract any features we like and then to combine them into anything we like to fit any world view that suits our personal beliefs, values, and purposes. Often this procedure acquires normative status and goes undetected because research scientists, like any established group, tend to share similar views and values (Longino, 1982) and their agreement with one another makes critical analysis seem superfluous. Such agreement can thus obscure what may be unexamined, unfounded, and probably unwanted theoretical assumptions. In addition, these habits of mind can have questionable ethical consequences. Clearly, if cognition is a matter of mental abstraction of separate parts, mental construction of those parts into integral wholes, and representation of those aggregated parts with internal schemas (rather than a process involving direct participation in and coordination with the world), then what passes for knowledge of the world can easily and unintentionally become the pawn of personal values and bias.

Consider the following example from a classic study on mental health (Broverman, Broverman, Clarkson, Rosencrantz, & Vogel, 1970). The study was designed to examine mentally healthy and unhealthy characteristics. Particular attributes were abstracted out of the ongoing array of possible human behavior and designated as mentally healthy. This mentally abstracted list included such traits as rational, objective, and unemotional. By fiat, intuitive, subjective, and emotional became negative traits for mentally healthy human beings. In a later part of this study, male and female characteristics were separated and compared. Not too surprisingly, rational, objective, and unemotional turned out to be male characteristics and intuitive, subjective, and emotional turned out to be female characteristics. Ironically, the choice of what traits might constitute mental health can easily be said to be intuitive, subjective, and emotional group decisions made in a cultural climate where the exemplar citizen has traditionally been male.

The use of separate traits that are a function of normative standards rather than real-world properties goes beyond the academic literature and creates ethical conundra in basic life areas such as work. For example, consider the Supreme Court decision in Dothard v. Rawlinson (1977). The court held that it was not an unfair employment practice for women to be barred from prison guard positions because of their vulnerability to rape. Such a vulnerability was deemed ''in the nature of women.'' First, as I have suggested, such designations tend to be a product more of unexamined prevailing belief systems than of actual evidence. Second, even if evidence could be found to support the actual existence of such a trait, research has shown that within-group variability is greater than between-group variability, and so deciding on a unitary "group nature" for one gender on the basis of separate traits can easily discriminate against individuals on the tail ends of either distribution. Third, and most important from an ethical standpoint, such "natural trait" attributions prevents the court from examining what might be done to combat vulnerability to abuse for both men and women. Thus, the court's adoption of prevailing assumptions about women's "traits" leads the court to both ignore possible remedies to violence that could affect men and women alike and to support unequal treatment for women (Littleton, 1983).

This kind of analytical problem can also lead to discrimination against men. Consider the U.S. Navy policy of allowing women more time to attain promotion because their natural traits make them unsuitable for the combat duty where most promotions occur (Schlesinger v. Ballard, 1975). The Navy does not examine either men's or women's suitability or intentions with respect to combat. The status of both men and women vis-a-vis combat is treated like an analytic statement, as part of the definition of what they are. Male conscientious objectors and female guerilla fighters the world over provide evidence to dispute this claim. The Navy practice clearly discriminates against both genders. Men must risk more injury and death in addition to qualifying for promotion faster. At the same time women are denied the choice to participate in many naval activities and are arbitrarily subject to slower advancement. The Navy uses atomistic traits that can actually be attributed to either gender but do not necessarily characterize any particular individual no matter what his or her gender, to make crucial decisions about peoples' lives.

Labeling people negatively using the mental magic of extrudable traits and claiming that the results are valid is not restricted to questions of gender. Skin color, height, weight, age, IQ, and various personality traits have all been isolated from integral people and used in a prejudicial fashion. This type of trait mongering is ethically deplorable but is reversible. In all fairness, much criticism has surfaced condemning such practices, and concerned people can use those critical tools to discredit such work. But the metaphysics of atomism, which supports the dissembling of whole items into separate parts, and the epistemology of mental schemas, which opens the way for arbitrary and value-laden decisions about which of these parts aggregate to match such schemas, have fueled much more dangerous ethical problems. They have provided a foundation for the belief not only that each plant, animal, or person is an aggregate of separate parts that can be abstracted and manipulated mentally, but more chillingly, that each group, and ultimately each nation, is separate from all other groups and that nations and can be treated as solitary units.

Thus we are all acutely aware of the differences between ourselves as Americans and the Russians, or the French, or the English, Arabs, or Israelis, and we seem to ignore our essential interrelationships and interconnections. The poverty of this conceptualization of reality comes home when one imagines one "separate'' nation dropping a hydrogen bomb on another "separate" nation and their separateness dissolving into one inextricably poisoned ecosystem and biosphere, a condition that is virtually irreversible but ontologically real.

There are many examples of this sort of atomistic thinking in our past relationships to the land. For example, we created the dust bowl across the great plains by ignoring the connections between soil type, rainfall, and wind patterns and by declaring that prosperity follows the plough (Wooster, 1977). The plough that "broke" the plains removed the tough sod that kept the soil in place during the well-known cyclical droughts that occurred in that area. Farmers added to this problem by ploughing straight furrows directly into the prevailing winds. When the rain stopped and the wind blew in the 1920s and 1930s, the soil, which was by then virtually "abstracted" from its ecosystem, was carried away in dust clouds so monumental that they obscured the light of the sun. Depression rather than prosperity followed the plough because rather than treating the environment as an integral whole, "prosperity" theorists and real estate speculators atomized and promoted the prairies into unrealistic parts.

We are plagued today by a similar problem that at present is not remediable— what to do with our increasing amounts of toxic wastes. We have produced goods from paint to power as if the excrement of those processes was a separable part and could be dealt with at another time. At present, uranium tailings scavenged from mine sites are permanently incorporated into buildings in Colorado and Arizona. The Navajo children living close by these same uranium mines are dying in disproportionately high numbers of cancer. Children in a tiny town in New Hampshire are dying of luekemia from chemicals transported far afield in subterranean channels that obey the laws of fluid dynamics not of ethical responsibility. We know that uranium tailings are radioactive and that underground water flows in lawful patterns. We have chosen to ignore those "parts" of the integral system in which they are embedded. What we do not seem to know, and what cognitive theories typically ignore, is that accurate knowledge involves whole systems that transform over time. Knowledge cannot be restricted to those parts of a system that are obvious, convenient, or profitable without epistemological decrement and ethical cost.

A metaphysics of atomism may be useful in particular types of scientific analysis. It is not appropriate for epistemological theories that purport to describe how we know reality because it conflates cognitive processes with scientific methods. Such a metaphysics confounds knowing the world with analyzing the world into its constituent parts as if it were part of a chemistry experiment. Focusing on constituent parts has often blinded us to available knowledge about the lawful and necessary connections among all things.

Thus even if the traits into which we tend to partition things could be proved to exist, they may be so inextricably and intrinsically connected to one another as to have no meaning if abstracted out of their reciprocal relationships (McCabe, 1984). Attempting to extrude parts from integral wholes in order to compare such wholes with each other on the basis of these extruded parts (as was done in the "healthy" traits study) can be nothing more than an ethically questionable mental exercise.

The boundaries that we believe actually separate nations have similar characteristics. They are mentally constructed political concepts that have come to roost in the physical countryside. This does not mean that national sovereignty has no meaning, but that nations as "parts" of the world have been created in the minds of men and those parts do not have priority status in situations that involve environmental hazards. That status belongs to a larger unit of analysis, the world itself. The land has no boundaries. It is a continuous expanse. The boundaries are boundaries in the mind. It requires a metaphysics of atomism to survey the world and be able to partition the physically continuous (though naturally varying) landscape into mentally constructed political and economic categories as if those categories were ontologically real rather than transitory political conveniences. It also requires a metaphysics of atomism to see ourselves standing separate and alone behind our arsenals of weapons, forgetting that although we inherited this land from our parents, we are borrowing it from our children, and we are putting those children, and their children, and unknown numbers of future generations at risk. Or in the words of a Nigerian tribesman, "I conceive that land belongs for use to a vast family of which many are dead, few are living, and countless are still unborn."

If we conform to the tenets of traditional metaphysical and epistemological theories, then we inevitably remain alienated from the world in which we live, able to know the world only as separate parts, and subject to our own frailties when we try to construct or infer larger wholes. By these lights, we will be continually subject to practical and ethical dilemmas as we constantly mistake the part for the whole and make decisions based on inadequate units of analysis.

One way to overcome this ethical conundrum is to examine the structure of knowledge from an ecological perspective. The notion, encountered repeatedly in this book, that we can track invariant structure over transformations, implies that we can perceive and thus know integral wholes. The previous chapters have reviewed research indicating that we can identify whole events, people, behaviors, and physical transformations from topological, biomechanical, and perspectival invariants (e.g., Alley, Frykholm & Runeson, Jenkins et al., respectively). Common sense tells us the same thing. We continue to recognize people even though they have changed by growing older or plumper. People preserve their identity over such physical transformations and we perceive that identity in spite of such transformations. We know a person as an integral whole, not as a set of separable attributes. Thus if one of their attributes such as size changes, we typically have little difficulty in recognizing them as the same person.

The ecological view gives us an attractive alternative to an epistemology based on separate parts and internal schemas. Rejecting separate parts as fundamental units amenable to constructive mental processes, we no longer need order imposed from without. We can then begin to conceive of order emerging from within—from, for example, the intrinsic coordinative properties of such integral wholes (McHarg, 1969; Thom, 1975). In addition, the notion that informative specifications are a property of organism/environment reciprocal units (affordance/effectivity structures) enlarges the appropriate unit of analysis to one not only with intrinsic order and specifiable properties, but with inherent meaning that reflects such order (Gibson, 1979). Thus order is not a function of some prior design, program, or schema but a property of the nested and reciprocal units of the world itself.

If organisms and their environments are lawfully entailed in nested and overlapping functional units that have epistemological properties, then knowledge of the world must be a function of one's own nested and overlapping participation in, coordination with, and fit to, those units and ultimately to the whole world. If cognitive theories are to reflect how we know the real world, and not simply give us license to construct the world in our minds, we must expand our vision from separated parts to patterns of connections, from constructions to detections, from observations to participations, from mechanistic processes to intentional acts, and from impoverished sense data to meaningful specifications.

Cognitive processes could not possibly have evolved to apprehend nonsense. Cognition and meaning must be reciprocally entailed. Because meaning is always for someone, it is a function of relationship. And so meaningful cognition connects to ethics as questions of ethics are implicit in questions of relationship. Any relationship, if it is to be preserved, entails ethical considerations. And the ability to perceive the moral responsibility inherent in relationships depends on accurate cognition (Herman, in preparation). If things in the world can best be known from the standpoint of relationship, but those relationships are discounted, then two things occur. First, only partial knowledge of the world becomes possible such as the kind of knowledge that is available from the scrutiny of separate parts. Second, such partial knowledge easily supports and rationalizes ethical violations of the integral world around us. Indeed, in ignoring our integral relationships to the things in the world we can know, we often destroy those things and then they are no longer in the world and no longer knowable. Thus cognition, like science, is not a neutral, value-free process. Knowing entails reciprocal relationships that entail ethical obligations. Indeed, legend has it that not knowing these facts about cognition and ethics led to the apple-eating episode (as if apples were separate items) that was instrumental in the exclusion of human beings from the Garden of Eden!

Consider the different ethical outcomes (with respect to the environment) that might result from cognitive theories with contrasting assumptions about the primacy of relationship. From an ecological view, one might assume that people see themselves in direct relationship with the world around them. Thus their actions in the world could easily be seen as affecting not only other people but their whole environment. How easy would it be for people who have this view to clear-cut the forests they use for recreation or pollute rivers that help temper their climate? Such a view is central to cultures that see themselves as participants in, rather than observers of, the world. The Dakota Black Elk, for example, perceive the world as a place where everything is inextricably connected. Thus no one thing has agency over another. The trees are their brothers, "standing people" in whom the winged ones build their lodges and raise their families, and who have equal rights to the land (Lee, 1959). Given such rights, the Dakota could not conceive of clear-cutting trees for profit. From a Western scientific view, such ideas might be discounted as animistic. Classical ecology, for example, considered trees from the perspective of "forest management" for optimal yield (Wooster, 1977). Management policies that treat integral forest ecosystems as if they are aggregates of separate "crops" often duplicate the attitude that created the dust bowl and produce ravaged landscapes subject to devastating erosion. (Wooster, 1977). The Dakota with their "animistic" views were long ago aware of ecological relationships that Westeners with their atomistic views are just beginning to notice. Recently a more realistic ecological view has gained purchase in the environmental movement and the legal issue of whether trees have "standing" (legal rights) has been raised (Stone, 1974).

From the world view of atomism, people can easily bypass relationships and see themselves as detached observers of a world quite separate from themselves. From this view, why would they not clear-cut the forests, strip mine the land, and plough up the prairies? But in so doing they would inevitably violate other people's rights to a livable environment, foul their own nest, and deny rights to generations to come. Such ethical problems easily arise when the prevailing view of reality gives priority to separate parts rather than to reciprocal relationships. A cognitive theory that accounts for relationships has less chance of supporting this type of ethically questionable outcome. And it is the hallmark of the ecological view of cognition that it proposes that we do not know something in a meaningful way by analyzing it into whatever parts we choose from the vantage point of detached observation. Rather, we know things by participating in intentional relationships and detecting what something means to us from specifications of reciprocal fit.

Such relationships, as has been argued, entail ethics. When cognition is characterized as a process that rends integral relationships into their possible parts, and cognitive theories focus on how those parts operate, relationship is discounted and it appears as if cognition, like science, can claim to be a detached, neutral process that is value free. The problem is that such neutrality can be gained only by eliminating relationship, which eliminates meaning, which virtually eliminates significance from knowledge. These practices, from both a cognitive and an ethical realist point of view, may best be described as sins of omission.

REFERENCES

Broverman, I. K., Broverman, D. M., Clarkson, F. E., Rosenkrantz, P. S., & Vogel, S. R. (1970). Sex role stereotypes and clinical judgments of mental health. *Journal of Consulting and Clinical Psychology, 34,* 1–7.

Dothard v. Rawlinson (1977). 433 U.S. 321, 335.

Gibson, J. J. (1979). *The ecological approach to visual perception.* Boston: Houghton–Mifflin.

Herman, B. (in preparation). *The practice of moral judgment.*

Lee, D. (1959). *Freedom and culture.* New York: Prentice Hall.

Littleton, C. (1983). Toward a redefinition of sexual equality. *Harvard Law Review, 95,* 487–508.

Longino, H. E. (1982). Scientific objectivity and the logics of science. *Inquiry, 26,* 85–106.

McCabe, V. S. (1973). The tyranny of grimping. *Human Behavior, 2,* 32–33.

McCabe, V. S. (1984). A Comparison of three ways of knowing: Categorical, structural, and affirmative. *Journal of Mind and Behavior, 5,* 433–448.

McHarg, I. (1969). *Design with nature.* New York: Natural History Press.

Paley, W. (1802). *Natural theology; or evidences of the existence of the Diety, collected from appearances in nature.* London: London.

Schlesinger v. Ballard (1975). 419 U.S. 498.

Stone, C. D. (1974). *Should trees have standing: Toward legal rights for natural objects.* Los Altos, CA: W. Kaufmann.

Thom, R. (1975). *Structural stability and morphogenesis.* Reading, MA: W. A. Benjamin.

Wooster, D. (1977). *Nature's economy.* San Francisco: Sierra Club.

Author Index

Subject Index